balance

LARGE PRINT

Praise for

Overcoming the Wall of Awful

"If you've tried all the strategies that should work but don't, *Overcoming the Wall of Awful* is the book for you. Brendan Mahan not only helps you identify why you're getting stuck, he offers the strategies, support, and compassion to get you going. As he says, this book will get you to the good things in life."

—Ari Tuckman, PsyD, MBA, author of *The ADHD Productivity Manual*

"WHERE HAS THIS BOOK BEEN?! If you are a neurodivergent human, the term 'the Wall of Awful' doesn't need much explanation, even if this is your first time encountering the phrase. We've all experienced it—that struggle to get started and do what we need to do. Now we have the instruction manual we have all been waiting for. Concise, compassionate, neurodivergent-friendly, and totally accessible."

—Dr. Carolyn Lentzsch-Parcells, the ADHD MD

"This book brilliantly and compassionately breaks down how every one of us can develop our own Walls of Awful, irrespective of any one diagnosis. Even more, it offers practical tips to nonjudgmentally analyze our personal Walls so we might create toolboxes to put a door in it, climb it, or smash it (only if we absolutely must)!"

—Raffael Boccamazzo, PsyD, clinical psychologist, Save Point Behavioral Health

"I've read plenty of books that explain why your brain won't cooperate; this one really helps you get unstuck. The Wall of Awful finally gave me language for something I have been struggling with for years, and it gave me a way to finally deal with it."

—Laura Klein, author of *Build Better Products*

"They call it 'writer's block' for a reason... almost every writer I know has experienced it and has struggled with finding a way to address it. The Wall of Awful is a perfect metaphor and a simple, clear, even fun solution for addressing it. I'd share this with all my clients."

—Cathy Yardley, writing coach of RockYourWriting.com

OVERCOMING the WALL of AWFUL

OVERCOMING the WALL of AWFUL

Why It's Hard to Get Things Done with ADHD, Autism, and Anxiety (And How to Do Them Anyway)

BRENDAN MAHAN, MEd, MS
with **ALEX HUGHES CAPELL**

balance
LARGE PRINT

Balance
Hachette Book Group
1290 Avenue of the Americas
New York, NY 10104
GCP-Balance.com
@GCPBalance

First Edition: September 2026

Balance is an imprint of Grand Central Publishing. The Balance name and logo are registered trademarks of Hachette Book Group, Inc.

The publisher is not responsible for websites (or their content) that are not owned by the publisher.

The Hachette Speakers Bureau provides a wide range of authors for speaking events. To find out more, go to hachettespeakersbureau.com or email HachetteSpeakers@hbgusa.com.

Balance books may be purchased in bulk for business, educational, or promotional use. For information, please contact your local bookseller or the Hachette Book Group Special Markets Department at special.markets@hbgusa.com.

The Wall of Awful is a trademark of Brendan Mahan.

Interior illustrations by Jesse Lundberg

Print book interior design by Bart Dawson

Library of Congress Control Number: 2026938506

ISBNs: 9781538778951 (hardcover), 9781538778975 (ebook), 9781538786024 (large print)

To my dad, Bill Mahan, who has always supported
my writing and without whom this
book doesn't happen.

And in memory of my mom, Peggy Mahan.
I wish you were here to see what all that
studying you helped me with led to.

CONTENTS

OVERCOMING the WALL of AWFUL

FOREWORD

by Jessica McCabe, creator and host of *How to ADHD*

The first time I heard about the Wall of Awful, I was sitting in an unassuming side room at an ADHD conference, nearly ten years ago.

Pre-pandemic. Pre-TikTok. Pre the world collectively realizing that maybe "just try harder" was advice akin to "burn out faster."

At the time, I was still early in my career as the creator and host of *How to ADHD*. I was there on my own dime, not because I could afford to be, but because I was desperate to understand my own brain—and to bring anything useful I learned back to a community that was just as hungry for answers as I was.

A handful of people were scattered around big round tables, surrounded by empty chairs, which made the space feel awkwardly oversized. This session had sounded amazing. I glanced around at the empty seats and quietly wondered if I was in the right place.

A short man with salt-and-pepper hair and

unmistakable teacher energy stepped to the front of the room. He stood beside an easel, paused, and scanned the room perceptively. He began.

"My name is Brendan Mahan."

He followed this with a string of letters and credentials that loosely translated to: *I know my shit.*

For the next forty-five minutes, Brendan did something quietly extraordinary.

He never touched the easel.

There were no slides.

No flash.

Instead, he put words to something I had lived with my entire life but had never been able to explain: the Wall of Awful.

He didn't frame our struggles to do tasks that "should" be easy as laziness. Or a character flaw. Or a lack of motivation. Or even an ADHD struggle.

He framed it as learning.

The Wall of Awful, he explained, is built from past experiences—shame, failure, frustration, criticism. Each brick laid, often unintentionally, by moments where we tried, struggled, and absorbed the message that we had failed.

He put a name to the moment where it looks—especially from the outside—like nothing is happening, even though, internally, plenty is: "We're Climbing the Wall of Awful."

As Brendan continued, I started thinking about the people I loved. The people I got frustrated with. The ones who took forever to start tasks I *knew* would be quick.

Tasks that didn't have Walls of Awful for me.

Tasks I didn't associate with guilt or failure.

I winced as I realized how often my attempts to emphasize the importance of a task had probably added bricks to someone else's Wall—maybe right as they were trying to climb it.

Brendan didn't stop at explaining the problem. He explained how we tend to approach it: the ways that don't work, the ways that work but hurt us, and the ways that actually work *and* are kind to our brains. He offered strategies without judgment and a framework instead of a mandate.

I left that room fired up.

This was something *everyone* needed to know.

My channel was—and still is—dedicated to helping people with ADHD and other executive function challenges work *with* their brains instead of against them. Metaphors are one of my favorite tools, because a good metaphor doesn't just explain—it gives you something to grab on to when things get hard.

The Wall of Awful was the most useful metaphor I had ever heard.

I asked Brendan if I could share it. We collaborated

on videos that reached millions of people all over the world, and we were careful to do the concept justice—because this wasn't just a clever idea. It was a reframe that could change how people saw themselves.

Over time, we became friends. When I finished my own book, Brendan sent me a bright yellow T-shirt with a red brick wall and words I still wear proudly:

"I Climbed my Wall of Awful."

Ironically, a Wall of Awful popped up for me while writing this foreword—because I cared so much about getting it right.

It's easy to assume that when people don't do something, it's because they don't care. But I've found the opposite is often true. The more we care, the bigger our Walls often become—and the more support we need to get over them.

That's why this book matters.

This isn't about forcing yourself through resistance or bullying yourself into productivity. It's about understanding what's actually happening when things feel impossible—and giving yourself options that don't involve shame as a motivator.

It's full of strategies you can use not just to get *this* thing done *today*, but to make your future Walls of Awful less painful. Less powerful.

Because the Wall doesn't guard the things that don't matter.

It stands in front of the things we value most.
Hey, Brendan?
You Climbed your Wall of Awful.*
And, reader?
You can, too.

—Jessica McCabe

* Dope.

MAKE THIS BOOK WORK FOR YOU

This book is written with neurodiversity in mind. So I've built in various supports to make it more accessible. If you need them, these supports should help. If you don't, they shouldn't hinder anything. As an example of a support, ideas that I think are particularly important are **bolded to make them easier to find**.

The text has a number of sidebars and bulleted lists, both to make the information easier to digest and to provide you with landmarks as you flip through the pages in search of ideas you want to revisit. There are even **landmarks at the chapter level**. Look for one-sentence summaries at the beginning of chapters and a "cheat sheet" (review) and action step guide at the end of each chapter. These will make finding information later easy.

This book is a web of ideas that does not have to be read in order. I will point you to ideas in other areas with **underlined chapter numbers** to make them easier to find, for example: see <u>Chapter 3</u>. I don't expect you to immediately hop over to that other chapter. I just want you to know where to find the additional information if you need it.

Engage with the book in whatever ways serve you best—get a friend to read and discuss it with you, grab a notebook and take notes on ideas it gives you, or draw pictures of the concepts, write notes in the margins when you agree or disagree with me about things, or fold corners. Read one chapter today and another in six months. In other words, do whatever you need to make it an interactive experience.

But don't stress. **You can always come back and read a section or sections again** in the future, and in fact, you might want to. Think of this book more like a manual than something you have to read once and know forever. **When you hit a Wall of Awful, go back through the table of contents** and see if you can find a section to read for ideas on how to get past it. This can be a toolbox if you let it.

INTRODUCTION

We've all been there. We need to write an email, but we can't seem to sit down to do it. We walk through our house and know we need to clean it, but we just...don't. Or we get up early on Saturday knowing that we have to do yardwork, yet somehow we find ourselves doing other things—anything other than yardwork. And then, finally, at ten in the morning, after waking up at seven, we start.

Why does it take hours to start the task we wanted to do?

We know *how*. The task *should* be easy. But we can't seem to start, and we don't know why. It turns out our negative emotions around the task, our fear, anger, disappointment, and judgment, have built up until there's an emotional wall blocking our way. We struggle, and that struggle can make us feel bad about ourselves. This is the Wall of Awful. It's the emotional barrier that makes the task *feel* overwhelming and impossible.

When we face the Wall of Awful without the tools to cope with it, we fall into strategies that don't work, things like staring at the Wall or trying to walk around it. We avoid the situation entirely, until the pain of *not* doing the task becomes greater than the pain of doing it.

As the task becomes more overwhelming, either because we mess up more often or we avoid starting at all, the pain we have to experience in order to start also gets bigger. Eventually the consequences are so severe that we lock up entirely, or we can only get the job done by acting with anger and damaging ourselves or those around us.

Fortunately, we don't have to depend on pain to get past the block. We can get past our Walls of Awful in other, healthier ways. We can take control!

This book is about the Wall of Awful, where it comes from, and what makes it bigger. But it's also about how to get *past* the Wall of Awful—in the moment, and in the long term—without having to depend on suffering. Consider it your cheat sheet to do the things you want to do.

WHAT THIS BOOK IS AND ISN'T

I'm writing about productivity but not in the traditional sense. This is not about how to go do another seventy-five not-very-useful things. Instead, it's about facing difficult things so that you can make progress on what's important to you.

Use the Wall of Awful as a model to talk to the people in your life about what's most difficult to you and them. Use it to talk to your spouse, your children, your friends, your employees, or your boss in a way that's productive and helpful rather than condemning. Talking about failure and struggle is hard. But everyone understands a wall.

The Wall of Awful is a reason for why things might be hard to do. It is not, however, an excuse to not do them. Use the ideas here to do more of the things you want to do *when* you want to do them. Consider using it to help others do the things they consider important, too.

You Are Worthwhile

I often feel like I'm splitting hairs when I talk about the Wall of Awful. Am I encouraging people to do the things they want and need to do even if those things are hard? Yes. I am. Am I trying to help people to rise to the challenges of their daily lives and push themselves toward a more hopeful future? Absolutely. Am I saying that I think your productivity dictates your worth? Not even a little bit.

There are a lot of people who embrace "hustle culture." They talk about *grinding* like it's a worthy pursuit, when it's really just a road to burnout. They place great emphasis on making millions of dollars, as though that somehow makes you a more valid person. (Side note: Most of the people making these claims are not millionaires.)

That's not my lens. I want you to read this book and use what you learn to be the best version of you that you can be. If that's being a millionaire—great! If it means that you're not going to be a millionaire, but you finally establish a solid sleep routine, have that hard conversation you've been avoiding, or regularly go to that yoga class you keep forgetting about—I'm just as proud.

Take from this book what is useful, and don't let the "Cult of Productivity" determine your self-worth.

WHERE TO START

This is a book about hope. So I want to start with encouragement and focus on solutions.

Because I wrote this book for people with executive function challenges (things like ADHD, burnout, anxiety, and depression, among others), it's not something you have to read front to back as a unit. Instead, it's designed to be **read out of order as needed**. Start in the middle or the end—or jump back and forth!—whatever works for your brain. I've even added some resources at the end of the book for additional help, including:

- Appendix 1—What the Emotions of the Wall of Awful Are Telling Us
- Appendix 2—How Do You Know If It's a Wall of Awful?
- Appendix 3—Decrease Your Anxiety and Get Ready to Climb Your Wall
- Appendix 4—How to Climb the Wall of Awful
- Appendix 5—Climbing the Wall of Awful Quick-Start Worksheet

If you're already familiar with the Wall of Awful, feel free to skip Chapter 1. Though you might want to read that part even if you are familiar—I've added things to that chapter that are not in the brief YouTube videos on the subject or on the various podcast interviews you may have seen or heard.

Of course, if you prefer videos, do a web search for the "Wall of Awful" and "How to ADHD" for a good introductory video to get started. Then you can come back to Chapter 2, on anxiety, Chapter 3, on skills and resources, or start anywhere else you'd like.

A PREVIEW OF STRATEGIES

Once I've finished setting the table by describing the Wall of Awful and its components, we'll talk about the five strategies people use to try to get past the Wall of Awful. Some are effective, and some are not.

- **The two strategies that never work** to get past the Wall of Awful are (1) staring at it and (2) going around it (both covered in Chapter 4).
- **An unhealthy strategy that *does* work** (while causing damage) is Smashing through the Wall (Chapter 5).
- **The two healthy strategies that work** are putting a door in it (Chapter 6) and Climbing the Wall (Chapter 7).

The chapters on change (Chapter 8), habits (Chapter 9), and planning (Chapter 10) round out the book by helping us understand and embrace long-term strategies to better manage our Walls over time.

We all face Walls—it's normal and natural to struggle—but we can overcome them with practice and care. This book is your toolbox. It's here for you whenever you need it; all you have to do is open it back up.

Your Walls of Awful may have felt overwhelming in the past. I'm here to make them easier. You *can* do this.

JUST FOR FUN: COOKIE SCAVENGER HUNT!

In retrospect, I talk about cookies a lot in this book. (They're delicious!) So, just for fun, I've added an icon to the pages where cookies come up. Consider this your notification of a cookie scavenger hunt!

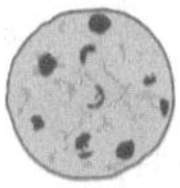

PART 1

THE WALL

CHAPTER ONE

WHAT IS THE WALL OF AWFUL?

> If you already know about the Wall of Awful from the YouTube video, you might want to skip to Chapter 2.

Sometime in 2015, I was in the kitchen of a coaching client, talking to her about her middle school son's challenges. While we were talking, I watched him take the notebooks and papers out of his backpack at a glacial pace.

"I don't understand why it takes him so long to get his stuff out." Mom was confused and concerned and looking to me for answers.

I understood. I was that kid when I was in middle school. I knew the dread that was building up in him as he had to do something that had already been a struggle for years. This time, though, I explained the problem in a way I never had before.

I'll never forget what I said. "It's sort of like there's a Wall of Awful between him and his homework." My brain immediately exploded with the idea. I went on to explain to Mom that there was a wall of negative emotions between her son and his homework. "He has to get past that Wall in order to start." It all made sense to her; she immediately identified situations in her own life where the idea applied.

A few months later, I went to a conference on autism and social thinking. I shared the idea at my table. One tablemate said, "That's great, but how do you get past it?" Of course! Identifying the problem wasn't enough. I had to help people solve it.

Soon, I was using the Wall of Awful to help my adult clients accomplish their goals, presenting on it at conferences, and sharing it on podcasts like the *Neurodiversity Podcast* and YouTube channels like *How to ADHD*.

Eventually, people began to tell me how much the Wall of Awful idea meant to them—they commented on social media, wrote about it on their blogs, and talked to me at conferences. Mental health clinicians, coaches, and social workers from around the world have told me how much it has helped their clients.

My idea from the kitchen that day has caught on so widely because **the Wall of Awful makes invisible**

struggles visible. It helps us recognize and talk about the emotions that get in our way. And it helps us talk about and overcome our challenges directly and without shame.

I Almost Forgot to Introduce Myself

I'm a former teacher and principal. I have some fancy letters after my name, but more importantly, I'm a mental health clinician turned ADHD and neurodiversity coach, consultant, and trainer. I've worked with adults and kids with a variety of challenges over many years; you'll read some of their stories throughout this book. (I've changed their names and other identifying details for privacy purposes.) And you probably know me as the host of the *ADHD Essentials Podcast*, where I interview experts on mental health, productivity, and relationships to help people better understand their unique brains.

I've coached clients through and given talks about the Wall of Awful extensively. The strategies that I cover in this book work. There are people all over the world sending me emails telling me that these strategies have worked for them. Odds are, the strategies and tactics in this book will work for you—or they will spark ideas to create your own strategies for your own situation. I wrote this book in an effort to make the world a little bit better by helping people understand the struggles of both themselves and each other. (I find that conflict is reduced when understanding increases.)

I'm also the husband of an incredibly intelligent and understanding wife (who I love to dance with!) and the proud father of two of the most creative and resilient twin sons a guy could ask for.

You've probably noticed another name on the cover; Alex Hughes Capell is my co-author. She's ghostwritten nineteen books with various business leaders and experts in their field. She's also the author of the science fiction mystery series Mindspace Investigations, published under the name Alex Hughes. She's a shameless nerd as well as a member of the mental health community, and the two together mean she knows a lot about psychology, health, and brain and behavior. Since Alex is used to being behind the scenes, in the rare cases she makes it onto the page explicitly, she speaks in the third person.

Alex and I have spent the last years having intense conversations about ADHD, mental health, neuroscience and psychology, the nature of reality, and how books work. When I invited Alex to work with me on this book, she was delighted to accept. The Wall of Awful is her personal nemesis, and she's extensively tested these ideas on both herself and her nine-year-old, with grand results.

EVERYONE IS DOING THE BEST THEY CAN

"Starting," what psychologists call *activation* or *task initiation*, is heavily impacted by emotions. Strong negative emotions can sit between us and the task, preventing us from activating.

These struggles are normal. Everybody—regardless of their place in life and how their brain works—has struggles. It doesn't make us less than, and it doesn't make us bad. However, if we give in to that desire to avoid our struggles too often, we are impeding ourselves. We stunt our mental growth, and we prevent ourselves from developing the skills we need to accomplish what we *want* to accomplish.

A core belief of mine is that everyone is doing the best that they can. Everyone wants to do well, and everyone wants to be included by the people around them.* So, when we encounter a Wall of Awful, we're not lazy or difficult. We're not broken. We're doing our best—we're just facing an emotional block.

---

* Shoutout to Dr. Ross Greene.

In the same way, if we're doing our best but we're having trouble with something, we don't have to give up. We also don't have to "try harder"—we can try differently. We can look for skills or resources that we presently lack so that we can get past the block. Just like any obstacle on an obstacle course, we can assume there is a way past it, no matter how overwhelming it *feels*.

The first step is recognizing the block. Once we do, we can work to see it clearly and plan to get past it. When we can see our Walls clearly, we *can* overcome them.

The Wall of Awful *is* real. It is painful and difficult. But that only matters as much as we let it. **All the good things in life are on the other side of the Wall of Awful.** And we can get to the other side.

The Wall of Awful and Mental Health

This book is not intended for anyone in a mental health crisis. If you're at the point that you can't seem to get out of bed, getting stable is probably your best first step. You'll need to find your way to talk therapy, medication, family support, or other help, until you can make your situation stable again. **There is hope, and it does get better.** Keep fighting, keep looking, until you find the resources you need to start to get better. Tomorrow will be different, and eventually, a day after that will be better. You'll find your way back to building a life you love—if you keep going. Focus there.

If you're not in crisis but are managing a chronic or long-term mental health condition or conditions, this book will serve as additional help. If you're stable enough to think ahead, to strategize to get past your Walls of Awful, *and* you have the spare capacity to do so, this book will give you the tools to do that. It's extra help to support you in your quest to do better despite your challenges.

Another book that we recommend if you're stable, and you need to get things done despite any kind of mental health challenge, is *Get It Done When You're Depressed* by Julie A. Fast (yes, even if your primary struggle is not depression). The strategies she details will complement the approaches we present in this book.

ACCEPTING OUR LIMITATIONS EMPOWERS US

Be aware that some of what I will ask you to do will not be easy. When dealing with the emotional overwhelm and blocks that are the Walls of Awful, sometimes you'll have to struggle. This is not going to be a magic bullet, and it will take time to see change. You can still do it.

That said, we all have limitations. When we figure out what those limitations are, we define our sandbox. Once we know what that sandbox is, we can play inside it all we want. We can learn to do the things we want within our sandbox and find ways to ask for help or build systems to help us outside of it.

Sometimes things are hard, and we all have limitations. But we don't have to let either of those things stop us from living a full life and doing what we need to do. We just have to accept that things may look different for us than they do for our neurotypical peers. Comparison is the thief of joy.

And we may find we are capable of more than we think, if we approach the problems differently.

DEFINING THE WALL

Imagine you're facing a task that you dread. You have to do it. But the idea of doing that task makes you feel stressed and anxious, even overwhelmed. And so you do anything to avoid it.

Or maybe you are facing a task that you don't dread at first. But the longer you avoid that task, the more stressed and anxious you feel, and the more dreadful it becomes.

In both cases, you are facing a Wall of Awful.

The Wall of Awful is the emotional barrier that

is built through repeated failure and struggle. It sits between us and the things we want to do, preventing us from initiating new tasks and/or taking risks. Everybody has a Wall of Awful, but most of us with ADHD, anxiety, autism, and other flavors of neurodivergence have several, because the way our brains work makes the Walls form more easily and more often.

The Wall of Awful can feel like a roil of emotions—uncertainty, anxiety, guilt, shame—getting in the way of our ability to start. At other times the Wall is simply a *lack of action*. We see the thing in front of us, and we are capable of doing it. We have the necessary resources and skills. We know how to do it. But we don't. The emotional energy needed to get started isn't there. The task just doesn't happen.

The Wall of Awful isn't just about ourselves, though. If we observe someone else's encounter with their own Wall of Awful, it might appear that they're not engaging—even if the task seems easy to do. We see the Wall of Awful when someone stress cleans instead of making a phone call, or when a kid takes forever to get their stuff out of their backpack before doing their homework. And we see it when someone sits staring at the wall rather than beginning a project that's already overdue.

So, this model doesn't just help us understand our own struggles but can also help us *talk to someone else* about theirs (or our own!).

TYPICAL WALLS

Here are some common Walls of Awful:

- **Money.** Whether it's budgeting, paying bills, or anything else, most people have a Wall of Awful around money because money is so often used as a (false) proxy for a person's worth.
- **Work-related and similar tasks.** Early struggles in school can lead to difficult emotions around work tasks as an adult.
- **Communication.** Being neurodivergent often means feeling like we aren't understood by the mainstream.
- **Friendships and other relationships.** Lifelong struggles with communication can lead to challenges in making friends and managing relationships into adulthood.
- **Employment.** If we've struggled in a job or if our employment history is checkered, we may have a Wall of Awful around finding a new job. We might struggle with performance or worry we're not making our employer happy.
- **Boring, repetitive tasks.** Particularly for neurodivergent people and those with ADHD,

doing repetitive tasks can feel painful and bring about strong negative emotions.

- **Things that are important but not urgent.** Many of us confuse urgency with importance. This leads to us putting out all the little fires of the day, while avoiding the more important causes of those fires.
- **Health and mental health.** People can develop Walls of Awful around going to the gym, doing self-care, or managing a chronic or mental illness.
- **Anything undefined or unclear.** The more vague or undefined the task we're facing, the more overwhelming it will be. If we don't understand the expectations, our uncertainty leaves room for anxiety to build a Wall.

This list is by no means exhaustive; Walls of Awful can come up in any category of life. Anything that triggers strong negative emotions is a place for a potential Wall.

WHERE THE WALL COMES FROM

Despite our best intentions, we struggle and we fail. We're human.

Every time we fail, we get a brick in the Wall that will stand between us and that task the next time we face it—a failure brick. Then, because we're likely to be disappointed in ourselves for that failure, we get a disappointment brick. And since we care about the opinions of others, we get a disappointment brick for everyone related to that task whose opinion matters to us and whom we may have let down. If the bricks pile up high enough, the Wall blocks our way.[1]

For example, if Hannah messes up a critical TPS report at work, she will get a failure brick. She'll also get a disappointment brick for herself. And she'll get disappointment bricks for anyone else affected by this mistake—her boss, her coworkers, her friends, her spouse.

Like the rest of us, Hannah worries that people will reject her if she disappoints them. That leads to rejection bricks on top of those disappointment bricks. And if she knows that her coworkers had to stay late to correct her mistake? Guilt bricks get added as well.

If this is a one-time mistake, odds are Hannah's bricks won't amount to much. But if it keeps happening, she'll start feeling ashamed—like *she's* the mistake. She'll move beyond guilt bricks and start getting

---

See Notes section at end of book for all numbered references.

massive blocks of shame. Blocks are bigger than bricks and are more emotionally charged. They make the Wall bigger and create more resistance as you climb, making it considerably harder to get to the other side of the Wall.

If Hannah fails at her task enough, she will have a hard time starting her reports. She'll stare at the screen for an hour and a half, unable to key in the first number. Her Wall for this task will become massive.

Sometimes It's Not a Wall of Awful—It's a Boundary

Not all emotional barriers are the Wall of Awful. Sometimes we get strong negative emotions because something is against our values. It's crossing an internal boundary that we need to respect.

For example, if someone is working at a company that is taking advantage of their customers through shady business practices, she might not be comfortable at her job. She may even find herself having trouble doing what's being asked of her. This person doesn't have a Wall of Awful for her job; her problems with engaging in those tasks stem from her morals and ethics.

Crossing her own boundaries to support the company will do her damage over time. Her best solution is *not* to try to talk herself out of the line in the sand she's facing, but rather to go find another job. Treating that line like a Wall of Awful would only prolong the problem.

It's not always easy to tell the difference between a Wall of Awful's negative emotions and the feelings we get when we are being forced to cross one of our own boundaries. But the difference will be obvious if we get clear on our own values. What do we, as a person, stand for? Are we comfortable on the other side with what we have done? Are we comfortable with how we have allowed others to treat us? If not, that's a strong clue that the line is a boundary, not a Wall.

On the other side of a Wall of Awful is relief, and likely a better ability to do the thing. On the other side of a boundary is a strong feeling of discomfort, and likely regret. We should never use the concept of the Wall of Awful to make ourselves or anyone else do things we find abhorrent. Walls should be climbed and boundaries respected.

WALLS BEGIN IN THE PAST

Our Walls of Awful don't just show up out of the blue when we're adults. They started forming in childhood, when we struggled to write an essay or couldn't understand the math assignment. They were built by failures—and the harsh feelings and judgments that came with them.[2] When we encounter activities similar to those we have struggled with in the past, we hit the Wall.

If someone struggled with math as a kid, they might find that paying bills is uniquely difficult for them as an adult. But the problem may have more to do with their feelings about math in childhood than their feelings about money as an adult.

Of course, Walls can also be built in adulthood. Walls connected to relationships are a good example of this. One of my clients had a very active social life until experiencing a terrible falling-out with his friend group in his late twenties. Now in his forties, he is much less inclined to risk that kind of rejection, and tends to interact with people online more than in person.

WALLS CAN INTERACT

My client Ashley was telling me about how she had a hard time discussing money with her partner. She tried to talk to him, but it took her half an hour to even begin the conversation. She was embarrassed about her struggles in managing money, and her inability to talk about those feelings was daunting and overwhelming.

She loved her partner and couldn't understand why she couldn't speak up.

In the course of our discussion, I reflected on her other challenges, which we had discussed in the past. I pointed out that her Wall of Awful made sense on a few levels: (1) Ashley had a math disability in school, and (2) had struggled financially in the past, having trouble earning enough money for many years. Historically, she had also (3) struggled to advocate for herself and ask for what she needed. No wonder she was having trouble engaging in a conversation that touched all three! It made sense that Ashley took thirty minutes to even start the conversation with her partner—that was ten minutes per Wall. Thankfully, she powered through that difficult situation, and her partner was both understanding and supportive.

When we're dealing with our own and other people's Walls, it's important to understand that the barrier in front of us may not be a single mammoth Wall. It may be a series of them. When facing more than one Wall of Awful, an apparently straightforward task can carry with it layers of hidden emotional triggers, as our Walls often interact with one another in surprising ways. Do not despair, though; dealing with each Wall in its turn, you can find your way to the other side.

THE WALL LOOKS DIFFERENT IN DIFFERENT PEOPLE

The Wall of Awful is an anxiety response (I'll discuss anxiety in depth in Chapter 2). Because of this, it looks different in different people. The *way* that anxiety manifests may vary depending on the day, and whether the person tends toward fight, flight, or freeze. In fact, the response may even change depending on the situation and whether or not they recognize the Wall!

One person might get frustrated and angry. Another person may become frozen and have trouble doing anything about the task. A third might just avoid the task altogether. When we dread a task, the negative emotions attached to that task make it much more difficult to engage. They're uncomfortable, and people generally try to avoid being uncomfortable.

In the short run, disengaging gives us relief from the intense discomfort and anxiety that come with the task. But avoiding pain in the short term won't help us get what we want (or need!) in the long run.

The Neurodiversity Penalty

Those of us who are neurodivergent—with conditions like ADHD, autism, obsessive compulsive disorder, or depression—are likely to struggle more with starting and continuing projects and develop stronger negative emotions around those struggles as a result. Instead of small, manageable guilt bricks, neurodivergent people regularly add large, immobile shame blocks. We often assume the problem is *us* rather than just the situation we face. Everyone has Walls of Awful, but for neurodivergent people who struggle more anyway, our Walls are generally larger, and we have more of them.

FACING THE WALL OF AWFUL

As soon as we realize that we are facing a Wall, we can start to be thoughtful and tactical about getting past it. We can do *something* to get ourselves activated. But if we don't realize we have a Wall, the Wall will tend to drive our behavior without us meaning it to. It will grow—and get worse—without intentional effort. Unless we are thoughtful about getting past our Walls, over time we risk our Walls becoming so large that we don't even notice them, like a fish that doesn't know it's in the ocean. When that happens, very little will get done, and we will tend to feel very frustrated with ourselves.

Noticing when we encounter a Wall of Awful is critical to getting past it, but it's not always easy. I literally created the concept, and there are still times I don't recognize that I'm facing a Wall. But you can become better at noticing and navigating your personal Walls.

Awareness is always the first step. And that's what this book is for.

Identifying a Wall of Awful

While there's no absolute process for identifying a Wall of Awful, try asking the following questions to help:

- **Does it feel overwhelming?** If the task gives you a headache, stomachache, or makes you feel tense or irritable, you're probably overwhelmed by it and may be facing a Wall of Awful.
- **Is the task hard to do or hard to start?** If it's hard to start but easy to do, you probably have a Wall of Awful for it. If it's both hard to start and hard to do, you might have a Wall for the task, or you might be low on energy.
- **Are there broad categories that you struggle with?** If you have trouble doing things that are related somehow, you might have a broader Wall of Awful. For example:
    - Things that feel icky—doing the dishes, picking up dog poop
    - Things that risk rejection—job interviews, making new friends

    - Things that involve money—buying expensive things, asking for a raise
    - Things that are loud—going to a bar, attending a concert
- **Is it something you've repeatedly failed at or been rejected for?** The pain of our repeated failures tends to echo when we encounter similar situations.
- **Are you having big feelings about something that isn't really all that big?** If you repeatedly feel frozen, furious, panicked, stuck beyond moving, or irritated out of proportion with the situation—all for the same task or category of tasks—you might have a Wall.

FAILURE HAPPENS TO EVERYONE

How we respond to failure is critical to managing the Walls of Awful that we have, and keeping new ones from forming. Rather than assuming that one failure means we can't ever do that task, we can assume that the problem we are facing has a solution. We just have to find it. If we can see failure as part of the process and if we can experiment with different solutions, we can learn from those efforts, whether they work or don't.

Rather than seeing our struggles as a value judgment

of our worth, we can see them as signposts telling us to look deeper.

Rejection Sensitivity

Rejection is hard for everyone. For many neurodivergent people, that challenge is amplified. We can react to even small rejections with huge storms of emotions. Rejection can lead to anxiety, self-doubt, shame, and feeling like we're inadequate or uniquely broken. These feelings can be so strong that we overcompensate by becoming people pleasers, putting massive amounts of effort into avoiding any *possibility* of rejection—and the feelings that result.

Further complicating things, we often see rejection where it isn't. For example, we often take constructive criticism as rejection. This can lead to overwhelming anxiety at work when a minor meeting with our boss regarding an area we need to improve upon leads to us thinking we're about to be fired. And our reaction runs the risk of becoming a self-fulfilling prophecy.

PEOPLE OFTEN UNDERSTAND

My client Kai had a spotty employment history. He lost a job during the COVID pandemic. He was so distracted and consumed by the pandemic that he was unable to focus.

Before too long, he got a job at a better company. Kai did amazing work for them, but two years later he hurt himself lifting weights. That same week, his wife was diagnosed with a terminal illness, and he completely lost his ability to focus—again. He became concerned about his performance at work and the risk of getting fired.

We strategized about what to do, and I told him he needed to get ahead of the problem. After a huge amount of emotional work Climbing his Wall of Awful on this topic, he finally sat down with his boss and told him what was going on. Kai was surprised to learn they would be accommodating. His boss told him that he could take two weeks off—paid—and he could even reduce his hours while he cared for his wife thereafter.

By getting past his Wall, Kai was able to learn that his new company had mechanisms in place to handle hard situations and that he could receive support. The Wall about his work performance is still there, and when tough situations come up, it still takes effort to climb it. But it does not take nearly as much effort at his new job as it did at the old one. Accepting our Walls sometimes means having hard conversations and giving people opportunities to show up for us. Sometimes, they do. Sometimes, they give us two weeks off with pay.

OUR BELIEFS CAN AFFECT OUR WALLS

Our mindset matters, and it can really affect a Wall of Awful. For example, if we are not careful, we may create self-fulfilling prophecies, where we are convinced we will fail and then, intentionally or unintentionally, take actions that cause failure. If, as I discussed earlier, Hannah messes up the TPS report, she may add several bricks to her Wall. If she messes up on, or even just fails to start, *many* TPS reports, she might begin to think she is incapable of doing TPS reports.

It isn't necessarily true that Hannah will always fail at her TPS reports. But even if it were true, writing TPS reports is a skill she can learn. But if she believes she will always fail at TPS reports and stops trying, it becomes a self-fulfilling prophecy. Hannah's belief might make it impossible for her to Climb her Wall without help.

Self-fulfilling prophecies can undermine the things we want. They create inaccurate conclusions that lead us down the road to anxiety and depression. Our mindset can make the Wall seem impossibly big and unmanageable. But it's not.

Our mindset is affected by the society and families we grew up in, as well as our experiences with friends, teachers, jobs, and, of course, books. It grows and changes as we learn and experience the world. We have far more to do with our Walls than we may first believe, and that's good. The more we learn about the concept of the Wall of Awful and the more we learn about strategies to get around our Walls, the better we can navigate our challenges.

The Wall is a barrier. It gets in the way of us doing hard things, but it's not impassable. We can Climb the Wall, we can put a door in it, or we can even punch a hole in it! But to do so, we first have to realize that progress is possible.

PUT DOWN THE WEIGHT

In one of my parenting groups, I had a parent whose son revealed to him that he'd done no homework all year. The son was a freshman in high school. First the parent group celebrated with the parent that they had built enough trust for the son to be willing to tell them what had happened—that was a huge win. But we then dug into the issue.

The parent asked his son why he hadn't done his homework. The teen said that he needed the weekend to relax, to hide in his room, because school was so stressful. I told the parent that I believed their son saying he needed to hide but suspected the reason wasn't because of school. The teen needed to relax because he was carrying guilt and shame. No matter how much he relaxed, he couldn't put down the homework assignments he hadn't done. Over time, they got heavier and heavier, and he got more and more stressed.

Some Walls of Awful are us carrying around tasks we haven't done. We never check the box, and we never know how it turns out. We just carry it. But if we would just engage with the task, even if it goes wrong, we might eventually be able to set it down.

Over the next weeks, my client supported his son through completing the assignments, and over time the son felt better. Soon he didn't have to hide in his room anymore; even though he wasn't able to make up all the grades he'd lost, at least he knew how it had turned out. He was freed from the weight of the uncertainty and fear.

Back when I used to work with clients on résumés and job search support, I saw people fall into the same trap. They would go on job interviews, then not hear back from the company. And it weighed on them! Or sometimes people were waiting for medical news that worried them. My advice was always the same—make the call. Even if the news was bad, the worst part would be over quickly, and they could figure out the next steps without the uncertainty.

A REASON IS NOT AN EXCUSE

The Wall of Awful is a reason why we might struggle to execute on a given task or tasks. It is not, however, an excuse to not do said task. If the task has been set for us, either by ourselves or someone else, and we feel pressure to follow it through, then we should assume the task is worth doing. We need to get past the Wall!

That means we will have to distinguish between a reason and an excuse. A *reason* is an explanation for why we might struggle to do something, or even fail to do it. Having a reason gives us permission to put down the emotional weight. It does not, however, give us permission to abdicate our responsibility to finish the task or clean up whatever problems happened as a result of our mistake. That's an excuse. The Wall of Awful is not an excuse.

The Wall of Awful model is intended to help us understand why we struggle in the areas we do. It gives us permission to put down many of the negative emotions created by those struggles that only serve to make things worse. The Wall of Awful model is not, however, intended to exempt us from our responsibilities to ourselves and to others.

ANXIETY LIES TO US

The emotional reality of the Wall of Awful is rooted in anxiety. The stories it tells us are frequently unhelpful, if not outright lies. The Wall tells us not to do the thing because there is pain in the thing. It claims that the task will be too hard or too overwhelming and that we cannot handle the thing, but none of that is true. We get *stronger* on the other side of struggle and even *more* capable of overcoming hard things.

The Wall also tells us that other people will not understand and that they will not care about us, but as you saw with Kai's story, this is frequently untrue. When we actively communicate and interact with our Walls, other people usually understand. When we give them an opportunity to support us, they often do.

Every instinct we have screams at us to stay on this side of the Wall, but those instincts are not helpful. They are not serving us, even though in some ways, it's a self-protective device. But here's the thing: Life is on the other side of the Wall of Awful. Even the hard things are better to wrestle with actively than deal with passively.

Since the Wall of Awful is an anxiety response, decreasing anxiety can provide some immediate relief. Therefore, it's helpful to understand where the emotion of anxiety comes from and how it works. Then we can work with our brains instead of against them and get past our Walls more easily.

CHEAT SHEET: WHAT IS THE WALL OF AWFUL?

1 When you avoid a task or a problem you dread, you're facing the Wall of Awful. You can have several Walls at once. Identifying each can help you overcome them. (See Appendix 2 for more information.)

2 **The Wall of Awful is the emotional impact of repeated failure and struggle** related to certain tasks. We all have Walls of Awful, but they're far more common in the lives of neurodivergent people.

3 The Wall of Awful is built from **strong negative emotions** and held together by **anxiety**. It shows up when we try to *activate* or begin or resume a task or project.

4 The Wall can look different in different people, from frustration and anger (fight), avoidance (flight), or being unable to do anything at all (freeze), no matter how hard the person tries.

5 The model allows us to quickly explain and talk about this struggle, which helps everyone involved to **stop feeling ashamed** and turn our attention to solving the problem.

6 Not all resistance is a Wall of Awful. Sometimes it's your brain's way of letting you know something is against your values. **Boundaries should be respected, but Walls can be overcome.**

ACTION STEP:

Make a list of any Walls of Awful you are facing now. Choose one that is bothering you, and read the rest of the book with that Wall in mind.

CHAPTER TWO

ANXIETY AND THE WALL OF AWFUL

> Anxiety changes the way the brain works in an attempt to protect you from danger. Unfortunately, the way it does that can cause problems for people who are neurodivergent.

Cleaning out a cluttered, messy bedroom is a process. In the beginning, we take out the garbage, pick up a few things, and it starts to feel better. But then we have to deal with the clutter. So we spread it out over the floor to organize what we have. If there's enough stuff, we might even move some of it to another room. The mess will feel worse than what we started with—to the point it's overwhelming. But, if we stick with it, throw out what we don't need, and then start creating space and systems, eventually we'll have a beautiful, organized bedroom. We'll be able to find what we need and literally sleep easier.

Our minds can work the same way. The Wall of Awful is an anxiety response intended to keep us safe. You can learn to get past the Wall—the rest of this book shares skills, resources, and strategies. But because the Wall is an anxiety response, it's worth spending a chapter talking about what anxiety is, how it works, and why it stops us. In other words, we have to pull out all our stuff and pile it on the floor.

Just reading about anxiety may feel a bit overwhelming. You can stop at any time, and come back when you're ready. And if you need some easy wins to get past your Wall in the meantime, feel free to jump ahead to Chapter 6 and come back once you're squared away. To get the most out of the book, though, and to get past Walls to do what we want, when we want, more consistently, we'll need the information in the next sections. There's a lot to it, but I've made it as short and practical as possible.

THE THINKING BRAIN IS DIFFERENT FROM THE SURVIVAL BRAIN

Below is a picture of the amygdala, a tiny organ about the size of a peanut sitting on your brain stem.*

* Yes, there are technically two of them. It should be amygdalae (maybe? It's been a long time since Greek class). But everyone in the ADHD/autistic, mental health, and neuroscience communities routinely says "amygdala" when discussing this part of the brain. So, we're being informal.

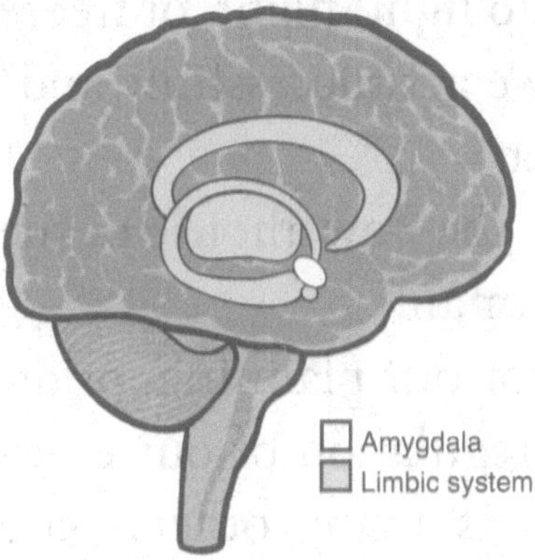

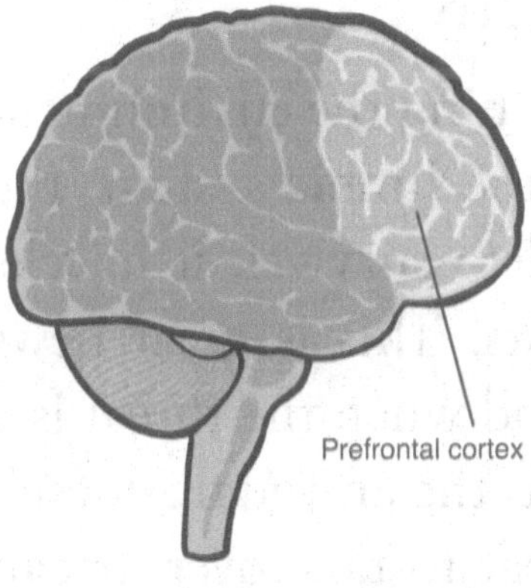

Evolutionarily speaking, the amygdala is in the oldest part of the brain, and we have it in common with lizards, birds, and dogs. When we perceive danger, the amygdala jumps into action and triggers massive brain and body changes designed to help us survive. Our information processing moves from the prefrontal cortex to the amygdala.* Adrenaline is released, causing our airways to open up and increase oxygen to our bloodstream. Our heart rate increases to pump that oxygen-rich blood to our

---

* The limbic system is a structure in the brain that contains many parts, including the amygdala, and is located below the cerebrum. It's connected to a number of things, like our sense of smell, hunger, and thirst. Critical for our purposes is the role it plays in our reaction to stressful situations, as it helps us process and manage our emotions, behaviors, and motivations. As stress and anxiety increase, the limbic system activates. If things get even more intense, then the amygdala will take full control from there. But for our purposes, the text simplifies to "emotional processing" and "fight or flight," sometimes blurring the line between the two.

muscles so we can act! We go into fight, flight, or freeze mode, and we stay there until we act successfully and/or get to the other side of danger.

This is the prefrontal cortex, the powerhouse of the brain, the part that makes us human.

This is the area responsible for our planning, prioritizing, sense of time, and the regulation of our emotions. These abilities—as well as many others—are sometimes jointly referred to as the executive functions, or executive function.

The Amygdala Is Obsessed with Safety

The amygdala is constantly scanning the environment for threats. Because it lies in the limbic system, the oldest part of the brain related to survival, it hijacks the brain when it senses threats. This is great news when we face a lion but less good when the threat is a scary email or your boss. In fact, the amygdala doesn't have to be right about the threat to take over. It can react to information it's misinterpreting, or even something you thought about in passing that's not based in reality.

When the amygdala activates, it can partially overrule the prefrontal cortex, making it harder to think rationally. If the threat is very strong and immediate, or if the amygdala senses multiple threats at once, it will outright hijack our processing from the prefrontal cortex. At that point, we are more of an emotional creature driven by our survival instincts than the rational, thinking human we strive to be.

This dynamic can cause problems for us in the long term.

ADHD, Anxiety, and Autism Make It Worse

Neurodiversity impacts how the prefrontal cortex and/or amygdala function. I have ADHD, which means my prefrontal cortex is not as developed as my wife's, because she doesn't have ADHD. Her prefrontal cortex is more powerful than mine, and it has more endurance than mine. My co-author, Alex, has an anxiety disorder, so her amygdala is hyperactive. It activates for more reasons and reacts more strongly when it does than your average person's. While the causes are different, the result for both of us is the same: Our amygdalas can take control more easily than they would if we were neurotypical, hers because it's more responsive and mine because I have more difficulty inhibiting that response.

This trend holds for most kinds of neurodiversity, just for different reasons.

- **With ADHD**, the prefrontal cortex is *underpowered* and the amygdala is normal.

- **With anxiety, OCD, and trauma disorders**, the prefrontal cortex is normal but the amygdala is *overpowered*.
- **With depression**, the prefrontal cortex (executive functions) becomes underpowered compared to how it used to be, potentially changing the balance of power in the brain toward the amygdala.
- **With autism**, the brain struggles to filter out sensory information, so the prefrontal cortex is more overwhelmed and the amygdala is more easily tripped than average.

Of course, many neurodivergent people have multiple challenges, and there are certainly other kinds of neurodiversity not listed here that can cause the same issue.

Fight, Flight, Freeze, and More

Different people react to the amygdala taking control in different ways. In fact, the same person may react differently in different situations. Here are some of the options.

- **Fight.** Someone acting out of this survival instinct will attack, either verbally or physically. (See Chapter 5.)

- **Flight.** This person will aggressively leave the situation, change or avoid the subject, and/or literally run away.
- **Freeze.** When freezing, someone will be unable to take action. They may or may not become physically still in practice; sometimes this results in feeling emotionally "stuck" and finding it difficult to think.

The three above are most directly related to the Wall of Awful, but these three are also common reactions:

- **Flock.** This survival strategy involves finding and surrounding oneself with other people. This may look like finding friends and allies, or it just might be finding comfort in a crowd.[1]
- **Fawn.** This strategy is common in survivors of complex trauma and involves lying, charming, and manipulating the dangerous person to decrease their threat. The fawn response breaks down at the highest levels of anxiety because it requires some prefrontal cortex ability to function.[2]
- **Fib.** Similar to the fawn strategy, when people feel under threat, they may lie to ease the tension or avoid the threat entirely. This mostly

happens in social situations, but even hiding is a form of fibbing.[3]

Anyone can use any of these strategies at any time—and often, several together. Individual people, however, tend to have one or two strategies that they go to first when under pressure.

THE WALL OF AWFUL BUILDS BY HIJACKING OUR SURVIVAL RESPONSE

The Wall of Awful is made of strong negative emotions, but the mortar that holds those bricks together is anxiety. Because facing difficult emotions and the situations causing them is hard, it is understandable that doing so might make us anxious. When the anxiety reaches the point that it's activating the amygdala, that's when the Wall arrives.*

Our brain gets in the way because it's trying to protect us. The amygdala is interpreting anxiety as a warning. But it doesn't care about long-term consequences

* You may or may not realize you're anxious, but the Wall doesn't arrive and stop you unless the anxiety is there with enough power to activate the amygdala.

and doesn't understand time. It only cares about keeping us safe in the moment, pushing us to punch back (fight), avoid that thing (flight), or shut down completely (freeze). Flight and freeze are the Wall of Awful. (We'll deal with fighting when we talk about Smashing the Wall in Chapter 5.)

It's important to remember that anxiety doesn't have any long-term plans beyond our immediate safety. If avoiding something will be bad later, anxiety only cares if the future pain is obvious and acute. If not doing something means we miss opportunities or stagnate instead of growing, anxiety does not care. Anxiety wants to keep us safe *now*. It only cares about later if failing to act means later will be much, much worse than now, *and* the anxiety is relatively low.

If the anxiety is turned up high enough, time has no meaning. There is only now, and if punching somebody in the face—or literally running away—feels like it would make things safer right now, anxiety is on board. Anxiety isn't thinking about getting in trouble later. This is why anxious people make seemingly bad choices; they struggle to think beyond now.

When it comes to the Wall, our brains are shutting us down or standing in our way because they are anxious and want us to be safe. But avoiding, freezing up, or endlessly procrastinating is damaging in the long term.

A Double-Edged Sword: Anxiety and Adrenaline

Many neurodivergent people who have trouble activating get into the habit of waiting until the last minute, turning urgency and anxiety into a short-term threat that allows the amygdala to get involved and release adrenaline. Because the threat is short term and concrete, the brain can focus and act to address it. Many people with ADHD, for example, come to rely on this burst of focused anxiety to get things done.

Unfortunately, this habit is a double-edged sword. It allows for action and creates motivation. But the amygdala can't see the long-term consequences, and relying on panic to start makes the prefrontal cortex become less practiced at getting us to activate without it. In the short term, someone relying on anxiety risks doing a terrible job at complex tasks that require deep thinking. Over the long term, relying on anxiety to act will result in burnout,[4] if not anxiety disorders, as other ways of starting fall out of use.

Too much anxiety, or the wrong kind, will turn regular stress into chronic stress and start triggering routine avoidance and shutdowns. A Wall of Awful will grow, and we'll have great difficulty starting. That's why people who use anxiety to activate tend to have more Walls than others and why their Walls grow bigger over the years.

It's also why neurodivergent people benefit from finding ways to activate *other* than anxiety and to use strategies to decrease anxiety and get past their Walls. Which is what the rest of this book is about.

WHAT MAKES ANXIETY WORSE VS. WHAT MAKES IT BETTER

Anxiety comes from four things, what I call the URPU model: uncertainty, rejection, powerlessness, and uncomfortableness. One can lead to another, and they often overlap. Being able to distinguish between them can help us feel more in control.

- **Uncertainty.** Anxiety worsens when you don't know what's coming next or you feel pressured to perform without being sure you can do it.
- **Rejection.** Even just the threat of rejection is at the core of a large portion of anxiety. We are often more afraid of the rejection that may come with failure than we are of the other problems our mistakes could cause.

- **Powerlessness.** Feeling powerless is stressful, especially when things are uncertain. The fewer choices we have or the less we feel like our choices have any impact, the more anxious we feel.
- **Uncomfortableness.** Being uncomfortable, either physically or emotionally, makes anxiety worse. Even just anticipating being uncomfortable can do the same. If writing an email creates difficult emotions, then the email makes you uncomfortable emotionally. And physical discomfort includes hunger, thirst, lack of sleep, pain, and uncomfortable furniture, among other things.

Thankfully, there are ways to oppose uncertainty, rejection, powerlessness, and uncomfortableness. The counter to the URPU model is CCAW: certainty, connection, agency, and well-being. We can leverage these things to decrease anxiety.

- **Certainty.** Understanding what's happening, why it happened, and what's coming next helps people feel safe and come back to their thinking brains.
- **Connection.** Humans are social creatures, so having trustworthy people around as company and support creates calm. Even the worst

situation becomes better with a loved one (or even a friendly, supportive stranger) next to us.

- **Agency.** We will calm down and start thinking more clearly when we can make decisions and see the impact of those decisions in a positive way. Feeling in control is empowering.
- **Well-being.** If discomfort adds anxiety, its opposite takes anxiety away. Anything that adds comfort, joy, or ease into a situation can help, from listening to our favorite songs, to snuggling up with soft blankets, to eating a good meal.

While URPU and CCAW are simple ideas, they play out in nearly every arena of life. When we use CCAW deliberately, we can turn difficult situations around in ways that would not be possible otherwise. **So these ideas will come up many times over the course of the book.**

In the meantime, I'll give you an example from my own life that illustrates how these concepts can play out in real life.

One of the things I talk to my kids about fairly often is the conflict between consuming and creating. It's a way to help them (and me!) get off their phones and spend less time doomscrolling. Doomscrolling is deceptive. It appears to provide connection and certainty, but in practice the constant feed creates uncertainty, rejection, powerlessness, and uncomfortableness. Even the positive moments do not have any lasting nutritional value. It increases anxiety and decreases mental health.[5]

Creating, on the other hand, provides lots of long-term benefits. Things like painting, writing, creating podcasts, or even playing games with friends are life-giving. They provide agency and certainty because of the decisions they require. They create authentic well-being and help us make connections when we spend time with other creators or share what we've made with others. They regulate our emotions and provide joy.

DIFFERENT KINDS OF ANXIETY AND STRESS

According to Lynn Lyons, LICSW, when we combine chronic **stress** with **worrying** about the future, we become **anxious**. Anxiety can be healthy in the short term. For example, if you live in Atlanta and see a black widow spider walking across your pillow once a week, anxiety about your sleeping location is normal and will save your life.

But if you move to a new home in Alaska and continue to worry about that spider, your anxiety has become unhealthy. (And if you worry about everything to this degree, you may have an anxiety disorder and need professional support. You are not alone.)

As a note, stress can *also* be healthy or unhealthy, and it can come from many sources.

Physical stressors include:

- **Unfulfilled body needs.** The body finds states like hunger, thirst, muscle exhaustion, and lack of sleep to be stressful.
- **Sensory discomfort.** Loud noises, itchy sweaters, and extreme temperatures are sensory irritants. Of course, there are many more!
- **Pain.** Regardless of source, pain feels threatening to the nervous system.
- **Illness.** If you're fighting off a cold, you have fewer physical resources to spend.

Mental stressors include:

- **Ongoing environmental issues.** Poverty, racism, survival needs, relationship conflict, and work pressure are all examples.
- **Short-term challenges.** Difficult projects at work, home repair, and travel can all add significant short-term stress.

- **Concern for loved ones.** Anything from our friend's chronic illness to our child's struggles in school can add to our mental load.

YOUR BRAIN DOESN'T KNOW THE DIFFERENCE BETWEEN STRESS, WORRY, AND ANXIETY

It sounds obvious when you say it out loud, but bear with me: You only have one brain. Your amygdala doesn't know the difference between different kinds of stress, worry, and anxiety. It will kick in at a certain level of input *regardless of the cause*. Perhaps even worse, those stress and anxiety numbers add up, and anything from pain to mundane worries can contribute to your overall score.

If you haven't slept or eaten in twenty-four hours, that's stressful to the body and will increase your baseline anxiety score. The same goes if you have a headache—pain triggers stress. Sensory discomfort, like an itchy sweater or a blaring fire alarm, particularly in people with very sensitive nervous systems, like Autistic folks, will increase the score too. *Anything* that puts extra stress on the body or mind impacts the anxiety scale. The calmest person in the world will still struggle if they haven't slept or eaten, have a headache, and are wearing an itchy sweater. If they are worried about an exam and then someone rejects them, that person will almost certainly have their amygdala take over; even the calmest person in the world will be much more reactive under those levels of stress.

For example, one night early on during the COVID pandemic, Alex was in lockdown in a small apartment with a four-year-old (a chronically high-stress situation). At one point, unbeknownst to Alex, a three-inch lizard wandered into the apartment from outside and made a normal rustling lizard noise as it walked. Alex had been worrying about COVID and the news and was overwhelmed with childcare responsibilities and work during the same time. Her baseline stress was high. So when the lizard came in and made the noise, it was the last straw for her amygdala, which kicked into high gear. She had a full-on anxiety attack and hid in her bedroom with her four-year-old for the rest of the night. The next morning, when Alex emerged and her stress level was lower, the lizard looked as harmless—and adorable—as it was, and she was able to catch it without incident. She has never, before or since, reacted so strongly to a lizard.

You have only one brain, and it can only handle so many stressful, anxiety-provoking things at once. So where you start matters. One of the best ways you can prevent meltdowns and blow-ups is to put a focus on self-care like sleep and food. And add routine soothing techniques to lower your baseline number. If that's not possible in your specific situation, give yourself some grace if your nervous system is currently overwhelmed.

THE ANXIETY SCALE

I like to use a picture to help communicate how anxiety works at different intensities. If you've seen a pain scale at the doctor's office, this works in much the same way.

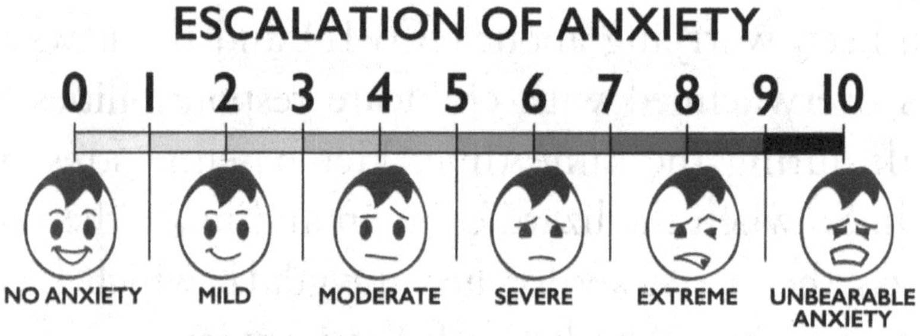

On the far left side, you have no anxiety at 0, and as the numbers increase, your anxiety in zones 2 to 3 is mild. You are still thinking clearly and can cope with nearly any challenge at this level of anxiety. At the other end of the spectrum, 10, your anxiety is overwhelming and unbearable. Anything at a 9.5 or above looks like shaking in the corner, unable to speak, literally running away, or fighting with force to get away. You are in fight, flight, or freeze mode, with the amygdala fully in charge. If you are thinking at all, you're thinking and reacting with your emotions alone.

In zones 0 to 2, your prefrontal cortex is still in charge. In zones 7 to 10, your amygdala and your emotions are in charge. In the middle of the spectrum, zones 3 to 7 are sharing control. You are processing emotionally more than cognitively in zones 5 to 7, but cognition still works somewhat. You are processing cognitively more than emotionally in zones 3 to 5, but the emotions are still in play.

Here's what that looks like.

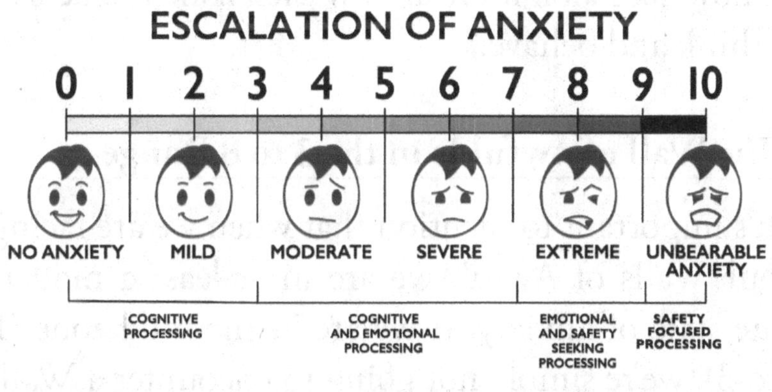

ANXIETY INCREASES AND DECREASES IN A PREDICTABLE WAY

We don't skip steps on the anxiety spectrum. The only way to increase anxiety to 8–10 is to go through the earlier stages, in order. It also normally takes time. If there is a true threat to our safety, moving up from a 2 to a 9 may happen in a few minutes or less. But often, the escalation takes longer than that—a half hour, a day, or even a few weeks, depending on our level of stress and worry. As we decrease anxiety, the same principle is true—we'll move through severe to moderate anxiety before we can reach calm, and the process takes time.

So, when you want to decrease your anxiety and put your prefrontal cortex back in control, start with emotional reasoning. I'll come back to that in a moment. For now, let's look more at how each zone impacts how we think and behave.

The Wall of Awful Is in the 3 to 8 Range

It's important to mention that when we are facing our Walls of Awful, we are in at least a moderate state of anxiety. If we are in the mild zone (1 to 3), we're simply not going to encounter a Wall, and if we're in the extreme or unbearable (8 to 10) zone, we are in crisis and too overwhelmed to care if we're doing a task or not.

That's not to say that the 8–10 zone doesn't require intervention—it does! But while I'll offer the occasional pointer, the key skills for living in the 8–10 zone and/or recovering from a crisis in this zone are beyond the scope of this book. If we're in this zone regularly, it's time to make changes in our lives and probably seek professional help and/or medication, if possible.

HOW PROBLEM-SOLVING IS AFFECTED

At every stage, anxiety has a different impact on our ability to function, based on how well the prefrontal cortex is working.

Let's say my toilet broke and I need to fix it. If I'm in the mild parts of the scale, I'm not emotionally involved. I can do research, go to Home Depot, get the parts, and try to fix the toilet. If I run into trouble, I can use logic to solve the issue. I might get mildly frustrated, but if I do, I take a few breaths and go back to logic. My executive function and prefrontal lobes are functioning normally.

If the toilet starts overflowing slowly, maybe I go into the moderate zone (3 to 5). I can use my critical-thinking skills, but my emotions have arrived on the scene. I feel flustered and frustrated, and I make more small mistakes until I untangle them.

If I worry excessively at this point, or the pipe breaks and starts spewing water everywhere, my amygdala takes over.[6] My reaction time to deal with immediate issues speeds up, and my senses sharpen. I notice and deal with threats faster if they're right in front of me, but I will overreact and yell at someone interrupting me. My heart beats faster, and until I calm down I will struggle to solve complex problems. I may not be able to focus on reading directions. I may make bigger mistakes and take longer to notice them. This is the severe zone (5 to 7).

In the extreme zone (8 to 10), I am moving all the way across the house in a few seconds to shut off the water. I can mop up the spill to save my house from water damage. Literally nothing else is getting done beyond that. I'm not functional except to respond to immediate danger. Once the immediate problem is solved, I will need to go for a walk or do something that convinces my body it's safe before I can deal with anything else.

IDENTIFYING WHERE YOU ARE ON THE SCALE

The first step to help yourself get past your Wall of Awful is to recognize what stage of anxiety you are currently in. This gets harder the farther up the scale you go, so it can take good observation skills and practice. What are your tells? What are the signals that you're escalating into moderate or severe? Pay attention to how you react.

There are both physical and behavioral clues. For me, when I get anxious I feel tension in my back. I grip my toes into my sneakers. I chew or clench my jaw, and I talk faster than normal. I've known people who first realize they are anxious on a low level because their fitness tracker tells them their heart rate is up. Others find their breathing gets shallow and they feel braced against something, or their hands literally shake, even if they ignore them.

On the behavioral side, anxiety can look like suddenly wanting to be alone or to be with people when it doesn't otherwise make sense. It can look like snapping at people, talking too much, or becoming very quiet. For me personally, if I'm eating a lot of cookies, I know I'm stressed. It means that my anxiety is higher on the scale than I think it is, and I need to go walk in the woods[7] and meditate.

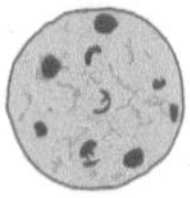

Those of us who are neurodivergent can easily think we're less anxious than we are and more functional than we are. If you think you're in the mild zone (1 to 3) when you're actually in moderate (3 to 5), or moderate when you're in severe (5 to 7), you won't work to calm down soon enough. You'll make emotional decisions instead of rational ones. You may hold it together until 6 or so, and then absolutely fall apart. Or, the extreme zone (8 to 10) will seem to hit you out of nowhere, and now it's an emergency for you and everyone around you. If you'd paid attention along the way, you would have had more time to de-escalate.

So, it's worthwhile to pay attention to your cues and learn what they are. And then take steps to decrease your anxiety *before* it becomes a crisis.

DECREASING YOUR ANXIETY

Most of us don't enjoy being at high levels of anxiety and would like to decrease that anxiety. That's easier said than done! Let's take a look at the scale in reverse, to represent what it would look like to decrease your anxiety from a high to a low level.

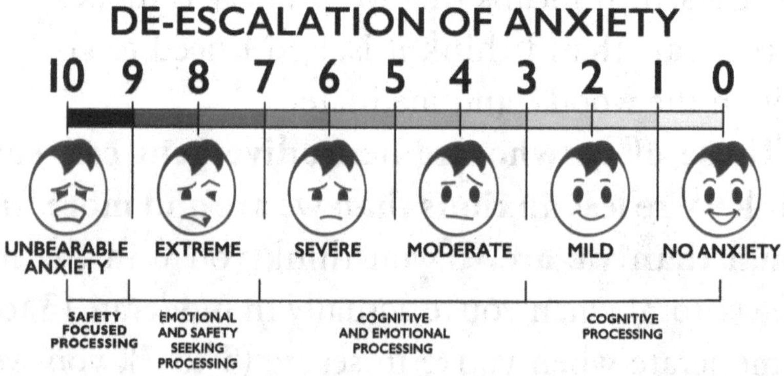

Because the prefrontal cortex and amygdala are in charge to varying degrees at different parts of the scale, a single set of strategies won't work at every point.

One of the biggest mistakes that people make when trying to calm themselves or someone else is using a strategy that's out of step with where they are on the scale. Deep breathing is great when you're in the moderate zone to calm you to mild, but it does almost nothing when you're in severe. Trying to use logic with someone panicking in the extreme zone (8 to 10) is also pretty useless; the emotional part of the brain can't understand logic, and gets irritated when you try. Logic can make the situation worse.

In the next chapters (and Appendix 3), I'll suggest strategies that will help you **decrease anxiety or side-step strong feelings** to get past the Wall. Right now, I'll share some general principles about how to decrease anxiety when you are in each of the following zones.

GUIDE TO HOW EACH ZONE WORKS

The Extreme and Unbearable Zones (8 through 10)

Primary driver: **SAFETY**
This zone is a crisis. The amygdala is fully in charge, and only interventions focused on *safety* and positive *social connection* will help.

How to Help Yourself: Get to a safe place, even if that's huddled in a corner, and then call a friend or listen to a podcast with calm people talking to each other in friendly tones. If the current situation doesn't feel safe, find one that does. Where it's possible, literally run away or hit a punching bag, to give the amygdala what it wants and let it calm down.

How to Help Someone Else: Don't try logic—it won't work. Instead, address only emotions and safety. Make yourself as nonthreatening as possible, and speak in a calm, steadying voice. Consider offering food or help reaching a place where they feel safer.

The Severe Zone (5 through 8)

Primary driver: **EMOTIONS POWERED BY ANXIETY**

In the severe zone, *emotions* are in charge.

How to Help Yourself: To help calm the emotions in this zone more directly, try *body-based strategies*, like stimming* or movement. Many Walls of Awful are in this zone, so we've given you strategies to calm yourself throughout this book. But for now, if you're facing fear or anger, ask yourself, "Why am I afraid?" or "Why am I angry?" If you're facing a problem, ask, "What is the

* Common in autistic people, this is a form of repetitive movement used to regulate emotions, focus, or physical discomfort. But anyone can stim! And in fact, ADHD people and others may call this "fidgeting."

next thing I have to do right now?" Remember, anxiety doesn't understand time.

How to Help Someone Else: In this zone, you should name the emotions and validate that it's okay to feel them, ideally in a gentle tone. You may be able to ask simple questions that focus on the present situation or the immediate next step to help the person feel calmer and in control.

The Moderate Zone (3 through 5)

Primary drivers: a mix of **ANXIETY** and **LOGIC**

How to Help Yourself: In this zone, *distraction*, *planning*, and *appeals to logic* can be very helpful, as they "turn on" the prefrontal cortex and "turn off" the amygdala. Try deep breathing, stimming, walking, and other body-based strategies. Planning and complex problem-solving are actively helpful and soothing in this zone. What is the next thing you need to do? What do you need to do after that? Write it down!

How to Help Someone Else: Give them permission to breathe, move, stim, and distract themselves. Schools give students in this zone math problems to help them calm, and adults can find podcasts or other materials that make them curious for the same effect. Also, helping the other person create certainty by making a plan can be profoundly soothing.

The Mild Zone (0 through 2)

Primary driver: **HIGHER THINKING**

When you are in the mild zone, you don't need an intervention; you are balanced and doing fine.

Action Guide: How to De-Escalate in Each Zone:

- To get from extreme anxiety (8 to 9) to severe (5 to 7), find safety and/or positive social connection.
- To get from severe anxiety to moderate (3 to 5), provide social support, move, and validate and comfort emotions.
- To get from moderate to mild anxiety (0 to 2), start thinking, planning, and moving.

Remember, the rest of this book will have details about exactly which strategies you can use, and where. I also have included a cheat sheet of de-escalation strategies in Chapter 6 (and at the end of the book in Appendix 3). So, don't worry if this feels too high level. I will teach you what to do with it over the course of the book.

DECREASING YOUR BASELINE ANXIETY SCORE

We've talked about how things like worries, not eating, poor sleep, and itchy sweaters can add to our anxiety score. But we haven't talked about where things start, our baseline anxiety scores. Given that you're reading this book, you probably don't start at 0.

Most of us have an elevated anxiety score. It's part of being alive. In fact, a little bit of stress and anxiety is healthy. It makes us want to do things and improve ourselves. The baseline anxiety score is a way to think about how much stress we might be carrying day to day, as well as how far we are from the amygdala hijacking things.

Let's revisit our graphic of the escalation of anxiety.

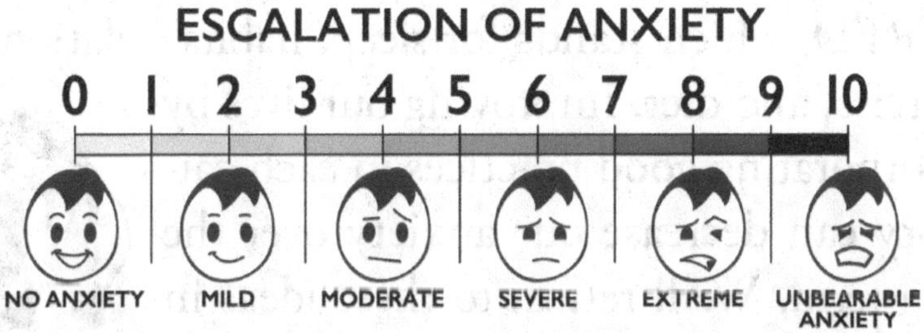

The more daily stressors we have, the higher our score will be. Because the things that cause stress in our lives vary in intensity, they do not all increase our scores by the same amount. A difficult project, a small-scale conflict with a loved one, or a child struggling in school might each increase our baseline by a half point, while a high-stress job, going through a divorce, or a child with chronic complex needs is likely to increase our scores by two or more points each. Most of us have more than one stressful thing going on at a time, and the points add up.

Thankfully, there are things we can do to reduce that baseline anxiety. Self-care is a good place to start. We can also use strategies to decrease the impact of negative influences on our score. If we regularly worry, don't eat enough, get poor sleep, and deal with itchy sweaters, our baseline score will be higher—but if we learn skills to manage worry, prepack a lunch and snacks, prioritize sleep, and swap out the itchy sweaters, suddenly our baseline moves to a less anxious place. I break self-care down into a model that I call SHRED, which stands for sleep, habits, relationships, exercise, and diet. Improving our lives by incorporating good practices in each category can decrease our anxiety over the long term. We'll return to these ideas in Chapter 3 and throughout the book.

ANXIETY CAN BE MANAGED

Now that we've pulled things out of our anxiety room and spread them out in piles, let's begin organizing.

We've established that anxiety is the mortar that holds our Walls of Awful together. So, the stronger our anxiety gets, the more likely we are to have our limbic systems take over, forcing us to default to emotional processing and short-term safety seeking. This makes our Walls of Awful much worse. Fortunately, the patterns are consistent, and we can respond better by understanding the anxiety scale. Anxiety can also be mitigated by using strategies that focus on improving our feelings of certainty, connection, agency, and well-being (CCAW). The more we build systems that apply the CCAW model into our day-to-day lives, the easier it will be to reduce our baseline anxiety. And that reduction will provide us with more space to absorb moments of stress and prevent our amygdala from hijacking our thinking. (See Chapters 9 and 10.) The lower our baseline anxiety, the easier it will become to routinely Climb our Walls.

In the remainder of the book, I get practical. I share five concrete strategies that people use to get past their Walls of Awful, discuss the pros and cons of each, and weave in tactics for anxiety management throughout. The Wall of Awful can be overcome! But to do that, we're going to need skills and resources. In the next chapter, we'll discuss how we can use them to help get past our Walls.

CHEAT SHEET: ANXIETY AND THE WALL OF AWFUL

1 Anxiety is our body's normal, and often useful, response to stress. It is characterized by feelings of fear, apprehension, and worry. It can be caused by both mental and physical stressors.

2 When you're in danger, the **amygdala** in your brain takes over, putting you in fight-or-flight mode so you can survive. This is important, and normal.

3 Since the Wall of Awful is made of strong negative emotions and held together by anxiety, facing the Wall activates the emotional processing of the limbic system. So problem-solving gets harder, and we're more likely to take things personally, avoid them, or become defensive.

4 **Four things make anxiety worse:** uncertainty, rejection, powerlessness, and uncomfortableness **(URPU)**. And **four things make anxiety better:** certainty, connection, agency, and well-being practices **(CCAW)**.

5 Depending on how strong your anxiety or stress is in the moment, **different strategies** will be required to calm you down.

ACTION STEP:

Make a list of three actions you can take when you are in each anxiety zone to calm yourself down. Then post the list somewhere you'll see it when you're anxious.

This might feel less important to do when you're calm, but do it anyway. It will make things easier later.

CHAPTER THREE

SKILLS AND RESOURCES HELP US GET PAST THE WALL

> However hard your life is (and however big your Wall of Awful is), you can always learn new skills and apply resources to make it easier.

"I don't know, maybe I'm just lazy."

My client Peter had been diagnosed with ADHD less than a year before. He was still in the middle of his journey to self-understanding, and he kept struggling with self-talk. He'd had his mother and two teachers telling him constantly not to be so lazy when he was a kid—and those words haunted him to this day.

I wanted to tell him that he wasn't lazy—he had ADHD! They're not the same at all. But my counseling training told me he'd hear it better if he got to that place himself. I validated the feeling. "I hear you. It's hard when your brain isn't doing the thing you want it to do. It's completely normal to worry that you're lazy or not trying hard enough. It's common, especially in that first year, when you're figuring out what ADHD means for you."

He agreed, and talked for several minutes about the situation he was struggling with before eventually coming back to this fear that he might just be making it all up. Maybe he wasn't trying hard enough. Maybe he was just lazy.

This time I put on my coaching hat and expressed an opinion. "I don't know, man. I don't believe in lazy."

Peter went quiet on the other end of the phone, then finally: "Why is that?"

"Because it's an answer without a solution."

"LAZY" ISN'T A USEFUL ANSWER

When I work with teachers, and they talk about a student being lazy, it provides a false sense of certainty. It answers the question of why the student isn't achieving but doesn't provide any useful information toward solving the problem, and it stops them from thinking more deeply about how to help that kid. "Lazy" shuts down the conversation.

That answer is just as useless when we think about ourselves. "Lazy" offers no information and no solutions. It adds bricks to our Walls of Awful and creates a story in our head for why we can't get past them. It makes us feel bad without helping us move forward.

If we take "lazy" off the table, how does it change our lens? We look deeper, and if we look deep enough, what we typically find is a lack of skills or resources.

I firmly believe that a lack of skills* or resources is the root of all our struggles, both large and small. Someone with plenty of extra money, family support, and good coping skills might be able to get through the health crisis of a cancer diagnosis without much secondary damage. Take away those skills and resources, however, and that same cancer diagnosis may cause a cascade of problems leading to job loss, mental health challenges, even bankruptcy. Cancer is hard in either circumstance, but skills and resources can help to circumvent second-level problems.

On a smaller scale, it could be very disruptive for a person living paycheck to paycheck, who just moved to a new

---

* According to Dr. Ross Greene, kids act out because they lack the skills to deal with their present situation. As he says, "Kids do well if they can." I believe this is true for adults, too, and that resources play a critical role because they can be used to solve so many problems. See Dr. Ross Greene. "Collaborative & Proactive Solutions," 2021. https://livesinthebalance.org/wp-content/uploads/2021/06/FAQ-21.pdf.

city with little to no social connections and zero automotive skills, to get a flat tire on the way to work. Such an event would present a significant disruption and might even cost them their job if they're unable to get to work. But if that same person has a AAA membership, supportive friends, or the skills to change the tire on their own, the situation becomes much less of an impediment. The resources and skills have helped to solve their problem.

SKILLS AND RESOURCES FOR THE WIN

Of course, we aren't at the mercy of the skills and resources we already have. We can find or develop more! We can also use the ones we have more deliberately to solve our problems and get us to the other side of our Walls of Awful. Sometimes we can hire someone to handle the task for us instead of having to Climb a Wall of Awful in the first place. We can apply other resources to make climbing easier. Or we can learn a skill that helps us take on both the Wall and the task more easily.

Skills and resources aren't as fancy as the metaphors in Part 2. But every strategy in this book will get better *and* easier to apply if we continue to add skills and use our resources more wisely. Skills and resources never stop being important to solving your problems and Climbing your Walls. In fact, half of this book will teach you the skills you'll need to know to get to the other side of your Walls sustainably.

ON SKILLS

You already have many skills, especially when it comes to the common challenges of your life. Recognizing our skills helps us to better manage the Wall of Awful because it supports the need for certainty and agency. When we enter into a tricky situation, being confident in our skills helps us feel more certain that we can handle whatever it is that we're facing.

As I share with clients, there are three broad categories of skills. All three kinds of skills are important, and all are most effective when used in concert with the others.

1. **Technical skills**
2. **Executive functioning skills**
3. **Social skills**

Let's start with the first, and most obvious, set of skills.

TECHNICAL SKILLS

Definition: Technical skills are the kinds of things traditionally labeled *skills*—the abilities to do tasks, often complex ones, that take learning to master.

Who struggles: Technical skills are learned. And anyone can struggle to learn things. However, those of us who are neurodivergent will be more likely to encounter learning challenges. It might be as specific as a learning disability related to math (like dyscalculia) or as broad as executive functioning challenges (like ADHD or autism), which can make learning harder in general.

Many technical skills are made up of layers of more basic skills. Writing a five-page essay by hand can't be done without the ability to understand written language, the ability to mechanically write the words, and the ability to maintain those skills over the course of five pages. It also likely can't be done without understanding how to plan and make an argument on the page. Most professional skills and life skills (like driving a car) are similarly complex and layered, which is why technical skills can take weeks, months, or years to master.

If a scientist doesn't have the specific technical skill, they may not be able to operate the DNA sequencer machine they need to run a certain experiment. That lack of skill might translate into them failing to do their job effectively. Similarly, if someone gets cut off in a Zoom call and doesn't have the technical skills to get back on the call, they face problems. The feelings of frustration and failure both feel as a result of these setbacks may lead to Walls of Awful. The situation only gets worse if they develop a Wall about learning the technical skills they need.

You Can Learn It

Almost anything in life can be learned and turned into a technical skill, including executive function and social skills. So, if you have a need to do something and you don't have resources, you *can* learn how to do it yourself with enough time. Many Walls of Awful are driven by simply not knowing how, and you can always *learn*.

EXECUTIVE FUNCTION SKILLS

Definition: Executive function is a broad group of skills that enable us to execute on tasks. It includes things like planning, prioritizing, mental flexibility, emotional regulation, focus, and self-control. These skills are often not explicitly taught, but they absolutely can be.

Who struggles: Executive function challenges are a major part of both ADHD and autism because the brains of people with ADHD and autism develop differently than neurotypical brains. Anxiety and depression, however, interfere with the person's ability to access their usual executive function.

Executive function skills are *skills*, in that they are learned, even though they are not always explicitly taught in school. But executive function *is also a function* of the brain. It takes time to develop as we mature from childhood to young adulthood, and that development is affected by our unique experiences and flavor of neurodiversity.

Executive function depends on working memory. This kind of memory is not the same as remembering an event in the past. It's the ability to hold in our heads what is currently happening, while thinking into the future to plan for what happens next. For example, if it's Sandra's night to make dinner, she will need to remember to take the chicken out of the freezer in the morning. Otherwise the family can't have chicken tacos that evening. At the same time, she may need to remember to email her boss about a project at work.

Keeping track of many things at once requires executive function. So does planning effectively, which typically involves breaking down the steps for a project and assigning those steps over several weeks. Other executive functions include emotional regulation, organization, regulating attention, inhibiting our impulses, and planning. When our executive function and working memory aren't functioning effectively, we will struggle to do all these kinds of tasks. We may also struggle with concept formation and learning new technical skills.

Most of the skills required for success as an adult depend on executive function to some degree. This is why depression, ADHD, and other mental illnesses have such a broad impact on our lives.

Why Did We Scroll Social Media for Two Hours?

We can't inhibit action without executive function.

A classic example is opening up our phone to look at the weather and ending up on Facebook. Our executive function glitched; we weren't able to prevent the lure of Facebook from pulling us away from the other tasks we intended to do.

Saying no to sugar or to other foods while on a strict diet works the same way. We use executive function to control our impulse to eat a cookie, but if our executive function is being taxed by too many stressors, that control gets harder.

The most effective inhibition strategies depend on creating layers of "friction" between us and

> something we *don't* want. It's easier to say no when it's harder to say yes. It's easier to avoid eating cookies if there aren't any in the house when we want a midnight snack. Good planning, after all, is *also* an executive function.

Executive Function and Willpower

Executive function is complex. No one is born with the full set of executive function skills. We learn them through experience, often because our parents and teachers model them and do much of the work with us until we can do it on our own. Over time, our brains develop further, increasing our biological capacity for executive function until around the age of twenty-five. We can also improve our executive function skills by training them intentionally in the same way we learn technical skills.

Willpower is our ability to delay short-term gratification for long-term gain, and it is closely related to executive function. In fact, many executive functions (emotional regulation, regulating attention, inhibiting our impulses) serve to support willpower. However, we can also look at willpower as a resource, which we will discuss later on in this chapter.

We are all limited by the amount of willpower we can utilize without tiring. Unfortunately, that amount varies from person to person. Some of us just don't have as much as others. Thankfully, we can train ourselves up! *And* it's often worthwhile to sidestep the easily tired functions of our brains with technical skills, speed bumps, and high-level planning (see sidebar above), which is why our parents and teachers model these skills.

Training the Muscle

Think of training your executive function like an athlete trains their body. An athlete can be skilled at ice-skating and train her body to be exceptionally strong at executing those skills. But if the athlete gets sick or injured, no matter how skilled she is, she will struggle to skate. The same goes for executive function as a "muscle"; no matter how well we train, it may fail if we are injured, under additional strain, or we might just have less of it than our peers.

In fact, those injuries and strains are common. Anxiety and depression reduce our availability of executive function at a chemical level. We can think of these as injuries, though not necessarily in a physical sense. The strain of overwhelming demands and sleep deprivation can also reduce our executive functions—which is why corporate executives[1] and parents[2] often struggle with consistent planning and decisions. And sometimes, as with ADHD and autism, there is just genetically less executive functioning "muscle" to go around.

Taking the Load off the Muscle

Fortunately, with practice, we can decrease the demands on our executive function "muscle" by moving more tasks from an instinctual planning-on-the-spot approach to the less energy-intensive technical skills instead.

We can learn organizational or planning skills, break tasks into smaller step-by-step chunks, and lessen the cognitive load. But we have to be intentional about this kind of training, particularly for those of us with neurodivergence. It can be a tricky trade. The development of those technical skills can have a high initial cost that many are unwilling to pay. It's important to remember that in the long run the initial investment is worthwhile because it reduces the overall cost and increases our ceiling for success.

Additionally, we can often get even more benefit out of our technical skills by applying them in a new area.

A client of mine struggled to keep up with personal and household tasks. He was able to (mostly) keep up with the demands of his job, thanks to the process documents his employer used. But things fell apart when he got home, which caused conflict when he failed to do the things he'd told his wife he would do. For example, she asked him every week to change the shower curtain—and six months later it was still lying on the floor. Something had to change. When he came to me, he was embarrassed that he couldn't seem to remember basic things at home. We tried many different strategies, but eventually he settled on a simple one that profoundly changed his life. Inspired by the process documents at work, he created a personal to-do list in a Google Doc shared with his wife.

The Google Doc increased his ability to handle the demands at home. Much like a grocery bag increases the number of items we can bring home from the store, the shared document increased the amount of information he could keep up with. Additionally, because he shared the document with his wife, it made communicating about these tasks easier, something they both had a Wall of Awful for. It didn't take long for them to start having regular Sunday meetings to discuss household tasks. The unexpected upside of the Google Doc was reduced conflict in the marriage! She could now see the effort he *was* putting in that had previously been invisible.

Sometimes we already know the technical skills we need to get past our Walls of Awful; we just have to apply them in a new way.

SOCIAL SKILLS

Definition: Social skills are the skills we use to interface successfully with other people, persuade others, advocate for ourselves, and get help and support. These skills are also not always explicitly taught.

Who struggles: Social skill challenges are most commonly seen in people with ADHD*, autism**, and (sometimes) social anxiety.

For many people, social skills seem instinctive. Others—like those of us who are neurodivergent—must learn some or all of the skills for social interaction intentionally. We lack some of the instinct, and so we are forced to make social skills technical skills.

As a note, when Alex has a question about a social phenomenon she doesn't understand, she'll go to an Autistic friend in their forties with relevant experience. Since they've had to learn social interactions as a technical skill, they can *explain it*. And often they can explain it with more nuance than a neurotypical friend.

Social skills are useful beyond just connecting with others, though. When we have a gap in our executive functioning skills or technical skills, we can lean on

---

* People with ADHD may miss social cues due to inattention, or behave in unexpected ways due to their hyperactivity.

** Autistic people often struggle with social cues due to the "double empathy problem." This is an issue where autistic and neurotypical people communicate and give cues in different ways; autistic people communicate with each other clearly and with connection.

others using social skills to make up the difference. We learn by talking to other people, and we succeed by getting some form of social support.

Of course, it's possible to learn technical skills without other people being involved. We can tinker and figure things out as we go, watch videos on YouTube to improve our skills, and discover new ways of looking at the world from the books we read. However, understanding a specific situation and how best to apply our technical skills to that situation is usually learned best with a mentor. There's no getting around the need to talk to another person eventually. So social skills are important!

Social Skills Open Doors at Work (and in Life)

Social skills aren't just about the ability to talk with a friend in a way that makes them feel heard. They can also be the ability to advocate for yourself or to talk to a group—and as such, social skills open doors. As my friend Caroline Maguire, author of *Friendship Skills for Neurodivergent Adults*, says, they are about being a "social spy." If we can walk into a place, read the room, and understand its norms and social structure quickly, we're far more likely to succeed.

Suppose you get a new job and arrive on the first day in khakis and a polo, only to notice that everyone else in the lobby is in a suit and tie. You'd have to figure out how to navigate that situation with grace. Maybe you'd avoid it entirely by learning the dress code in advance. Those kinds of skills are what we mean by "reading the room," though that skill is only one of many.

Social skills, or "soft skills" as they're often called in business, get someone in the door. To stay in the job afterward, the person will generally need technical skills and a strong work ethic. Of course, sometimes social skills are also needed for success on the job.

I had a client going through a difficult social transition at work. Aliyah's small company had been bought by a large corporation. As a scientist, she was expected to come up with topics to research. But the new direction of the company had not been communicated to her yet, so she was anxious she might choose the wrong research arena. Aliyah worried she'd go down a rabbit hole and lose her job as a result.

To navigate this moment successfully, Aliyah needed to determine who in her office was safe to talk to, in a situation where corporate politics were costing people jobs. She worried that bringing up the questions to the wrong person could prove detrimental, but she needed the information to do a good job. So Aliyah came to me for guidance navigating what felt like a social (and emotional) minefield.

She had a huge assortment of technical skills. But if she didn't navigate the situation with excellent social skills, it could blow up in her face. We worked together to help her figure out who to trust and how to get past her Wall to ask for their help. Then we worked on how to ask the coworker for information in a way that didn't come off as anxious or risk undermining her position. Thankfully, she was able to do that and used the information she got to make a good choice for her research.

LEARNING A SKILL EXPLICITLY

Every skill can be learned. Often, learning a skill explicitly, as a technical skill, can be profoundly helpful in getting past a Wall of Awful.

A former client of mine, Chris, struggled with presenting to his team at work. He had a Wall of Awful about public speaking, and that was our main focus. He could continue to approach public speaking as he had been, where even the thought of it left him anxious and worried about his career, or he could create a safe space to practice and skill up.

I pointed Chris to Toastmasters, where he could speak publicly but in a low-stakes environment. No matter how bad he was, those speeches would not hurt him. He was able to relax and focus on the technical skills they were teaching, working through the steps of a good speech over and over until he felt better about going onstage.

When he needed to present at work, he built in extra

time for himself beforehand. He practiced in an empty room or in front of a friendly coworker, so if he made a mistake he could fix the problem in advance. Public speaking never became comfortable for him, but he was able to become comfortable in the discomfort. Eventually his confidence in his skills grew, and he was able to Climb his Wall more easily.

Getting Past the Wall Is a Skill

Many of us need to increase our skill set to get past our Walls more effectively. But having the skills alone may not be enough. Sometimes we may already have skills and just need a reminder that they're there. Or we may need to get more practiced at those skills to make them easier to implement. My kempo sensei, Master Phil Pritchard, often talks about how if we ever have to use our martial arts skills in a self-defense situation, we can expect to perform two to three belt levels below our rank in the dojo. In a high-stress situation, the amygdala gets in the way of our higher-order skills. Even though I've developed a long list of strategies, both in martial arts and in Climbing my Wall, I'll still sometimes have trouble using them under pressure. It's just part of the process.

> Often, the higher-skill options to get past our Walls won't be instinctive. We will have to exercise them with intention, practicing them until they *become* more natural, and we can use them with the confidence of well-worn technical skills.

Social skills are *skills* with people, but people can also be considered resources. In the same way that resources can lead to using skills in a better way, skills can lead to using resources more effectively. **Skills and resources are linked.**

Now that we've looked at skills, let's turn our attention to resources.

DEFINING RESOURCES

I define resources more broadly than most people. I include literally anything we might need to initiate or complete a task. Time, money, and food are resources, but so, for example, are brain chemicals. I am diagnosed with ADHD, and that diagnosis means (among other things) that my brain lacks dopamine. I lack an important biological resource that would make task initiation, planning, short-term memory, and other executive functions happen for me as easily as they happen for other people. I struggle more because my brain doesn't naturally provide me with all the resources I need. Thankfully, the medication that I take for my ADHD (another resource) helps to solve this problem.

People with depression face a similar (if different) struggle also based in the brain.* Depressed people find they have less brainpower and energy and less ability to get things done. They may experience more physical and emotional pain[3] and less enjoyment,** and struggle to bounce back from adversity. The same goes for people with anxiety and OCD,*** to some degree.[4]

If a neurotypical person has never suffered from depression or anxiety, they might look at someone who is struggling with it and judge them. But people with depression have a fraction of the executive function, energy, and mental resources of people without it.

---

* While people used to think that depression was caused by a lack of serotonin in the brain, recent studies have called that understanding into question. However, *something* happens chemically in the brain of someone with depression that limits their executive function (and other kinds of function) biologically.

** A common symptom of depression is **anhedonia**, a loss of interest or enjoyment in everyday things. See list of depression symptoms here: Elizabeth A. O'Connor, Evelyn P. Whitlock, Bradley Gaynes, and Tracy L. Beil. "Table 1, Primary DSM-IV Depression Disorders, Criteria for Adults—Screening for Depression in Adults and Older Adults in Primary Care," NCBI Bookshelf, n.d. https://www.ncbi.nlm.nih.gov/books/NBK36406/table/ch1.t1/.

*** Anhedonia is a common symptom of many mental health conditions. See Cleveland Clinic Medical. "Anhedonia." Cleveland Clinic, October 8, 2025. https://my.clevelandclinic.org/health/symptoms/25155-anhedonia.

It's not their fault. Their struggle makes sense, but can easily cause more failure and shame, adding bricks to their Walls of Awful.

Fewer Resources Lead to More Challenges

Of course, brain chemicals aren't the only kinds of resources. More traditional resources include money, time, education, social standing, and support from friends and family. A stable living situation is a resource, as are physical and emotional supports. Someone with financial challenges will struggle more often, for reasons beyond their control, as will people dealing with bigotry or institutional violence. A single mom may not be able to progress as far in her career as someone with a spouse at home. If she doesn't have external support, she may be forced to take off work whenever her child has a problem. The need for flexibility will likely mean she has to take jobs that don't pay as well, and she will likely have fewer opportunities for promotion.

Of course, challenges tend to compound. The single mom forced into jobs that don't pay well will have less money. Less money means less ability to weather difficult circumstances, like a car breakdown, without going into debt. And debt will lead to other challenges.

In a similar way, someone who is neurodivergent (ADHD, autism, CPTSD, OCD, bipolar disorder, etc.) and has abundant financial and social resources will be more likely to overcome their challenges. Someone with the same challenges plus poverty or family dysfunction may end up with significant struggle. That said, some people are able to do better with limited resources than others. Individuals vary in their coping skills and abilities.

Some resources can compensate for the lack of others. If the single mom has a large network of family and friends in town, she may have people to watch her children. So, she may have time to learn skills to make herself irreplaceable at work. If a person with ADHD has good health insurance, they will be able to get medication to support their executive function. The medication might unlock the ability to finish school and open up other life paths.

Common Resources

While we can define a resource as literally anything needed to start or complete a task, the same types of resources tend to pop up again and again. Here are the most common resources we encounter in everyday life. Hopefully this list will provide a new lens on some resources that you might be overlooking:

- time
- money

- food
- family
- social networks
- emotional support
- professional support
- tools—computer, phone, printer, notebook, pen/pencil, lathe
- values, purpose, faith
- knowledge—books, the internet, anything in your head
- a healthy body and/or mind (and the energy that comes with them!)
- regular sleep
- a stable place to live
- a reliable source of transportation
- "can do" attitude

Certainly there are other resources, but these are the ones we tend to encounter most often. When in doubt, if it's not a skill and you need it, it's probably a resource.

RESOURCES INCREASE CHOICES

My friend Tung has a job that he hates, but he's good at it. His boss is a jerk, the hours are terrible, the responsibilities change without warning, and he doesn't like one of his main daily tasks. Every day he stays, Tung's Wall of Awful grows, but he doesn't have the money to move.

Because he has fewer resources, it's harder for him to make changes. He has less cushion if things go wrong. So Tung keeps banging his head against his job, because he needs the money it gives him.

If he had better-resourced **connections**, his mom might give him a free place to stay, or his uncle might hand him three months' salary. He would suddenly have choices, more **agency**. He would have **certainty** that he'd be okay in the short term. He could throttle back his effort at work and look for a new job instead, maybe finding one with better pay, responsibility, and hours. With less to lose, it would become easier for Tung to make decisions that increased his **well-being**.

Resources and Skills Lead to CCAW

Remember the characteristics that decrease anxiety that we talked about in the last chapter? Each one can (1) act as a resource to reduce your anxiety and also (2)

be a positive thing that can happen as a result of using resources and skills. Certainty can improve well-being and give someone more agency or confidence in using agency, and so on.

- **Certainty.** Executive function skills can be used in the form of self-talk and perspective taking to reassess a situation and increase our certainty.
- **Connection.** Social skills and connection are inextricably linked. The better our social skills, the stronger and more varied our connections.
- **Agency.** Technical skills are often the best way to increase our agency because they lead to status, power, and higher-paying jobs. Status and power are nearly always the result of turning social skills and executive functions into technical skills.
- **Well-being.** Well-being is mental and physical health as much as anything else. Maintaining both requires skill and effort.

STARTING WITH THE BASICS

Every now and then I'll have an ADHD client (for example) who feels so overwhelmed that they cannot conceive of changing *anything* for the better. But they still want to work with me. They *want* to believe they can succeed, even if it feels impossible.

At that point, I start by looking at their health, their stressors, and their unmet needs, rather than jumping straight to ADHD strategies. While I do take into account their diagnos(es) of ADHD, anxiety, and so on, often the biggest issue is life circumstances. It can also be a negative cycle; their symptoms are making their needs harder to meet, and the unmet needs are making their symptoms worse. So we start with the basics and try to increase their well-being.

Are they sleeping? Is their living space clean *enough* that they don't worry about bugs or finding a clean dish? Do they see others *enough* to avoid loneliness? Is their mental health good *enough* to let them focus for a few hours? We use the SHRED model as a great place to start answering these questions.

Once the foundation is in place, we start looking at managing their ADHD (and/or other diagnoses) more effectively and use the CCAW model to get them moving toward meeting their additional goals.

Depression, anxiety, and other overwhelming challenges can cause us to focus on the scarcity of our resources and to miss the positive things we do have. When we're overwhelmed to the point that progress feels impossible, we have to come back to the basics. Work on our resources. Get the food, water, and sleep we need and begin to get other basic needs to a good enough, stable place. Then and only then can we address the Wall of Awful.

THE SHRED MODEL

Over the years I've found that people who have a "good enough" version of my SHRED model tend to have the bandwidth to work on other beneficial changes. Those who don't have the basics covered need to work on those first.

SHRED stands for:

- **Sleep.** On the low end, we can get *enough* sleep to get through the day. For even better results, we can sleep enough to support deep work, regulated emotions, and the patience for hard things.
- **Habits.** Basic habits mean we get up and get dressed in enough time to get to work or school. For more advanced systems and habits, see Chapter 9 for a deep dive on how we can use them deliberately.

- **Relationships.** On the low end, we can see the people we care about enough to stave off loneliness. On the high end, we can build supportive, nourishing relationships with trusted people.
- **Exercise.** Our bodies need a certain amount of movement for basic health. More exercise can provide additional focus, energy, strength, and enjoyment.
- **Diet.** Eating enough food and drinking enough water helps our brains and bodies stay on track. Including nutritious food (like vegetables) and minimizing junk food is even better.

The magic of SHRED is that a "good enough" version of all these things is enough to get started. Leveling up each of these areas from the baseline gets us *more* energy, more bandwidth, and more ability to work on hard things.

Even small improvements over time can add up, and the additional mental bandwidth we get from SHRED over time can pay off in big ways.

FINDING OTHERS LIKE US

For those of us with ADHD, autism, and/or mental health struggles like depression or CPTSD, our challenges may be specific to our diagnoses. A good first step in overcoming those challenges can be finding a group of people we can be open with. When we are around other people like ourselves, we can be accepted for who we are and not criticized for who we aren't. We can let go of the "stuckness" and tackle our challenges—and our Walls of Awful—without the weight of shame.

The same is true of other struggles to a lesser degree. Paying off debt is easier when we surround ourselves with other people also paying off debt. Giving up alcohol is easier with regular AA meetings full of other people in the same boat. Founding a business is easier with others surrounding us in entrepreneur mastermind groups. Having other people in a similar situation to ourselves around for support and to help us brainstorm solutions to problems can be priceless.

A Word about Systemic Issues

I am not dismissing the real struggles people face, nor saying that everything can be fixed by calling a friend. We *can* become more resilient, find additional resources, and work through difficult situations. We *can't* resilience our way out of systemic problems. A toxic workplace is not a place to learn resilience; it's just a place to leave.

"Try harder" usually isn't the best answer, but "try different" might be. Think more flexibly; apply different strategies to the obstacles until something works. Someone with a learning disability related to math may decide not to pursue math as a career, and choose sales or art or something else. And that's the right call. That said, someone with a learning disability in math deciding they're never going to pay bills is making the wrong call. Everyone still has to pay bills. Their diagnosis is a reason something is hard, but it's not an excuse to not try.

Racism is real, as are poverty, ableism, and other profoundly unjust situations. When we face a systemic problem, we're allowed to be frustrated by it, and angry. But we still need to keep moving forward in *some* direction.

When we are the ones facing the systemic problem, our only responsibility is to get through it as best as we can. Resilience is not complacency or being a doormat; it's continuing to progress in the face of hard things, in a direction that ultimately serves us. Sometimes resilience is taking a rest before moving in a different direction. Sometimes resilience is trying a new strategy. Hard things are hard.

But just because something is hard doesn't mean it has to be hopeless.

SKILLS, RESOURCES, AND THE WALL OF AWFUL

Typically, when we're encountering a Wall of Awful, it's because we lack skills, resources, or both. Sometimes the thing we're lacking is obvious, like needing a tire iron to change a flat or not knowing how to port over apps and numbers to a new phone. Other times it might be less obvious, like when we don't realize that our lack of social time has led to us feeling lonely, or when our poor emotional regulation skills lead to us avoiding things due to emotional overwhelm that could be worked through if we knew how.

When it comes to figuring out if we should start with skills or resources when confronting a Wall of Awful, my friend and fellow ADHD coach Dusty Chipura has a problem-solving sequence she uses with her clients that can serve as an excellent framework for addressing our Walls in certain situations.

Neurodiversity Problem-Solving with Dusty Chipura

1. **Is this even a problem you have to solve?** Are your expectations wrong? Are societal expectations like ableism coloring your view?

2. **Can you reduce the size of the problem?** Either by lowering the bar or by reducing the impact of the issue at hand? What do you have to do vs. what do you think you have to do based on societal expectations (ableism) that likely don't apply?
3. **Can you solve it with resources?**
   - Can you solve it with **money** (hire it out or buy another solution)?
   - If not, can you use **other resources** to go around the problem or make it easier to solve? (Who can you ask for help? Can you trade for help? What research can you do?)
4. If that doesn't fix it, **what skills do you need to develop** to avoid (or reduce) the problem going forward?
   - Repeatable Skills / Systems (cooking)
   - One-Shot/Infrequent Skills (how to change a tire)

FINDING RESOURCES

All Walls of Awful are made worse by a lack of resources, so getting more resources or using the resources you have more strategically is critical. Creativity and exchange are always worth considering. When Alex was very small, her dad worked long hours, often multiple days at a time, and her mom was several states away from family support. There was no money for babysitters, no matter how tired her mom got, or how much she needed to go to a doctor's appointment or to take a nap on her own. So Alex's mom figured out how to trade childcare with another mother in the neighborhood to get breaks. Watching four kids who liked playing with one another turned out to be not much harder than watching two, and in exchange she got a full day off every other week. Those days saved her.

Can we find similar solutions? If we're good at plumbing, or cooking, or anything else, can we trade that skill for something else we need? Can we pool resources with family or friends? Can we meal prep, work ahead, or work together with others to get farther than we can on our own? Can we ask a friend to sit with us while we do something hard, in exchange for supporting them later? Sometimes these creative solutions aren't possible, but they *are* worth considering, just in case.

We can often make up for the *lack* of one kind of resource with the presence of another.

HOPE

I believe that, no matter how hard a challenge we are facing, we can reach the other side—if we do not give up. Whether we find the success we wanted on that other side or we don't, we get through it, and we learn. We come out of each struggle a little more knowledgeable, a little more resilient, and a little more able to problem solve the next issue.

That's success, even if it might not be the kind we were looking for. On the other side of our challenges, we understand ourselves better. We *know* that we can struggle and overcome. We understand our strengths and weaknesses better, and we can use that knowledge to apply our efforts—including our strengths—more effectively in the future.

There is dignity in struggle, and there is power in knowledge and understanding. No matter how many or how few resources we have, we can always learn new skills and add them to make it easier the next time around. Our Walls of Awful *can* become less scary with familiarity; they *can* become easier to climb as we become more skilled in climbing them.

If the Walls become larger and more numerous with fewer resources and skills, they become easier to overcome with more resources and skills. So collect resources where you can, and spend the time to level up your skills as you go. Then use the strategies you'll learn in Part 2 of this book to Climb your Walls and get to the other side.

CHEAT SHEET: SKILLS AND RESOURCES

1 **"Lazy" is a dead-end answer** because it doesn't provide a solution. Instead of beating ourselves up, we need to add skills or resources to solve the problem.

2 **A skill** is our ability to do something well. We can learn skills intentionally or pick them up naturally. They can be grouped into three broad categories: **executive functioning skills, social skills, and technical skills**.

3 **Resources** are anything we need to initiate or complete a task, including, but not limited to, **time**, **money**, **sleep**, **values**, **and brain chemicals**.

4 When in doubt, work on improving SHRED factors: **sleep**, **habits**, **relationships**, **exercise**, **diet**. When these resources are high, everything else becomes easier.

5 When facing a Wall of Awful, **leveraging resources is generally the best place to start**. If they can't solve the problem, move on to applying skills.

6 Our Walls of Awful become larger and more numerous the fewer skills and resources we have, and they become easier to overcome when we increase our skills and resources.

ACTION STEP:

Make **a quick list of five to six skills or resources** that might be useful in tackling the Wall of Awful you identified earlier.

Then apply one skill or resource to the Wall—does it help?

PART 2

HOW TO GET PAST THE WALL

CHAPTER FOUR

STRATEGIES THAT DON'T WORK

> Staring at the Wall of Awful and trying to go around it are strategies that feel good, but they never work. Here's how to identify and avoid the ineffective traps.

Part of overcoming the challenge of the Wall is figuring out which strategies *don't* work so that we can do fewer of them. (We also need to figure out what *does* work, but that comes later.)

Often, we don't notice that we have a Wall of Awful until we realize that we've been avoiding something for a long time. Avoidance, or procrastination, is the most common response to the Wall of Awful, but it does nothing. So we first need to talk about waiting, why it happens, and why it's ineffective.

When faced with a Wall of Awful, the instinctual

response from most people is to try waiting. When the waiting is passive, I call it "staring at the wall." When the waiting takes the form of frantic action, I call it "going around the Wall." This can look like doing something, anything other than what's needed, or doing a related task that seems like it should make progress against the problem but doesn't. These strategies *feel* satisfying and helpful in the moment, but in reality they waste precious time and energy with false hope and often make the situation worse.

No matter what form the waiting takes, active or passive, it almost never overcomes a Wall of Awful. Walls are built over multiple months or years of strong negative emotions, and a little waiting won't relieve such strong negative emotions by itself. Spending the time to calm down and then coming back to the Wall just means we have to get past the Wall again. Doing that process six times in a row only adds increasing bricks of frustration and shame to the Wall.

Waiting alone just doesn't work. It's too easy for it to become a trap!

WHY DO WE KEEP DOING THIS?

So why do we keep staring at the Wall and trying to go around it? Our instincts drive us in this direction; the approach *feels* natural. And if we try these strategies enough times, very occasionally we will stumble into similar strategies that work. But just because it worked once doesn't mean it's a good plan. Getting past the Wall by climbing or putting a door in it are the only effective, nondamaging strategies. So, if we don't know how to get to those strategies on purpose, we will keep coming back to waiting, hoping we'll stumble to the other side of the Wall again. But the magic isn't any of the failed strategies in this chapter—the magic is in the *successful* strategies in Chapters 6 and 7. The good news is that the successful strategies can be accomplished at will, much more quickly than someone might expect, and don't require waiting for a happy accident to happen!

The ineffective strategies, then, have little to no upside: They are simply traps to avoid. Once we understand exactly how they look and feel, we no longer have to spend as much time being stuck. We can identify them and avoid their false promises. Instead of waiting endlessly to get past a Wall, we can learn to recognize what we're doing faster and pull ourselves out faster—to reengage with actions that *will* get us past the Wall. Ultimately, we'll be able to deliberately replace the habits that aren't serving us with the habits that do.

The first step, though, is to fully understand how these traps work.

Taking Time to Recover

We only have so much executive function and emotional energy in a day. Sometimes walking away from a Wall of Awful and coming back in the morning makes sense. We'll have to get past it again, but if we've returned with renewed energy and better strategies, it's a good idea—if there's time!

Walking away is okay if it's done on purpose, for good reason. Walking away to avoid something we need to do is not.

THERE'S A REASON

There's always a reason we wait, or procrastinate, endlessly. Whether we're conscious of it or not, **procrastination is our best attempt to solve a problem related to emotions**. And remember, the Wall of Awful is built of emotions.

When we feel anxious, overwhelmed, or have similar negative emotions around a particular task, we try to avoid it because we don't want to feel that way. Instead of doing the thing or managing our emotions by processing and dealing with them, we procrastinate. We numb ourselves or do something, anything, other than what we're supposed to be doing.

For example, watching television is a numbing behavior. It doesn't have to be, of course; television shows often act as entertainment. But if we're using them to avoid a task, we're using them to avoid emotions we don't want to deal with. We're numbing. We're watching television or doing other things while we wait for better emotions to show up. We're waiting to be "in the mood" for the task—waiting for the right time, the motivation, or for some mysterious person to show up to help us feel ready. We wait.

Numbing and Avoidant Behaviors

All of us participate in behaviors that numb us from our feelings or allow us to run from them. Common ones include:

- doomscrolling social media
- watching TV/YouTube
- eating
- playing video games
- drinking/substance use
- reading
- staring off into space
- obsessive exercise or cleaning
- revenge bedtime procrastination*

* A loose translation of the Chinese term for when you stay up super late in anger or resentment of the day, only to make tomorrow harder from lack of sleep.

Inherent in the waiting (and the activity) is an implication of hope. We secretly believe that if we wait long enough, we will eventually feel ready. The Wall of Awful will magically disappear. Or the future version of us will swoop in to tackle the task with courage, skill, and absolutely no fear of negative emotions. (Future us is a superhero.) Unfortunately, hope isn't enough on its own. Hope needs engagement to be able to activate. The longer we wait, the more we frantically take the wrong actions, and the higher the anxiety builds. The longer we sit, hoping and waiting, hoping and waiting, the more we lose trust in ourselves. The more we stare at the Wall of Awful, the more we try to go around it, the more it grows.

No matter how good it feels in the moment, avoidance doesn't help long term.

Waiting Brain

All too often, those of us with neurodivergent brains fall into the "waiting brain" trap.[1] We're humming along, moving toward a goal, when—bam!—we have to wait for something important to happen, and we get stuck in waiting mode.

For example, I had a client who wanted to get in shape. One week I helped him make a plan to that end, including finding a personal trainer. The next week he was still waiting for various trainers to call him back and hadn't done anything else on the plan. He had stalled. I coached him to start with small actions he *could* do on his own while he waited for the calls—like eating an apple instead of that extra piece of pizza, going for a walk, or doing some push-ups. He wasn't actually dependent on a trainer calling him back.

To make things even more confusing, sometimes what we're waiting for isn't even connected to the tasks we're trying to do, like when we lose half a day because we have a doctor's appointment in the afternoon. "Waiting brain" is a trap. It often absorbs massive amounts of time and energy that could go toward actually making the problem better. Thankfully, knowing about it can help us avoid it.

STARING AT THE WALL

Staring at the Wall is an internal process based in the amygdala's *freeze* response. In response to feeling threatened by big emotions and big anxiety, we become overwhelmed and stuck. Sometimes our bodies literally feel heavy, like we're moving through mud. Small tasks feel increasingly hard. And since we can't activate on our tasks, we become passive. We literally sit on the couch (or in front of the screen) and do nothing.

But staring at the Wall can happen while in motion. Some people stare at the Wall while they do something that's rote and mindless, like scrubbing their kitchen countertop or folding laundry. Still others engage in numbing behaviors—mindless television, alcohol, or anything else that shuts off the mind.

Dopamine Rabbit Holes

Staring at the Wall and trying to go around it are ineffective strategies. They don't help us get past a Wall of Awful, but they feel instinctively correct. When faced with emotions that feel threatening, we try to avoid, escape, and ignore them, or we wait for them to leave. But in doing so, it's possible to get caught in a "dopamine rabbit hole." Dopamine is a neurotransmitter—the brain's anticipation and reward chemical. It makes us want to do things and rewards us when we do them. But in the modern world, we can "get stuck" chasing the wrong things in a self-reinforcing cycle.

We start watching television to relieve the difficult emotions, but the streaming service keeps offering us another episode. We start scrolling social media to distract ourselves, and the endless scroll captures our attention, providing us with so much dopamine that hours pass. Neurodivergent people struggle to regulate attention and disengage from distractions more than other people do. When we're facing a Wall of Awful on top of our usual struggles, dopamine distractors become even more tempting. The more we avoid our Walls, the worse we feel about not doing the task, and the stronger the pull of the distractions—especially those that make us feel better—gets. Before long an entire day goes by without doing that one critical thing.

Rather than immediately trying to numb emotions with distractions and risking a dopamine rabbit hole, try going for a walk or playing music while you do another useful task. The immediate hit of the dopamine reward chemical will be less, but you will also avoid becoming trapped in the rabbit hole. Of course, you have other choices. You can put on a timer to limit the television or doomscrolling, or use one of the strategies shared later in this book to put a door in your Wall. You can intentionally change your emotional state and get to the other side. (See Chapter 6.)

GOING AROUND THE WALL

Imagine you're standing at the base of a gigantic Wall of Awful. Rather than trying to punch a hole in it or Climb the Wall (both hard), you do what any self-respecting owner of a brain would do to get past the Wall: You decide to walk around it. After all, why work hard when you don't have to?

The problem is that the Wall moves with us. The negative emotions we've built over months and years aren't going away. No matter how long we walk, the emotions still block our path. We can wear ourselves out with frantic action that gets us nowhere, and the Wall will still be there.

Trying to walk around the Wall is an instinctive strategy based in the amygdala's *flight* response. We feel threatened by big emotions or big anxiety and want to run away. We avoid the problem in the hope it will disappear. We do something, anything to distract ourselves from the reality of these overwhelming emotions and seemingly impassable obstacles. But when the dust settles, the task and the Wall are still there. No matter how far we run, our overwhelming emotions follow us.

From the outside, going around the Wall can look like one of three things.

Churning

Churning is an active form of anxious procrastination. When we churn, we do things over and over that are *related* to the task or goal we need to accomplish but that don't actually help us do it. Churning looks like useful action, but it's not; we're spinning our wheels. Nothing related to the task moves forward, despite a great deal of action.

I've watched many new entrepreneurs fall into this trap. They might need to create a website and have a good understanding of how to do it, but instead of getting started, they sign up for yet another online course or buy another book on web design in order to learn things they mostly already know. They need to sit down and start building. They know this, but they instead waste time talking to three *more* colleagues about what their website should do.

They might look busy from the outside, but they're avoiding the problem just as much as someone who's spending all day watching television. Often people who do this have big emotions about presenting themselves in public. Maybe they're worried about embarrassing themselves with the new website and losing customers as a result. If these new entrepreneurs are moving to self-employment from a more traditional career, they may very well be terrified of going out on their own. (I know I was!) After all, once they publish that website, their traditional career is really over.

I don't mean to invalidate anxious feelings. They're real and they matter. But as long as we're churning, we're trapped with the feelings. We aren't interacting with the Wall. No matter how much activity we do, we'll never get past it. We can spend all day exhausting ourselves planning that metaphorical website out one more time or taking one more course, but if we aren't doing the one thing that will move us forward, we'll stay where we are. Churning is exhausting, and all the frantic effort does nothing to address the real problem.

Perfectionism Is a Silent Killer

Sometimes, the more deeply we care, the higher the Wall becomes, and the more we get stuck churning. We know enough, but we can't stand the thought of it being imperfect. So we disregard "good enough" and let perfectionism stop us cold.

High standards or quality are good things, but perfectionism isn't either of those. Perfectionism is a fear response.[2] Even when it doesn't cause someone to freeze up entirely, it still stalls forward progress. Churning *can* look like endless planning or learning without making headway. But it can also look like "rearranging the deck chairs on the *Titanic*" or making endless changes past the point of reason.

Let's return to those new entrepreneurs and their websites. If they are secretly not sure that they're ready for self-employment, they might churn even when they've finished that website. They might change the fonts and colors of the site for the fourteenth time rather than start marketing their business. They're stalling even if they don't realize they are—pretending to engage with a new business without actually launching it. I know I did similar things when I first started out. Eventually I learned that churning, this constant effort without any forward progress, doesn't work. All it does is bog people down.

Puttering

Churning is a mostly internal effort focused in the direction of our task or goal, but the effort ultimately goes nowhere. Puttering, on the other hand, is productive, external effort focused in the wrong direction. The great rallying call of the putterer is "I need to do this other thing first!"

Productive procrastination, where you avoid something you're anxious about while you do something else that's useful, is similar to but not the same as puttering. If you're crossing off the rest of your to-do list while you wait to "feel like" doing the next most important thing, that *can* be a viable strategy to life management as long as it doesn't go on too long. (Keep in mind, though, that it may not help you get to the other side of the Wall of Awful, and you may need to use the strategies in the rest of this book deliberately at some point.)

Puttering is different because it's ultimately counterproductive. Mary needs to launch a website, but first she has to get her business cards made despite having nowhere to use them. Then she has to go to three weddings to notice how *those* photographers are doing wedding shots. Then she has to help her mom clean out her attic and her sister pick out a new car—all before she can launch the website. Then she has to find a new client—but she puts that off too, because she has to do something else before *that*. Soon all the work Mary has put into the photography website goes to waste, and despite accomplishing many small goals, months later she still hasn't launched her website or her business.

Puttering can be difficult to spot from the inside. Often it takes three or four rounds of "But first I have to..." before we're able to spot the pattern of avoidance. If we need to mow the lawn, but first we need to get the dog's toys off the lawn, that might be legitimate. If then we need to move the rocks away from the fence and fill three holes and trim the bushes and take a call from a friend before we can mow the lawn, eventually we need to accept that we're avoiding it.

How to Avoid the Waiting Traps

We all fall into staring at the Wall and trying to walk around the Wall sometimes, myself included. These behaviors are instinctive! The key is to check in with yourself, so you can identify these traps early. Make sure you understand your task clearly and the goal you want to accomplish. Then check in with your current level of action. What are you doing, and is it getting you closer to your goal? If not, you might be churning. If all of the effort is getting you to other goals, you might be productively procrastinating, or simply puttering, spending a lot of effort in the wrong (and unhelpful) direction.

Once you know you're staring at the Wall, or trying to walk around the Wall, you're in a better position to abandon that unhelpful strategy. Then you can intentionally apply the strategies in the rest of this book to get past the Wall successfully.

YOUR INSTINCTS POINT TO EFFECTIVE STRATEGIES

Effective and ineffective strategies to Climb the Wall of Awful can end up looking similar. The difference is *intention*.

Often when we procrastinate, we're using an unintentional system or structure to try to solve a problem. For example, my client Cody tends to sit on the couch and watch TV rather than starting his difficult college assignments. This approach is an attempt at solving an emotional problem—Cody's lack of desire to do homework. Watching TV on its own will not get Cody to do what he needs to accomplish, but it has the seed of something that *could* work. So we've been working on approaching his TV watching more intentionally. A Marvel movie is not as useful for motivation as a documentary about Shep Gordon. Cody likes Shep Gordon and finds his documentary engaging and inspiring. Watching part of it changes Cody's emotional state, leaving him feeling pumped to start the difficult homework assignment. Cody has turned his initial strategy of staring at the Wall, which was ineffective, into a similar but more effective strategy that puts a door in his Wall (see Chapter 6).

When my client Emma faces a Wall of Awful, she often finds herself processing her emotions unconsciously. Typically, she paces around her house and half-heartedly spot-cleans instead of engaging with an overwhelming but important task. I wondered how we could help her process those emotions more intentionally. If she needs to use her body, could she walk in the woods behind her house? That helped a little but not enough. So we added music to her walk, songs she enjoyed that would help manage her emotions. It worked. The music, nature, and mild exertion of the walk helped her process her emotions and get herself regulated for the task at hand. The walks give her time to think about what she is intending to do, and she often comes back feeling energized with a clear plan.

FACING THE FRUSTRATION

Trying to get past the Wall of Awful by way of the "staring at it" and "going around it" strategies can be incredibly frustrating. It can feel shameful, when other people seem to be able to get started, and we can't. We can feel stuck in a very, very dark place. But there is hope. The better we get at identifying our unhelpful instincts, the easier we can avoid the traps. If we recognize the habits that aren't serving us, we can begin to change them. We can always start over when we inevitably make a mistake. Awareness is always the first step.

None of us will ever do this perfectly, and that's okay.

There is no such thing as laziness. Most of us facing a Wall of Awful are trying our very best—sometimes using incredible reserves of energy—and still may not be getting where we want to go. Adding judgment to the situation doesn't help; it just adds new bricks to the Wall. Instead, be kind.

Show compassion. Give yourself permission to mess up. When you catch yourself staring at the Wall, or trying to go around the Wall by puttering or churning, accept the reality of what is happening. Then stop yourself gently and try something that may work better.

Even when we hit setbacks, we use every experience as an opportunity to learn. Nothing is ever wasted when we approach it with curiosity and learning. Even failures can provide some useful information to make things easier next time and help us understand ourselves better.

CHEAT SHEET: STRATEGIES THAT DON'T WORK

1 The reason we procrastinate when facing a Wall of Awful is because **procrastination is often our best attempt to solve a problem related to emotions.**

2 For many of us, the instinctive response to a Wall of Awful is to wait. When the waiting is passive, we're "staring at the wall." When active, we're trying to "go around the Wall."

3 When we do things related to the task at hand (like learning a thing we already know how to do about the task) but don't actually start, we're churning.

4 We're puttering when we actively procrastinate by doing things that are pointed in the wrong direction—"First I have to check the weather; then I can pay the bills!"

5 **The more we care about a task, the higher our Walls can become.** And when we care deeply, especially about the outcome, perfectionism can stop us cold as we lose sight of the fact that **done is better than perfect**.

6 None of us is perfect, and that's okay. When we catch ourselves hitting a Wall and using one

of these strategies that don't work, **we always learn from the experience.**

ACTION STEP:
Think about the Wall of Awful you're facing. Have you caught yourself staring at it or trying to go around it? What could you have done instead to get started? Write it down.

CHAPTER FIVE

SMASHING THROUGH THE WALL

> Smashing works temporarily, but it comes at the price of damage to ourselves or others. There are healthier choices long term.

In the last chapter, we talked about staring at the Wall and going around the Wall, the strategies people use to get past the Wall of Awful that don't work. Now let's talk about the first strategy that gets us past the Wall: Smashing through it.

Smashing uses strong negative emotions, most often anger or anxiety, to punch a temporary hole in the Wall. Smashing requires less skill than the other (better) options we'll discuss in later chapters, so people often find and use this strategy instinctively. The problem with smashing is that it can be just as destructive as it is helpful. Smashing causes damage to both ourselves and our relationships. And, in the long term, when used too often, smashing eventually stops working at all.

WHAT SMASHING LOOKS LIKE

In one session, my client Martin told me that over the previous week his boss had asked him to update a database. Martin hated updating databases and had a Wall of Awful for it. He spent hours avoiding that task. His boss had to ask him a second and a third time, and eventually Martin got angry about it.

He ended up clicking out of a Zoom meeting, angrily saying, "Fine. I'll do the update right now!" He updated the database, muttering and cursing the whole time. It was a strategy that had worked for him; anger gives us energy to smash through obstacles, and Martin used it successfully to Smash through his Wall of Awful. Unfortunately, his boss took his angry outburst badly, and it damaged Martin's standing at work.

Anger often creates the need for action. It drives us to our goals and lets us punch holes in our Walls. Unfortunately, those holes don't stick around, and we'll have to deal with that Wall again sooner or later. We'll also have to deal with the rubble our smashing left behind.

OTHER NEGATIVE EMOTIONS HIDE BEHIND ANGER

Anger is an easy emotion to access, particularly for men and boys (myself included). That's because anger can cover up other, more vulnerable emotions.[1] When people experience humiliation, anxiety, rejection, or fear, those emotions will often get papered over with anger. We want to avoid those vulnerable feelings underneath because most of us are uncomfortable with that vulnerability. Our anger makes us feel powerful and often makes other people feel vulnerable. But our other negative emotions are still there, no matter how angry we get, just hiding underneath the anger and biding their time.

The emotions we've papered over will cause problems if we don't deal with them. (See Chapter 7 on Climbing the Wall to learn how to deal with these other negative emotions sustainably.) When you feel anger, are you really feeling anger? Or is the anger covering up other negative emotions that are harder to deal with? The answer will help you overcome your Walls.

Other Negative Emotions and Smashing

While anger is the most common way to Smash through the Wall, other strong negative emotions can also do the same work. Anxiety, frustration, and defiance, for example, can build up in a person's system to the point they also provide smashing force. The damage that anxiety causes tends to be more internal, but the experience can otherwise be the same as the experience of anger smashing.

SMASHING THROUGH

When explaining the smashing strategy to kids, I like to use the image of the famous green superhero Hulk. When he's angry, he turns bright green, gets giant, and if there's a wall in front of him, he smashes through it. Of course, when he smashes through the wall, it hurts him. Bricks go flying in every direction, some hitting and hurting others. There's no getting around that.

Smashing can be weaponized anger. When we're angry, we're in our fight response. We aren't going to let obstacles get in our way. We'll crash through those barriers, even if the barrier is a Wall of Awful. If we're angry enough, we may even enjoy the chaos and destruction we're causing.

When we Smash, we get through the wall at any cost. We aren't being elegant about it. We aren't considering the consequences of our actions or trying to be thoughtful about the nervousness we have around our

Wall. We've moved into our fight response, and our amygdala only cares about now.

An Instrument of Blunt Force

As we talked about in Chapter 2, the prefrontal cortex—the skilled "thinking" part of the brain—can power down when we experience strong emotions. In those moments, processing is moved to the amygdala. This is our "fight or flight" response, and anger is *fight.*

In fight mode, our prefrontal cortex struggles to function. We can't think clearly about the consequences of our actions, and we won't be able to access complex skills nearly as well. That means we'll tend to make more mistakes and rely on blunt force to solve problems when a more skilled approach would be better. Tasks that are done won't be done as well with high levels of anger or similar emotions in our system. We may *feel* powerful, but we are typically less capable under this pressure.

Anger has its place. It can get us to take action and can be an effective short-term solution in that way. But if we lean on anger more and more over time, we're keeping our amygdala primed and ready to fight. Our only tool will be a hammer, so everything around us will look like a nail. We're likely to overuse our anger, causing damage to ourselves and others in a self-reinforcing cycle.

SMASHING HURTS

All smashing comes at a price. Sometimes the damage is outward, as we scream at our spouses, children, or coworkers. We snap at the person making a request of us or berate someone who interrupts us.

Sometimes we take our anger out on people who have nothing to do with the specific Wall we're facing, just because they're there. If Roxanne intends to do the slides for next week's financial presentation but hasn't started yet, and a coworker asks her about the Jones account, she might growl at them, "Can't you see I'm doing something?" That coworker had nothing to do with her stress, but they interrupted her, and the anger gave Roxanne more energy to Smash through her Wall. Unfortunately, accessing that energy may have caused damage to that relationship.

Not every "Smash" is external—sometimes we turn our anger, frustration, and especially anxiety on ourselves. We ask, "What's wrong with me? Why do I suck? Why can't I just do this?" We may threaten ourselves, saying if we don't do this, then we deserve to lose our job, or a date, or the promotion we've been working for. We might use shame, self-loathing, or toxic words to smash inwardly. But the cost is rarely worth the benefit.

Shame and Self-Loathing

Two of the most difficult bricks in the Wall are shame and self-loathing. If guilt is when we feel like we caused a problem, shame is when we feel we are the problem. We can feel overwhelmed, like we are inadequate or disgusted with ourselves. If we are smashing inwardly, odds are we're experiencing some degree of shame.

Self-loathing is when we don't like ourselves—but taken to the extreme. We overcriticize ourselves, looking only at our flaws and failures, disregarding our strengths and virtues. Self-loathing often comes with shame, causing us to feel like we deserve to be punished. That makes smashing inward *seem* like a good idea, but its long-term costs are real. It intensifies mental illness and makes us just generally have a hard time. There are better ways to get past the Wall!

Taking stock of the positive things we bring to the world is a good way to start moving out of both shame and self-loathing. Sometimes that means we will have to ask our loved ones for their perspective, or seek the help of a therapist, coach, or other trusted adviser. It's worth doing.

INTENT MATTERS

Talking to ourselves strongly doesn't *necessarily* mean we're smashing inwardly. Motivating ourselves by appealing to our integrity can look similar, but they are not the same. If we tell ourselves, "If I can't do X, then I'm not worthy of a black belt," and the black belt is the goal that is motivating us, that *can be* different. Being motivated by a goal may or may not carry with it some degree of sacrifice, but inward-facing anger hurts us every time.

Similarly, some people can talk to themselves with enough humor and affection that even harsh words don't carry the same meaning. "What's wrong with you?" said with humor can have a very different effect for those people.

The difference between smashing inwardly and using integrity or humor to motivate ourselves is largely about how the process makes us *feel* and therefore whether or how much we damage ourselves.

Smashing inward isn't sustainable in the long term and can contribute to burnout and negative mental health spirals, making anxiety, depression, and other conditions worse. Over the long term, choosing kind, compassionate, and sustainable ways of motivating ourselves is the healthier option.

Smashing Doesn't Always Work

Sometimes strong emotions *don't* result in Smashing through the Wall of Awful, and in that case, attempting to smash results in the worst of all worlds. We get nowhere, but we still take damage from the attempt.

Outward smashing that doesn't get us past the Wall is a tantrum. Inward smashing is either self-flagellation or perhaps a fawn response.* "I'm sorry, I suck, I'm sorry, I suck," proves as ineffective at getting past the Wall as a tantrum. It can also do damage to relationships if it is continual and unchecked.

Whatever we do, we should try to avoid smashing that doesn't work. Taking damage without benefit is a fool's errand.

MAKING IT PERSONAL

If we smash inward, we're making value judgments about ourselves. If we smash outward, we're making value judgments about the problem we're being asked to address and the person asking. We're making the problem personal.

---

* A note on the fawn response: The fawn response attempts to decrease the impact of threats by appeasing them. As a result, people with CPTSD and related experiences may fall into this pattern even in healthy relationships. Fawning *is* helpful in dysfunctional relationships and trauma situations, but that is not the scenario I am talking about here. Additional information is beyond the scope of this book.[2]

We're using resentment and anger toward the other person as fuel to act—but those negative thoughts and words damage our relationship with that person.

For example, there's nothing personal about doing the dishes; it's just a mundane chore that everyone has to do. But if our partner asks us to do the dishes and then we stomp off, growling, "Fine, I'll do the dishes if you just shut up," we're *making* the situation personal. We might be assuming that our partner is judging us, personally, for not having done the dishes. Or we may be judging ourselves.

The same is true about nearly any other task we get angry about. A large portion of the anger may not be from the task at all—a dirty dish is simply a dirty dish, not an indictment of our character. But when we make the situation personal or read into a request that the situation is personal, we'll feel defensive. If we assume they think less of us, we may resent them (and the task) unnecessarily. Of course, if the other person is, in fact, judging us, if they are making the situation personal, then they're the one damaging things from their side.

Smashing can damage relationships in a couple of ways. First, as we subconsciously look for that aggressive energy to solve our Wall, we may assume that things are personal when they aren't. We may walk around feeling judged all the time just so we can be angry or offended and activate. From the other side, people who have caught the brunt of our failures and subsequent smashing may indeed begin judging and find us wanting. Either way the anger isn't helpful and often makes the situation worse. If we feel like we're in the middle of an emotional arms race, we might be tempted to strike at the other person first. We might feel better, but they will feel worse, and the cycle continues—often because of a small task like dirty dishes that are easily cleaned.

Thankfully, if we can find our balance and respond calmly rather than react with anger, we can avoid or mitigate the relationship damage. Responding with compassion and intention allows us to have these interactions in a healthier way.

IF WE DON'T CARE, WE DON'T GET ANGRY

Anger is an important signal that whatever made us angry matters to us in some way. In other words, if we're getting angry about something and there's no boundary or value involved, we should take that anger as a clear signal that either the task or the person making the request matters to us. Even if the task only matters because something bad might happen if we don't do it, like losing our job, it still matters.

Anger focuses and activates us because it's our body's

way of making sure we pay attention to and take action toward something critically important.

Smashing Can Be a Worthwhile Strategy (Sometimes)

Just to be clear, I'm not *completely* vilifying this strategy. Smashing through the Wall is an effective tool, and there are times when smashing is a reasonable choice, maybe even the best choice.

For example, if you need to smash in order to go online and pay your rent and not doing so would result in you being thrown out on the street, Smash your Wall! The internal or external damage is less than the damage of losing the roof over your head. For another example, if everyone at your job aggressively Smashes through their Walls, sitting and staring at yours may lose you their respect. Matching their energy may serve you in that specific environment—you may be promoted if you're seen as someone who doesn't let barriers stop you. But you may pay a price for burning so much anger or anxiety for fuel—your health and personal life may suffer.

Make the choice of whether to smash or not as intentionally as possible, with a full understanding of the cost.

THE HIDDEN COST TO OURSELVES

Motivating ourselves with weaponized judgment, anger, and resentment hurts us in subtle ways. It is one of the biggest costs of long-term smashing.

The human mind has a negativity bias—we're hardwired to remember the bad story over the good story, so we avoid bad things in the future and keep ourselves safe. If we tell ourselves a negative story over and over again, it shapes how we view the world. Eventually, we won't see our strengths or give ourselves credit for being as amazing as we are. And if we can't see our strengths, we'll miss chances to act on them and lose out on opportunities that align with our best selves. We may miss out on adventures, promotions, personal growth opportunities, or even people that we might have loved.

Even more concerning is the risk of anxiety, depression, and other mental health conditions. If the story we tell ourselves is that we're not good enough or that we're the worst parent, friend, or business leader in the world, eventually we will believe it and decide we can't improve. Even if we point the blame elsewhere, and tell ourselves that all of our mistakes are someone else's fault, we still can't improve. The negative thought spirals waste time and eventually undermine us subconsciously.

TOO MUCH SMASHING LEADS TO BURNOUT

The body isn't meant to live in fight-or-flight mode all the time.[3] If we get used to living on adrenaline and hitting the smash button to overcome every problem we encounter, we'll eventually burn out. We'll stop responding as strongly to the anxiety of it all, and our smashing will stop working. If smashing is our only way of getting past our Walls, burnout can be devastating.

During and after the height of the COVID-19 pandemic, I had three long-term family emergencies overlap: (1) In response to the school disruptions of the early pandemic, I made the choice to homeschool my twin sons while also running my business. Shortly thereafter, (2) a family member had a significant mental health crisis, leading to an OCD diagnosis, and then (3) a different family member was diagnosed with cancer. Both family members required significant support as a result.

The stress of juggling so many overlapping crises took its toll. Soon I began relying on anxiety to activate and get past my Walls. I didn't have the bandwidth to use any higher-skilled options. Every day I relied on anxiety to survive and get the bare minimum of things done.

Unfortunately, relying on anxiety is a terrible long-term plan. I stopped sleeping well, I stopped managing well, and eventually it didn't matter that I wasn't taking care of myself, seeing my friends, or participating in the world around me. It didn't matter that I hadn't made a podcast in so long that people may have forgotten about me or that I wasn't making enough money. No matter how much anxiety I felt, I couldn't activate. I couldn't make myself do anything that wasn't an emergency. I was unable to move forward. One day my wife took me aside and told me our financial situation couldn't go on. I had to run my coaching groups again.

Fortunately, by then the worst of COVID was over, and my family members had gotten the help they needed. But I was still burned out, and smashing was not an option. I am fortunate that my love for my wife and my children was enough to motivate me at that moment. I was able to reach for, and apply, more skilled options to Climb my Wall. (I'll teach you these options later in the book.) My motivation in doing those things was no longer based on anxiety, however. It couldn't be. This time I had to tap into my values for motivation—ultimately finding it in a place of integrity, of doing my part to ensure that my wife wasn't carrying our financial burden by herself, and helping others.

Many of us share this kind of story, though the details may vary. Alex, the co-author of this book, also had this experience in the middle of COVID, parenting a four-year-old in a small apartment on lockdown while also trying to make a living. When the motivation of her anxiety finally failed, she had to go on antidepressants and get family support to find her way out again.

What is true of anxiety is also true of anger. We can only live in fight-or-flight mode for so long before our bodies fail, our relationships with ourselves and others take too much damage, or both. The cost of Smashing through the Wall is real and adds up.

Anger Leads to Dopamine (and Getting It Done)

Smashing sometimes looks like picking a fight. We see this a lot with kids, where they pick a fight with mom or dad about doing their homework before eventually caving and doing it, but we adults do it, too. Sometimes the fight isn't even related to the task at hand, like when someone argues about the chances of their favorite team winning that night's game, only to suddenly sit down and write the email they've been avoiding all day.

It may not make logical sense to get angry *at* something in order to do that thing more easily. But anger feels good and sets off a cascade of brain chemicals (including dopamine)[4] that make decisive action easier.[5] Anger engages our attention and keeps us focused and moving.[6] It's inherently motivating.*

Whether we use the dopamine from a fight to activate consciously or not, we eventually learn that fighting works to push us through our Wall and help us get started. If we aren't careful, we'll fall into a pattern of picking a fight with friends or family every time we need to get started.

POSITIVE AND NEGATIVE FUEL

Anger can provide us either positive or negative motivation, so it's important that we learn to understand the difference.

For example, if someone tells me I can't write a book, I might react in anger. I might yell, "F that noise! I can absolutely write a book. Just watch!" If I am out of control and letting my anger take control, I'm probably not going to write the book.

On the other hand, if someone tells me I can't, and I take the opportunity to prove them wrong out of a

* It's important to state that the ease of getting started or deciding what action to take doesn't necessarily translate to making *good* decisions or actions while angry.

place of control, I might say the same words. "F that noise! I can absolutely write a book. Just watch!" But the tone and the nonverbal cues will be different. If I'm in control of my emotions, I'm not at the whim of spite or wounded pride. I'm using determination to move forward, and odds are I will write that book.

In the same way, some relationships have a joking competition about them. If one person at the gym says, "You can't do fifty push-ups," and the other responds, "Shut up. I can too," that interaction can be angry, or it can be meant playfully and in the spirit of motivating competition.

When in doubt, become curious about our emotions and their intent. If we are trying to play, or to be positively competitive, we should make sure the energy we have around that stays positive. Play and competition are healthy as long as they are well managed and don't become toxic. If, on the other hand, we are angry but in control of our emotions, we may be using anger to get to determination, and determination is positive fuel. If our emotions and anger are in control of *us*, it's smashing. That anger is serving as a negative and unhealthy fuel. We should take a step back, calm down, and find another approach.

An Example of Intent

At a recent ADHD conference, I attended a baby shower for my friend Jessica McCabe. I had just done four hours of interviews for the podcast, and I was having trouble doing the activity that was next at the shower.

I was sitting there, looking at the card I was supposed to be writing with advice to the mom- and dad-to-be about parenting. Out of light-hearted frustration, I said, "I've got nothin'. Why am I so dumb right now?"

One of the other attendees, Dani Donovan, spoke up. "Stop being mean to my friend!"

I'm usually the one calling people out on their self-talk, and for some reason I was caught completely off guard. The truth was that I had meant it playfully, expressing frustration as a way to validate how I was feeling and get myself moving. I know I'm not dumb, but in that moment I wanted to make space for my note to not be as good as I felt it could be. I knew I was fried from all the interviews I'd done that day. In a way, I was trying to playfully lower the bar for everyone, to banish perfectionism.

If we can relate our self-criticism to a personal strength, we can avoid the damage it might otherwise cause. In that case, it's more of a climbing strategy than a smashing one. But the outside observer may not be able to tell the difference—and we might not either. When we say negative things about ourselves, it's important to pay attention to our intent so we're sure that we're not smashing inwardly in a way that does us harm.

BUILDING HEALTHIER RELATIONSHIPS

Paying attention is also the first step in building healthier relationships with others. If we are repeatedly smashing in a specific relationship, that should be an indication to us that the relationship might not be healthy. Perhaps we are responding to unhealthy pressure, or perhaps we are causing unhealthy pressure. In any event, the dynamic isn't good for us.

A few years ago, I was helping a fourteen-year-old client with his homework at his kitchen table. Despite the Walls of Awful that William felt around homework, he was doing well, typing away at his Byzantine Empire assignment. Then his brother walked into the room, and William lost focus on what he was doing. Eventually, he picked a fight with his brother before getting back to work. It became clear over the next few weeks that whenever his brother came into the room, William would get distracted and then pick a fight. William had a Wall for doing things when his brother was around and was using the fights to Smash that Wall and get back to his homework. Eventually William went away to college, and the two were able to mature and come back after time away from each other to have a healthier relationship.

If we're always battling with a boss, coworker, or spouse, we might need to take that as an indication that something about the relationship is unhealthy. If we're battling with everyone, and smashing is our only approach to solving problems, then it's time to look at ourselves. We're the common denominator. What does our constant anger mean about how we operate interpersonally and what our expectations might be?

FINDING BETTER CHOICES

Smashing works, but it is the least skilled method to get past our Walls. It *can* be the right choice in certain circumstances, but there's always a cost. If it's the only tool we have to get past our Walls, we're in for a harder road than necessary. Fortunately, there are several strategies to get past the Wall that are just as effective, with fewer downsides. The rest of the book is about how these approaches work.

CHEAT SHEET: SMASHING THROUGH

1. Smashing is an effective (but damaging) strategy to punch a temporary hole in our wall by using strong emotions to hit the fight part of the fight/flight/freeze instinct.
2. **Smashing works to get us past the Wall of Awful, but it often damages relationships.** When we smash outwardly, we damage our relationship with other people, and when we smash inwardly, we damage our relationship with ourselves.
3. The anger we feel when smashing is often covering up other, more vulnerable emotions—fear, shame, humiliation, anxiety, rejection, etc. But our anger gives us the illusion of power so we don't have to face our vulnerability.
4. **If we didn't care, we wouldn't feel anxious or angry** about the task. We might care because a boundary is being crossed, because a value is at play, or because there is a strong negative consequence connected to the task.
5. If our only strategy for getting past our Walls is to Smash, **we will eventually burn out**. The

body isn't meant to live in fight/flight/freeze response all the time.

6 Smashing is the least skilled approach that gets us past the Wall of Awful, and it can do damage to ourselves and others if we're not careful, but it is still a valid strategy. It just shouldn't be the only tool we have in our toolbox.

ACTION STEP:

Let's return to the Wall of Awful you've been considering throughout the book. Have you Smashed this Wall in the past? Was it inward or outward? Was the price worth it?

CHAPTER SIX

PUTTING A DOOR IN THE WALL (AKA EASY MODE)

> Because the Wall of Awful is made from strong negative emotions, changing our emotional state can "put a door in the Wall" and get us to the other side quickly. Be cautious, though: You will have to Climb the Wall sooner or later.

About halfway through writing this book, Alex mentioned in passing that her then-six-year-old daughter Audrey was resisting bedtime. Me being me, I had to know details.

Her daughter was trying to do "one more thing" for ten to fifteen minutes at a time, or just refusing to go upstairs and brush her teeth entirely, despite multiple warnings. After as much as twenty minutes of struggle and delays, Alex would get frustrated—and yell.

Yelling worked in the short term but made Audrey associate bedtime with yelling, which made her (understandably) avoid it that much harder. It was a bad cycle.

So I suggested a new plan. Instead of going upstairs and immediately trying to brush teeth, Audrey would get to play her favorite music—the *Bluey: Dance Mode* album—and the two would have a three-song dance party, complete with stuffed animals.

"Here's the thing," I told Alex. "You have to really be silly and dance full out to make it fun. Like, dance with the stuffed animals. If you get frustrated, it won't be fun, and it won't work." After three songs, she needed to dance over to the sink and help Audrey start brushing her teeth while dancing.

"Also, a lot of kids don't like the sensory experience of certain toothbrushes or toothpastes. If you can, buy a few kinds and see which Audrey tolerates best."

Alex, who would try anything at this point, executed my advice to the letter. There was a dance party to Bluey music. There was dancing teeth brushing with unicorn toothpaste. And Audrey got to check off items from the bedtime checklist with a marker.

Within two days, Audrey no longer tried to sabotage the beginning of bedtime—it was fun now! And with less frustration on everyone's part, Alex and Audrey snuggled in to read books at the end of the night more consistently.

A little music and a little silliness had gotten over the Wall of Awful.

THE MORAL OF THE STORY

The bedtime struggle had lasted more than two years, and Alex had tried everything. So why did *Bluey: Dance Mode* and a stuffed animal dance party instantly solve the problem? It's not because I'm magic (though I try to be)—it's because the dance party worked to "put a door in the Wall." The fun, the joyous dance music changed Audrey's emotional state in a positive way. The barrier she was facing became less important, and even toothpaste felt less intimidating. Play is the opposite of anxiety.[1]

The Wall of Awful is built of negative emotions, so changing our emotional state also changes the Wall—temporarily. The Wall is still there; our negative experiences with the tasks are still there. But changing our emotions and the state of our nervous system opens a temporary door in the Wall, just big enough for us to quickly step through.

FEELINGS ARE LIKE THE WEATHER: THEY CHANGE

Emotions are temporary. No one is always happy, and no one is always mad—even if it sometimes feels that way in the moment. If we recognize that our emotions are going to change, then we can start to take some agency over how they change. We gain *some* control over how we feel in the moment.[2]

Of course, that control can be limited. My client Danielle lost her husband a few months ago, and the sadness and devastation she feels are going to linger. But it also doesn't mean she has to always feel sad. She's allowed to have moments of joy and wonder, even if they don't hang around as long as they otherwise would. People experience the whole range of emotions, day by day and hour by hour—and this is particularly true for those of us with neurodivergence and mental health conditions.

Because change *will happen*, we can make that change work for us. Whatever makes us feel happy, or motivated, or powerful is something we can use as a cue. We can act with the goal of sparking different feelings. We can put a door in our Wall.

HOW THE DOOR WORKS

Up to this point in the book, we've done the hard work of defining anxiety, talking about skills and resources, and discussing the strategies that don't work—and the strategy that works but with damage as an unavoidable side effect. Putting a door in the Wall is different! This chapter is designed to be a breath of fresh air, to help you get to the other side of the Wall of Awful *quickly* and without any damage.

Let's look at the principles and practical hacks to do just that.

Fair Warning: The Door Is Temporary

Putting a door in the Wall can give us quick, easy progress on our hardest challenges, and it's worth doing! But it's not a long-term solution.

While there are *many* different ways to change our emotions and get the dopamine we need to start, each way only works some of the time—and a single tactic tends to stop working if it's repeated too much. The Wall is also still there, still blocking our way. It continues to cause friction around our tasks and weighs down our lives. Eventually we *must* Climb the Wall (see the next chapter) if we want to resolve the issue long term.

Of course, climbing takes time and effort, which we don't always have. So if we need a short-term solution to get started *now*, this is it! Just keep in mind that the easy wins won't last forever.

Putting a door in our Wall is about changing our emotional state. This change can come in one of two forms (sometimes both!): (1) we **soothe** our nervous systems into a state of reasonable calm, or (2) we add excitement, fun, or positive emotions to **motivate** ourselves. In the words of the ADHD community, we add dopamine—we create the conditions that **make our brains *want* to activate.**

Then we start with an "easy win," a small, concrete action that helps us start toward our goal. Once we activate, the rest of the task gets easier.

Of course, some Walls are bigger than others. For small Walls, soothing or activation strategies will work on their own. **Larger Walls will require both**, in order, plus planning. To put a door in a *huge* Wall, we might have to line strategies up like marbles, and hit them one after the other. Even then, putting a door in that Wall will still be faster than climbing it.

Putting a door in the Wall, even when hard, is always the faster solution.

QUICK-START SOLUTIONS

Before we get started on soothing and activation strategies, let's take a minute to run through some fast hacks.

Satisfy Biological Needs. Unmet biological needs increase our anxiety.[3] It can be surprising how much easier getting started becomes after eating a snack, drinking some water, or going to the bathroom.

Listen to Music. Music is emotional communication. The *job* of music is to make us feel a certain way. So if the way we're feeling is not conducive to what we want to do, we can often change the way we're feeling with the right playlist.[4]

Watch Inspirational Videos. The same goes for videos. If we need motivation and we know a YouTube clip will inspire us, we can turn on the video! As long as we're careful not to lose momentum with an endless scroll afterward.

Seek Support. As mentioned in Chapter 3, we can often avoid our Walls entirely by getting the help of others. We might ask a friend or neighbor to help with tasks we struggle with, or hire someone to do the things we're less skilled at or just don't like doing.

Get Moving. Sometimes just going for a walk around the block is enough to get us into a more engaged state of mind. After all, action leads to more action. You might also try stretching, calisthenics, or a dance party.[5]

Try a Podcast. Listening to a good interview discussing the problem we're facing can not only give us new ideas, but hearing people talk about overcoming a similar challenge soothes and motivates us.

Use a Body Double. The ADHD community has long known that asking a friend to sit with us can get us unstuck. An actual friend in person is best, but an online service like Focusmate, Caveday, or Focus 101 can be almost as good. Finally, we can use peer pressure to our benefit!

Change Your Location. There's a reason so many people write in coffee shops. Going to a new location can help give us a fresh perspective. A public place also adds implied accountability.

DOOR #1: SOOTHE THE ANXIETY

Remember anxiety in Chapter 2? The Wall of Awful is made of *many* strong negative emotions, but the mortar that holds them together is anxiety. Anxiety overwhelms us and makes us freeze up, fight, or run away. Because of our strong emotions, our brains and bodies inaccurately take the thing we need to do as a *threat*.

Our brains are built to help us survive. As long as there seems to be a threat in the immediate environment, dealing with that threat will be the number one priority.

As long as we believe on a deep level that our task is a threat, approaching (or doing) it will be hard. We're fighting our survival instincts. So the first and best thing to do for most people is to soothe the anxiety. Regulating our emotions this way helps the brain and the body calm down and feel safe so we can take action.

Once the amygdala no longer sees the task as a threat, we can open a door in the Wall of Awful. After all, the best things in life are on the other side of that Wall. So we have to decrease the anxiety and help our survival instincts see that we are safe.

Just Walk Through

Putting a door in the Wall can, from the inside, sometimes feel a lot like smashing. The Wall of Awful was blocking our way, and now it's gone. We're able to do "the thing" in ways we couldn't a few minutes ago. But smashing is a destructive, low-skilled approach. The strategies that put a door in the Wall require a little more skill, but they're fast, and they're healthy. Like the music and dance party bedtime, they often add positive feelings or dopamine to the situation to help us initiate the task.

Instead of using anger, anxiety, or shame to push through the Wall with negative emotions, putting a door in the Wall works *with the brain*, using positive emotions to make the starting cost cheaper. And walking through a door often is much gentler than smashing through it.

How to Soothe Anxiety: Your CCAW Reminder

As a quick review of <u>Chapter 2</u>, there are four things that make anxiety smaller, which I call CCAW:

- **Certainty**—decreasing the uncertainty of the situation and adding things we can know for sure.
- **<u>Connection</u>**—adding connections with other people for emotional support.
- **Agency**—actions that make us feel more in control of our lives.
- **<u>Well-being practices</u>**—actions that connect with our bodies and directly soothe our nervous systems.

A few caveats: I've underlined connection and well-being practices because these categories are easiest to start at high levels of anxiety, 6 or above on the scale reprinted below. That said, if you have autism and/or social anxiety, you may find that starting with certainty and agency may give you better results. Try the suggested way first. Then try it with certainty and agency—at the end of the section—and see which approach works best for you.

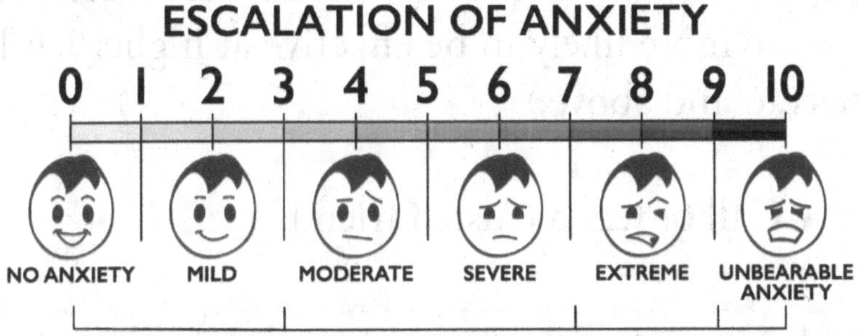

As we saw in Chapter 2, at the highest anxiety levels, our amygdala is in charge. So using logical approaches doesn't make sense, because the amygdala doesn't understand logic. But it does understand the presence of a friend! It also understands running or walking away from the problem, and it can be reasoned with emotionally.

The following quick guide contains ideas for soothing anxiety and increasing our sense of safety in the moment. (You may also want to check out Appendix 3 for additional ideas.)

Soothe with Connection

Connection with other people is a highly effective method of decreasing anxiety, even when that connection is not in person.* Humans are social creatures, and when we connect with people, we often feel safer immediately. Almost any threat is less dangerous when faced in a group!

While there are many ways to add connection, here are a few that work quickly. (Items that start with a star ★ are more likely to be effective at higher levels of anxiety, 6 and above.)

- ★ Call or text a trusted friend.

---

* Social connections are literally good for us and decrease anxiety and depression over the long term. See J. Holt-Lunstad, "Social Connection as a Critical Factor for Mental and Physical Health: Evidence, Trends, Challenges, and Future Implications," *World Psychiatry* 23, no. 3 (October 2024): 312–332. doi: 10.1002/wps.21224. PMID: 39279411; PMCID: PMC11403199. They also have short-term impact, as anyone who has ever seen a mother comfort a toddler or an adult comfort another adult can tell you. And an "in person" connection doesn't seem to be required. In a recent study, young people who found **meaningful connection with other humans through digital means** found significant improvements in mental health including depression and anxiety scores. See L. Dewa, E. Lawrance, L. Roberts, E. Brooks-Hall, H. Ashrafian, G. Fontana, P. Aylin, "Quality Social Connection as an Active Ingredient in Digital Interventions for Young People with Depression and Anxiety: Systematic Scoping Review and Meta-Analysis," *Journal of Medical Internet Research* 23, no. 12 (December 2021): e26584 https://www.jmir.org/2021/12/e26584 DOI: 10.2196/26584.

- ★ Have a trusted spouse or parent give you a hug or rub your back.
- Have a friend come by and body double with you.
- ★ Talk with a counselor, a spiritual leader, a teacher, or other supportive person.

If we can't lean on a trusted person we personally know, that's okay. Sometimes we can use the brain's baked-in social instinct to "borrow" calm from other people**—the same part of the brain that gives in to peer pressure will give in to calm if we ask it to.

- ★ Listen to two calm people joke with each other on a podcast or TV show.
- Go to a coffee shop, library, or park and sit quietly, paying attention to the people around you and how calm they are. Tell yourself you, too, are safe.
- ★ Connect with a special interest or beloved book, TV show, or other media.

---

* This principle is widely understood and discussed within the anxiety circles of the mental health community. It's also reasonable, based on neuroscience's current understanding of emotions as contagious. See Desautels, L. (n.d.). *Contagious emotions and responding to stress.* Digital Commons @ Butler University. https://digitalcommons.butler.edu/coe_papers/94/.

(For more ideas for decreasing anxiety quickly, visit Appendix 3.)

Soothe with Well-Being Practices

We only have one nervous system, so any practice that increases well-being or decreases physical stress also decreases anxiety. (Again, items that start with a ★ star are likely to be effective at higher levels of anxiety, 6 and above. Ones **without** a star are NOT likely to be effective with high anxiety.)

- ★ **Play music** we like, loudly or softly. We can experiment with using different musical emotions at different volumes to see what our anxiety responds to best.
- **Clean your house, whittle, or knit** while listening to a podcast or calming music. The repetitive movement is calming to the body.
- ★ **Go for a walk**—bonus points if it's in nature. Both walking and nature are soothing at a visceral level.
- ★ **Exercise.** At high levels of anxiety, try running or hitting a punching bag. Often, the amygdala wants to run away or fight to resolve the situation. Letting it will help it let go.

Consider yoga or weight lifting (at lower levels of anxiety). Both seem to decrease anxiety over time, and weight lifting tests well as an intervention for PTSD.[6]

- **Do deep breathing exercises.** My wife, Amy, taught me diaphragmatic breathing. She learned it to help manage an asthma attack, but it works for anxiety, too.

  Get comfy, putting one hand on your chest and the other on your belly. Inhale deeply through your nose, focusing on expanding your belly and keeping your chest fairly still, for a four count. Exhale slowly through your mouth for an eight count, letting your belly fall. Repeat several times, keeping the same rhythm, until you feel calmer.

Sensory Regulation Strategies

Dr. Alice Nicholls is an expert on helping Autistic people recover from burnout. Because of this, she's gotten very good at helping neurodivergent people calm their nervous systems using their senses.

The approaches she recommends to soothe the nervous system[7] include:

Linear vestibular motion—such as walking, jumping on a trampoline, swinging on a swing, rocking chair, swaying, yoga/martial arts/dance.

Deep pressure—such as weighted blankets, carrying a heavy backpack or toddler, compression clothing, deep tissue massage, squeezing hands, wrists, fingers.

Proprioceptive input—such as weight training, squeezing a stress ball, clay/slime, LEGO, housework, craft activities, pushing or pulling, yoga/martial arts/dance.

Oral motor stimulation—such as eating crunchy foods, chewing gum/toffees, sucking water from a bottle with high resistance, chewing jewelry.

Retreat—going somewhere for a break from overstimulating sensory input, such as taking a break in your car, or ducking outside from a busy social event. A soothing, low-stimulation area at home or work might also be helpful, or use earplugs and hearing protectors to reduce ambient noise.

Adding sensory strategies can work not only to decrease anxiety in the moment but also to decrease the nervous system's arousal over time.

Soothe with Certainty and Agency

Adding practices that support certainty and agency also decreases anxiety. If we reduce the anxiety enough, we can put a door in the Wall.

- **Add Certainty:**
    - Describe the situation out loud to yourself or someone else. Putting it into words will decrease your anxiety. Anything with a name gets less scary.
    - Break down big, complicated tasks into a manageable list of specific, actionable next steps.
    - ★ If you don't know how to do the task, find someone to help you learn the needed skills. (This strategy also potentially adds connection.)
- **Add Agency:**
    - ★ Do one small action that's helpful—right now.
    - Get clear on the things in our situation that we can control, and act on them.
    - Instead of worrying about someone else's action, plan what we will do to respond.

Soothe with Play

One of the first things I do when coaching someone is change the language we use. They describe a big, heavy problem that's been eating at them, and the first thing I do is ask, "Can I play?" A small choice of words makes a big difference.

Play immediately makes the situation lighter. It opens possibilities and reduces expectations. It throws open the doors of creativity and allows for fun and experimentation. There is no failure in play, and there are no stakes.

Playing with hard problems doesn't invalidate them. But it does make them easier to handle emotionally. I invite the person to play with me, and together we approach the problem in ways we couldn't when it was heavy. Anxiety shuts down creativity and curiosity. Inviting creativity, play, and curiosity allows anxiety to loosen its grip.

On the Threshold of Activation

The higher our anxiety, the more important it will be to soothe *first*, before adding activation strategies. Otherwise the Wall of Awful will stay stubbornly closed.

Of course, for many neurodivergent people, it's not enough simply to be calm. We must *also* have enough dopamine—and enough interest—to activate.

Understanding Social Expectations Puts a Door in the Wall

Social expectations are the things other people (or society) tell us we "should" do. They come from outside of us, and for neurodivergent people these expectations can be particularly difficult to navigate. Depending on the person and the expectation, they can feel huge and overwhelming or be so subtle that they're completely missed!

Sometimes these expectations are real and matter. We might have to dress a certain way or have a certain hairstyle to get a job and then behave in a certain way to keep that job. Other times the expectations are in our head. Just because the people on our favorite sitcom have a spotless house doesn't mean ours has to be perfect as well. After all, no one is filming a TV show in our home! Even our favorite YouTubers and TikTokers put thought and effort into what the room looks like behind them. Getting clear on what is real and what is an illusion is a great way to keep bricks out of the Wall.

If you don't have to do the thing, maybe you can *not* do the thing?

DOOR #2: ACTIVATE

According to psychiatrist and ADHD expert Dr. William Dodson, neurodivergent people (and especially people with ADHD) have a hard time activating under the conditions that commonly motivate others. Mundane tasks, extended timelines, and importance don't mean as much to us. Instead, we have what's called an "interest-based" nervous system. We are motivated by and activated by things we find *interesting*.

In his upcoming book, *The Recognition and Treatment of ADHD*, Dodson says the ADHD brain is motivated by five things, what he calls INCUP.[8] I would argue that all neurodivergent brains work in much the same way.

- **Interest**
- **Novelty**
- **Challenge**
- **Urgency**
- **Passion**

While these "buttons" are strongest for ADHD and autistic people, they exist for *everyone*, and I would argue that they're especially important for people with mental health challenges. Anxiety, responsibility, and obligation—even if they work as motivators—are heavy. They're hard. INCUP, on the other hand, involves the parts of the brain linked to our old pal dopamine, which feels lighter, and exciting. Dopamine makes it easier to activate and to enjoy the task we're doing.

The best part about this model is that we use INCUP on purpose to get ourselves activated when we're stuck.

Interest Is Activating

My friend and fellow ADHD coach Jonathan Hassall tells a story about a couple he worked with. They were discussing chores and how the husband (who had ADHD) tended not to do them. In response, the husband said to his wife, "Yeah, but you love doing the dishes!" The wife was stunned, of course. Eventually it came out that the husband struggled so mightily to do things he didn't enjoy that he assumed she must enjoy it. Needless to say, they both learned a lot about each other from that session.

Everyone engages more easily with things they find interesting, enjoyable, or that spark their curiosity. For those of us with ADHD, autism, or similar neurodivergencies, **finding something interesting *about* the task can be critical to our ability to start it**. Thankfully, it's not the only thing that can help us get started.

Novelty Is Activating

Neurodivergent brains are excited by new things. Approaches or tasks that we don't do frequently can catch and keep our attention—provided the newness feels interesting and not intimidating. (A challenge that is overwhelming or intimidating—especially if we didn't choose that challenge—probably sparks anxiety, as it feels uncertain and out of control.)

A new challenge that feels interesting helps us engage. The same goes for adding novelty to an old challenge. For example, when my kids were little, we struggled to get them to expand their diet. If it wasn't chicken nuggets and mac and cheese, they wouldn't eat it. But they would eat tacos, and they would eat blintzes stuffed with eggs, berries, or peanut butter. We realized that being able to construct their own food was novel and engaging. Alex's daughter wouldn't eat shelled pistachios, but she would shell pistachios and then eat them, because the process of shelling them was interactive.

The same goes for adults. Going to a different place is another way to add novelty. This is why so many people work in coffee shops or libraries. It's also why so many people go to conferences. They become highly engaged with new material in novel surroundings and bring that enthusiasm back to work. Having traveled somewhere, spending all day doing workshops and networking, makes their job fresh again.

If you're having trouble getting something done, and you don't feel too anxious about it, try adding novelty. Go to a different location even if it's a new room in your house, chew different flavors of gum for different projects, play unusual music, or add a timer, clicker, or sticker chart to measure what you're doing. You might also try using a deck of cards to randomize your task order.

Additional Resources to Put a Door in Your Wall

A good resource for how to put a door in your Wall using INCUP methods is Dani Donovan's *The Anti-Planner: How to Get Sh*t Done When You Don't Feel Like It.* She uses drawings, games, novelty, and fun activities to get you going when you feel stuck or overwhelmed—for example, the "How to Speed Clean Like a Boss" challenge.

I'll also give examples in this book of potential INCUP methods, and you can easily try approaches and build your own.

That being said, if you get stuck in a particular situation and soothing alone isn't solving it, consider working with a qualified ADHD coach (yes, even if you're not ADHD). We solve problems with INCUP all day, every day.

Challenge Is Activating

Competitions and challenges can be extremely motivating for neurodivergent people. We want to see if we can do hard things. We want to see if we can win, or win against ourselves. A toddler who hates putting on shoes will gladly race to do it faster than Dad. An adult who hates cleaning their house will get excited if they make it a game. For example, I've done cleaning contests with friends. We take a picture of the room when we start, we clean it, and then we take another picture for the group chat when we're done to see who finished first and who did a better job.

If you're having trouble focusing on a boring or routine task, add some competition. Time yourself and see how many emails you can answer (successfully) in ten minutes. Can you beat yesterday's number? If you're struggling to get started on your gym goals, join a public challenge and log your progress. Or set yourself a big goal that excites you, and check off your progress in a visible way.

Urgency Is Activating

Earlier, I talked about urgency in the context of anxiety. Many neurodivergent people get used to pulling this lever to get started. They wait until the last possible second, when the anxiety of the impending deadline is enough to activate, and *then* they do the thing. It's great! Until it's not. The cycle can become a trap that leads to surprising success and then disastrous mistakes and burnout. Inevitably, something happens, and they're unable to deliver—which starts a Wall of Awful around that task.

If urgency and the anxiety of the last minute are your go-to motivators, realize they aren't healthy long term (and may lead to burnout). But if your brain likes urgency, there are other ways to get it! Try the Pomodoro Technique,* where you race the clock to finish a task by the end of a timed period. Set up accountability, where you have to email a friend by a certain time. Or ask for an earlier deadline just so the task won't expand to fill the time you have, at the expense of other important things.

Passion Is Activating

Long-term consequences may or may not feel real to us as neurodivergent people. But today does. One of the best ways to motivate ourselves consistently is to connect today's action back to a larger passion (or perhaps a value) we have.

---

* In its most common pattern, the Pomodoro Technique involves taking a timed twenty- to twenty-five-minute work "sprint," with a five-minute break afterward, before doing it again.

We can have behavior-driven values, for example, expecting ourselves to be honest or generous when we interact with others. Or we can value money, status, free time, or other rewards in a way that drives us to act in the pursuit of them.

Many neurodivergent people have a strong feeling of right and wrong, often referred to as justice sensitivity. We can use this sensitivity to help us activate in the service of fairness, or doing the right thing, without using anxiety. Sometimes we can also harness special interests or passions we have for organizations or ideas larger than ourselves. By using our values, passions, and special interests, we can orient ourselves and activate by heading toward a positive value we hold. This is why it's valuable to take time to reflect to determine what our values and passions are. I'll return to the idea of values many times over the course of the book, as it's one of the best ways to motivate ourselves before making a change or cementing a habit.

For now, when you face a Wall, consider: Who do you want to be in this moment? What value helps you choose how you want to act?

INCUP + Dopamine

Remember from Chapter 2 that dopamine is the brain's anticipation and reward chemical. When

dopamine is abundant in the brain, we feel motivated. We're anticipating that we'll get a reward if we act, and so we find it easy to activate. When dopamine is low, we struggle to *want*. We feel unmotivated, and it's hard to activate.

On the other hand, when dopamine is released in the brain in anticipation of doing the thing, it stays around for a short period. For a while, the dopamine from one thing will actively help us begin another task. This is why people with neurodivergence often have to *start* with fun or easy things before moving to the harder ones—they need to build up the "want" to do the hard thing.

Most of the INCUP model is related to dopamine. Competition and novelty increase the anticipation and reward chemicals available to the brain. But so does arguing with someone, which is why the unhealthy smashing strategy works. Dopamine can be as harmful as it is good—addiction cycles and social media scrolls *also* work on dopamine, and people can get trapped in the negative anticipation cycles.

As of the time of writing, it is believed that ADHD is tied to a lack of dopamine in the brain. This is why ADHD people find it hard to activate more often than others. The same *may* be true for other neurodivergent people, such as those with depression or autism. Even people with anxiety may find it helpful to increase the anticipation of reward to overcome everyday fears. But keep an eye on how the dopamine strategies are working for you. Are you acting in a healthy or unhealthy way to get started? Is dopamine working for or against you?

For neurodivergent people, it's often not enough to soothe our anxiety alone. We must also have a reason to **activate** on the task, so that we can open a door in our Wall. Rather than trying to convince ourselves of the task's importance or timeline—things that don't effectively activate neurodivergent brains—we want to work *with* our nervous systems. We want to add interest, novelty, challenge, urgency, or connect with our passion and values.

Fidgets to Focus

Sometimes tasks aren't sticky. We have trouble staying with the task, and every time we pop out, the Wall of Awful is back. Then we have to put another door in it. Fidgeting, on the other hand, tends to fill up the brain and let us stay with the task* without the Wall of Awful returning.

* See the book *Fidget to Focus* by Roland Rotz.

Neurodivergent people are more likely to get distracted and more likely to have Walls of Awful. So neurodivergent people need more fidgets, more often.

A fidget can be a traditional fidget cube or a stress ball. It can be standing up and pacing—though not walking to the kitchen to get a bagel, just pacing. The brain continues to work on the task while the feet move. The same goes for tapping fingers, doodling, folding paper, or using other fidgets.

Many people will play music in the background while they work, because it serves the same purpose; it's an audio fidget. Part of our brains stays in the song while we're moving in and out of the task.

DOOR #3: PLAN TO DO BOTH

Creating a door in the Wall of Awful is quick and easy—if we remember to go through the steps. Remembering steps when we're under the influence of strong emotions is hard! So the best approach is to pre-choose. If we can anticipate which Walls of Awful are likely to come up, we can make a plan to overcome them.

I'll return to the idea of planning in Chapter 10, but here are the basics.

Plan Ahead

Neurodivergent people often have a loose understanding of time, so we fail to commit to *when* we will take a specific action. Picking a time and committing to that action makes success more likely. But be aware—all of these strategies work best when dealing with one Wall at a time.

Once we've decided on the Wall we will tackle first, we schedule a *realistic* time frame. **Build in more transition time than you think you need.** Dealing with a Wall of Awful, even with a door, is hard. Don't rush the process in the beginning; create the space to regulate your emotions and to execute the plan. By doing so, we create Certainty and Agency. A good rule of thumb is to add an additional 50 percent to whatever your initial time assessment is.

Here are some questions to answer when you are starting to plan:

- What will you do?
- Which strategies will you use to open a door?
- Where will you do them?

- How long will it take?
- What help will you need?

Once you've answered the questions, schedule some time and add additional buffer time to be sure.

We should **use resources** and lean on people as part of the plan (see Chapter 3). If necessary, we can hire someone to help or to provide accountability. Schedule a friend to sit with us as a body double or to call us to check in on our progress.

Commit to the Plan

Once the planning is done, we commit. In the words of the great philosopher Yoda: Do, or do not—there is no try.

When the time comes, we do what we said we were going to do. We pre-choose, and keep the commitment, even if it's hard. Again, it's great to schedule body doubling and accountability buddies if we need to; keeping promises to ourselves creates momentum and helps us trust ourselves more. It makes us more powerful against the Walls of Awful we face.

Plan to Remember

Those of us who are neurodivergent should plan on *not* remembering the plan. The last step of making sure we can open a door in a difficult Wall is to create a system to help us remember the plan.

Here are some questions to consider before you're done planning:

- **How will you *remember* to do the plan?** Set reminders using your phone and physical space.
- **How will you remember which strategies to use?** Write down the steps somewhere obvious.
- **Can you access the list where you will need it?** Make multiple copies if needed.

Note: This planning to remember step is a version of what I called a pre-mortem. I talk about the pre-mortem at length in Chapter 10.

YOU CAN QUIT—INTENTIONALLY AND THOUGHTFULLY

We are in charge of our own actions, and we *can* quit a goal. But we should never quit due to the emotion of the moment. Breaking a promise to ourselves will only damage our self-esteem. It makes us feel less powerful and makes our Walls bigger and more intimidating.

> If you quit, always quit thoughtfully and intentionally, with integrity. Choose another path instead. Make it right with anyone you have let down. Then make a plan for a new path—and keep *that* promise to yourself.

REMEMBER, THE EMOTIONS ARE STILL THERE

Even if we can open a door in the Wall when we want to, we still have to eventually Climb the Wall. Often, the door helps but doesn't solve the struggle completely. The emotions are still there, and sidestepping them with the door doesn't do anything to meaningfully address them. If we climb, though, we do the hard emotional work that makes the Wall easier to manage over time.

The door also doesn't solve ongoing problems. If Emil is asked to create a report at work that isn't part of his job, he may resent it. But with work, he can put a door in that Wall and do the task perfectly well. The more he is asked to do that report, though, the more his resentment will build, and his Wall will grow. Eventually, he may start feeling angry just from thinking about it. He may start out putting a door in his Wall, but because he hasn't addressed the underlying emotions, he will end up smashing.

If, on the other hand, Emil faces the problem head-on and accepts that the new report is now part of his job, he can come to terms with the new reality. Maybe he gets to the point where he can do the report without a Wall. Or he can start addressing the issue with his boss or find a new job. The door solved the immediate need for the task, but the door won't solve the real problem. Emil has to do that.

Be aware that the door is temporary. Even if we can get to the other side of the Wall, until we deal with the Wall, our negative emotions will continue to wear on us. They'll drain our energy, and they may eventually lead us to burnout. So even though it's harder, it's worth it to climb—which is covered in the next chapter.

CHEAT SHEET: PUTTING A DOOR IN THE WALL

1 **Emotions are temporary.** If we recognize they're going to change, we can take steps to help them change in the direction we want. This gets us to the other side of the Wall temporarily.

2 Some Walls require **soothing our anxiety** or other hard emotions before we move forward.

3 To soothe ourselves, we should **increase connection**, whether to people or a special interest. Then add **well-being practices** like exercise, deep breathing, or music, or try other methods from CCAW (Certainty, Connection, Agency, Well-being).

4 If we've soothed our emotions and we still can't get started, **we should try adding INCUP strategies** (interest, novelty, challenge, urgency, or passion/values) to make the task more fun and help our brains activate.

5 Fair warning: Just like the emotions are temporary, so is putting a door in the Wall—it will

eventually stop working. We'll have to climb sooner or later.

ACTION STEP:

Think of activities that (1) soothe your anxiety and that (2) make you want to take action. Write down a list of at least five options for both.

Then return to the Wall of Awful you're considering for this book. Pick a soothing activity and an activating activity—and go do both (in that order.)

CHAPTER SEVEN

CLIMBING THE WALL

> Climbing is the best way to reliably get to the other side of the Wall of Awful over the long term. It requires skill and resilience, but you will feel lighter and more accomplished afterward.

Odds are, THIS chapter is the reason you bought this book. In fact, I'd give even odds that you've skipped other chapters to read this one first. (It's cool. I'm going to point you to where the ideas in this chapter are expanded on in other parts of the book.)

Just like Chapter 2, parts of this one might feel a bit heavy. But you've got this! After all, you know what it is to face the strong negative emotions of the Wall of Awful. Think of this chapter like a toolbox. Take the pieces that help *now* and come back for more tools as you need them.

NOW, LET'S GET STARTED

Ever been to an indoor rock climbing gym? You can *see* the difference between new and experienced climbers at a glance. New climbers struggle to put on their gear and spend long periods of time looking at the easiest walls before they make their first move. They go up slowly, carefully, and often with a great deal of fear—heights are difficult for just about everyone at first.

Experienced climbers are a different story. They tie the knots on their harnesses, looping the ropes quickly and smoothly. They attack difficult walls with confidence, using the appropriate gear and skill to fight against gravity seemingly without effort until they get to the top. An established climber looks like a dancer going up the wall, with rarely a foot placed wrong. When they settle back onto the ground, you can see the muscle in their arms and the hard-won strength that makes that dance possible. They are calm the whole way up, because they've climbed long enough to lose their fear.

You've read this far in the book, so chances are you have a Wall of Awful you need to get past. You want to do the thing—you're intrinsically motivated—but you're having trouble. That happens to us all! No matter how good we become at climbing, the Walls do not get smaller.

What happens is you get *stronger and more skilled* at Climbing the Wall. Like a climber at an indoor rock gym, the more you practice your techniques and the better the equipment you use, the easier the climb gets. You'll build emotional muscle as you continue to climb. And the skills you build will let you climb harder Walls with more confidence in less time—*if* you persist.

WHAT I MEAN BY CLIMBING

Since the Wall stands between us and the goal, and the Wall is made of emotions, the work we do to climb must also be emotional. To climb, **we sit with the emotions**, **come to terms with them**, and **move forward**—*while feeling* the emotions we've accepted. In other words, if the emotion we feel in the moment is fear, we do it afraid. If it's anxiety, we Climb the Wall while we're anxious.

Research by the Gottman Institute has found that 69 percent of ongoing conflicts in relationships are never resolved.* Healthy partners are just able to manage those conflicts well, while treating each other with

* As discussed extensively in Gottman's work. See the Gottman Institute's article here as an example: Feuerman, M. (2025, May 6). *Managing vs. Resolving Conflict in Relationships*. The Gottman Institute. https://www.gottman.com/blog/managing-vs-resolving-conflict-relationships/.

love and respect. The Wall of Awful is just a conflict within ourselves. Just like in the Gottman Institute's research, we may never resolve the conflicts in our relationships with ourselves, but we can manage them in a healthy way. Climbing the Wall is about those internal conflicts. It's about facing our emotional bricks, managing them, and moving forward to the task at hand.

What If I Have a Wall of Awful About Climbing My Wall of Awful?

I get this question from clients, frequently coming from a place of guilt or shame. Often what they're really saying is that they feel "less than" because they're facing a Wall of Awful in the first place. But here's the deal: Everyone has Walls of Awful, and they're nothing to be ashamed of. You're allowed to struggle. Sometimes things are just hard, and there's no getting around it. Instead, put a door in your Wall, or climb it, and do the hard thing. You can do it. I believe in you.

PRE-WORK: GETTING READY TO CLIMB

Climbing gets easier when we know what's on the other side of the Wall. Even if we know what the task is or what the outcome of that task will look like, it feels hard. The uncertainty only adds blocks to our Walls. Adding certainty helps us engage.

My favorite way to add certainty is by getting clear on the values that doing the task will serve. That way, I know what I'm heading toward on the other side of my Wall. After all, the emotions that make up my Wall often push me away, *so I need something on the other side that draws me forward.*

Finding the values we want to move toward will sometimes be as easy as a mother's love for her child. But often, if we are facing a particularly difficult Wall of Awful, we won't know *why* we need to do the task. In that case, finding the right set of values can be difficult, but we can start with two questions:

- ***Who do I want to be* in this situation, and how does this task fit in?**

  Sometimes a value comes from how we want to show up in the situation. If we promised to do a task, and it's important to us to keep our promises, then integrity is the value affected by our Wall. If we want to be an honest person, then when we make a difficult phone call to tell someone the truth, we're practicing honesty. We might even simply have the value that we finish what we start. Climbing a Wall of Awful to finish the project means we're following through on that value.

- **How does this task give me what I need—in the short term or long term?**
  I have a client with chronic health conditions. She had a Wall of Awful for contacting her doctor. We worked on ways to help her make that call, and in the end, what got her there was that her health didn't change regardless of whether she talked to the doctor or not. What changed was whether or not she had the information she needed to take effective action. She valued making her own choices, and when she realized that talking to the doctor gave her more agency, it became easier for her to do the hard thing.

Discover Your Why

Take a moment and write down the Wall of Awful you're facing. What task is causing the problem? What values will you satisfy if you make it to the other side of the Wall and do the task successfully? If you notice emotions during this process, write them down, but stay focused on the *values* in this pre-work.

Once you have a *why*, you're ready to move on.

➜ **But what if you have more than one Wall?** If you have more than one, write down all of your Walls. Number them and then roll a die to pick which one you'll tackle first. But listen to your gut! If you rolled a six and wanted a three, work on three instead.

→ **What if you don't know how to move forward?** If you still need more certainty about what's on the other side of the Wall of Awful after defining your values, *spend a little time getting clear on the next step*. What's the goal? What's the first step you'll need to take on the way to that goal? Call a friend, do research, or try an online tool that helps you break down a big task into small steps. (See Chapters 8 through 10 for help if you need it.)

THE WORK: CLIMBING THE WALL

I hate to say it, but it's true. Since the Wall of Awful is built of difficult emotions, Climbing the Wall means we have to deal with those emotions. If we swim across a river, we will get wet. To get to the other side of the Wall of Awful, we have to engage the emotions that make up our Wall, so we might get drenched by them. The hard emotions may feel *awful*—at least at first. But just like we dry after swimming, those hard emotions won't stay with us forever.

With time and practice on a specific Wall of Awful, we'll get stronger and more skilled, and it will get less uncomfortable. We'll also know how to deal with the discomfort like a swimmer in the water.

Name the Emotion

Emotions are a lot like Rumpelstiltskin. **Once we say their name out loud, emotions lose much of their power.**[1] Names let us understand and address reality. We can soothe ourselves, regulate our feelings, and eventually find ways forward. But it begins with a name or names.

Learning to name our emotions is a skill in itself. Some of us have learned that skill in depth from our parents, a coach, a therapist, or even a teacher. Others of us haven't had that chance yet. Most of us know basic feelings words like *happy*, *sad*, *angry*, *afraid*, or *anxious*, but there are many other feelings that may be useful. To help you find the words, I've included a helpful emotions wheel. Use it to find the emotions that are getting in your way, as well as the ones you want to move toward. See if you find any of your feelings on this wheel, or look up other wheels on the internet if you need to.

To name and understand your feelings, try asking yourself the following questions:

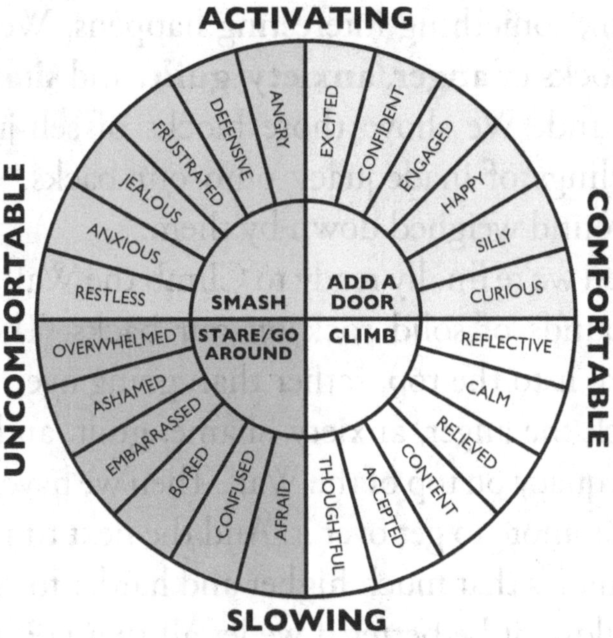

- What emotions are you facing? Use the emotions wheel if you are having trouble identifying them.
- Where do the emotions come from?
- Do you still think those emotions apply to you today? Do you want to carry them forward, or let them go?

(For more on emotions and what they tell us, see Appendix 1.)

Piling Up Bricks in the Backpack

The Wall of Awful is made of hard emotions—and when we avoid those emotions and judge ourselves for them, something interesting happens. We pick up extra blocks of **anger**, **anxiety**, **guilt**, and **shame** from the ground. We shove those blocks of self-judgment and feelings of inadequacy onto our backs. Then we walk around weighed down by them.

When we're finally ready to Climb the Wall, we have fifty pounds of solid rock on our backs. Then, once we make it to the top, rather than going over, we stop. We stack the anger, anxiety, shame, guilt, and feelings of inadequacy on top of the Wall. Then we have to climb a little bit more to get over it. And the next time we face this Wall, it's that much higher and harder to climb.

Wouldn't it be better if we let all that go? The Wall is tall enough—and the emotions are hard enough—on their own!

Ignoring our emotions doesn't get rid of them—it sticks them on our back, weighing us down and making climbing harder.

Sometimes Understanding Is Enough

Many years ago, I was enrolled in grad school. I was working on the final project for my degree, and I was struggling to start. I knew how to do it and had successfully completed plenty of similar assignments in the past. Eventually, a light bulb turned on, and I realized what was going on. I had a Wall of Awful, just not for the assignment.

It wasn't a productivity Wall—it was a personal life Wall. My mom had died while I was in the middle of my grad school program. Completing this assignment, and therefore the grad program overall, would mean that the last season of life that had my mom in it would be over, too.

Sometimes the process of identifying a Wall alone makes that Wall easier to climb. (For more help identifying what your emotions are telling you and how they could make up a Wall, see Appendixes 1 and 2.) My grief over my mom was still there. I would still have to process all those emotions at some point. But I realized grad school had nothing to do with that. I was able to separate my feelings from the assignment and get it done. The Wall let go, and I was able to do what I needed to do before returning to my emotions about my mom.

In the next two sections, I'll walk you through passive and active climbing. You may only have to do one of the two. But hard walls might require both, and the two techniques work great together.

OPTION 1 (OF 2) OF CLIMBING: PASSIVE TECHNIQUES (SLOW)

Let's start with passive climbing—it's cool because it can happen automatically if we make space for it. Passive climbing is easier than active climbing—it can literally work while we're asleep—but it's slow. The trick is the "default mode network," which activates when we allow our minds to wander.

The default mode network is the brain's secret powerhouse working "behind the scenes." It processes our emotions, helps cement our learning, and makes connections between ideas.[2] The default mode network is why we will often score *better* on a test if we study a few days beforehand and then sleep several nights, rather than staying up all night cramming for the test. The brain connects the information to what we already know in a way that sticks.

According to a conversation I recently had with neuropsychologist David Nowell, PhD,[3] we use different parts of the brain when we worry actively than we do when we're at rest. During our brain's rest period, the default mode network* kicks in. We learn, make connec-

* Recent research has *suggested* that ADHD brains may have default mode networks that kick in more quickly and quiet less easily. This may suggest that rumination is easier to fall into, and daydreaming may be more dangerous as a result. Autistic brains also seem to have differences in default mode networks. This doesn't necessarily apply to all forms of neurodivergence, but it's interesting.

tions, form memories, and—the critical part for our Wall of Awful—process emotions and challenges without even realizing it. It's our mind wandering. With everyday problems, eventually an idea or solution will spring to mind, and we'll be able to move forward. Spending time in the default mode network helps us process difficult, lingering emotions and Climb our Walls.

As a note, ADHD and autistic people connect with the default mode network better **while in motion**.[4] This may or may not be the same for other types of neurodivergence, but when in doubt, don't sit in one place. Go for a walk! You may think better.

We Have to Steer It

Passive climbing works automatically—*if* we "set the course" in advance.

We have to steer ourselves in the right direction before we allow our brains to coast, or they'll take us in the wrong direction. This is especially true for neurodivergent people. If we don't spend some time setting a positive tone for our default mode network, we run the risk of getting stuck on our negative thoughts and feelings*—adding bricks to our wall. Or our brains can go to work solving a problem that isn't a priority instead of facing our harder, stickier Wall(s). So we need to "set

* The technical term for this is rumination. New vocabulary word, yay!

our course" deliberately, priming our brains to work on the right problem, and Climb the right Wall.

So how do we set our course? We probably already do without realizing it. When we encounter a Wall of Awful, it's because we already intend to do something. (The thing we have the Wall for.) The intention is already set, but we're stuck. Taking a "soft fascination break" helps clear the barriers to our progress, and if we plan on returning to our task afterward, odds are the default mode network will work on the problem in the background while we take our break.

If I have to do my taxes and hit a Wall of Awful, going to take a walk immediately will help Climb the Wall. If I decide to check my email and *then* take a walk, for example, now my brain is working on email problems, too. I might make *some* progress on my taxes Wall, but I might not. The distraction has pointed my default mode network in the wrong direction (possibly several!). To get back on track, I need to set the intention of climbing my taxes Wall when I start the walk.

SOFT FASCINATION BREAKS

Our default mode networks work better when we're in a "soft fascination" state. Soft fascination is a mental state that involves gentle engagement with our environment. This state soothes the nervous system and sets a more positive course for our minds.[5] There are many things that can create soft fascination (though your mileage may vary):

- Getting into nature
- Doing simple chores
- Coloring
- Taking a walk
- Sitting around a fire
- Listening to soothing music
- Showering
- Looking at clouds
- Making art
- Gardening

How to Support the Default Mode Network

The most important thing to do to support the default mode network is to reduce the amount of time we spend using our deliberate attention, also called "hard fascination." We use deliberate attention when we solve problems at our jobs, listen to podcasts, work on projects, and when we doomscroll. We spend much more of our time using our deliberate attention than our ancestors did. It's a major reason we get the Wall of Awful phenomenon so often in modern life.

So, how do we spend less time directing our attention and more time in the "mind wandering" default mode network? I'm sorry to say it again, but the less time we spend in front of a screen, the better. If we're taking a break from work or waiting in line at the grocery store, we shouldn't immediately hop on our phones. Ideally, we can design our breaks so the default mode network can do its job.

Here are some practical ways to support the default mode network in everyday life:

- **Prime the system.** In quiet moments, name and claim the hard emotions you're processing from that specific Wall of Awful, so that you can better face and move through the feelings involved.
- **Let your mind wander.** When you leave space for quiet moments, the brain's default mode network kicks in, allowing for deeper processing.
- **Get moving.** Movement often improves processing in people with ADHD and autism. So give yourself bonus points if you let your mind wander *while* you do repetitive actions, such as weight lifting, walking, knitting, coloring, or swinging on a swing. (Doomscrolling is NOT mind wandering.)
- **Use music to steer it.** We already talked about using music to change our emotional state and

put a door in our Wall. When we're climbing, we can use music to help us process the emotions we're facing. It's why we listen to sad songs when we're bummed out or aggressive songs when we're angry.

- **Check in.** Every few hours or days, ask yourself if you're moving in the right direction. Are you feeling more settled after the processing? Do you have a clearer sense of where to go? Are you more able to take action? If not, change the supports, or try climbing actively. Alternatively, have a friend check in with you and ask you these questions.
- **Prioritize sleep.** The default mode network does powerful work when we're asleep. So make sure you're sleeping enough—maybe even a little more than usual, if your Walls are especially challenging.

Don't Get Lost

Passive climbing should be productive, and possibly unnoticeable. It may lead to some levels of stress or anxiety, but it should be manageable. If you find that your mind wanders to overwhelming levels of anxiety, it's important to add some of the support activities mentioned above to help point yourself in a more positive direction. (I tend to start with music, a walk in the woods, or karate forms.)

If you find yourself ruminating on the same things over and over, it's probably time to do something about those things. Meaning, you need to take action to address whatever problem is leading to those thoughts. (Action reduces anxiety!) If that doesn't work, bring the line of thought to your counselor, coach, or therapist.*

What Is Steering You?

Our subconscious minds are powerhouses. Pointed in the right direction, they can carry us naturally to our goals without special effort. But our thoughts are not the only things that steer us.

Everything we take into our minds will steer our subconscious to some degree. If you're talking with a wise friend, their advice will influence you. The same goes for listening to podcasts or music, reading books, or watching television.

Scrolling social media, however, can be particularly damaging to our progress if we aren't

* If you can't afford a therapist, some people get benefit from at-home therapy workbooks using ACT (acceptance and commitment therapy) or DBT (dialectical behavioral therapy).

careful. Social media constantly barrages us with (negatively) emotionally charged content—and switches us to a new thought, over and over. It's enough to wear even on ADHD-powered brains! High levels of social media use exhaust our deep-thinking capacity[6] and executive function, as well as increase stress and worsen mental health.[7]

We want our subconscious minds to move us in the direction *we choose*, not the ones the algorithm chooses *for us*. When we're trying to change something about our lives, we should periodically ask ourselves: Is something steering us in the direction we want to be going? Is it helpful? Or should we take a break and choose better resources?

Transition Time

It's pretty straightforward: Neurodivergent people typically need more transition time than we think we do. Allowing for more time between activities gives our brains more space to "catch up" to what is happening. It decreases the demands on our executive function. It keeps us from getting as tired—and the extra transition time opens space for our default mode network to operate away in the background, processing emotions and situations to our benefit.

One of the most beneficial things we can do for

ourselves if we have a Wall of Awful is to simply allow for more transition time in our day. Leave space and resist filling that space with mindless scrolling. Can we do a small chore in that time instead? Can we sit and breathe?

Passive Climbing Works

Passive climbing happens during the boring times of our lives—standing in line at the grocery store, raking leaves, and waiting at the doctor's office. If we don't allow ourselves to be bored—and learn how to be comfortable with it—our Walls will be harder to climb. Even worse, passive climbing might happen at inconvenient times. (We might not be able to sleep when we want, because our brains are trying to catch up on processing time!) Building small chunks of time into our day for passive climbing, even just a few minutes here and there, will go a long way to helping us overcome our Walls of Awful.

ACTIVE AND PASSIVE FOR THE WIN

People process information on two levels, emotional (feeling) and cognitive (thinking). Both are important, but you may have to "turn on" your cognitive or thinking brain deliberately to get the best effect. For example, as I'm trying to figure out how to write this sidebar, I'm encountering a Wall that's giving me low levels of anxiety (feeling). I can *feel* the emotion show up in a need to work my jaw muscles (biological response). When this happens and I'm not aware of it, I instinctually try to go around my Wall by eating foods that I shouldn't. I react emotionally to the stimulating event without thought. Thankfully, I noticed the urge this time (cognitive) and was able to respond deliberately and cognitively to it by grabbing a piece of gum off my desk to chew. (It's peppermint.)

To get the most out of our climbing, **we will need to engage both parts of the brain**. Our emotional processing is powerful because it resolves difficult emotions without us having to use willpower or executive function—at all. It's lower cost. The problem is, our emotional system doesn't always bring us in the right direction. So we will sometimes have to use deliberate thought (cognitive processing) to get to the right answer, like I just did with the gum. Had I gone upstairs to get a cookie, I would have lost the thread of this section. But I had gum in easy reach and was able to think through the sidebar instead!

OPTION 2 (OF 2) FOR CLIMBING: ACTIVE CLIMBING TECHNIQUES (FAST BUT HARD)

Active climbing, as the name implies, means we deliberately face the emotions that make up our Walls with the intention of getting past them. It is both faster and more challenging than passive climbing. It's worth the effort, though, because the more we do it, the stronger we will become.

Broadly speaking, there are four strategies to apply when actively Climbing our Walls of Awful:

1. Accept the Situation.
2. Change Your Self-Talk.
3. Keep Moving Forward.
4. Build Support Systems.

While these steps *can* be done in any order, this is the typical sequence.

1. Acceptance

Acceptance does *not* mean that you are happy with reality, only that you agree it exists, even if it sucks. Probably half of the work I do with clients is around acceptance. Once clients can see their Walls of Awful, feel their feelings, and accept those feelings, *everything changes.* They let go of resisting and become lighter.

Acceptance makes climbing easier. When we accept the reality of our emotions, we let go of the heavy weight of their burden. With that weight off our backs, we naturally climb faster and with less effort.

Acceptance is hard. When we accept, we allow ourselves to feel our feelings without running—even the *awful* ones. We allow ourselves to see the reality around our Wall of Awful clearly, and we let go of telling ourselves things should be different. If we struggle with paying bills, we accept that reality. Every time we pay bills, we will struggle unless and until we change something. (But once we accept, then we can change something!)

We May Feel More Emotions During Acceptance

Acceptance often comes with huge emotions. We may be angry, or sad, or resentful about the reality we allow ourselves to fully see. We may mourn the missed opportunities or the way we thought things would be. But we also let go of the suffering we feel when we cannot do the things we believe we "should" do.

When we accept, we become lighter. We also become able to see patterns *as they are.* We stop expecting every month to feel like that unrealistically easy month three years ago. We stop expecting our reality to look like what our mom *said* it should. Instead, we accept our real abilities. We forgive ourselves for our mistakes, and we move forward. It's a game changer.

Nothing about our situation may change as a result of our acceptance—or at least, not yet. We may still be stuck halfway up the Wall. But *we* change, and we become empowered to deal with reality as it is, from a place of flexibility and forgiveness. And that changes everything.

Working Through Acceptance on All the Layers

There are three layers to acceptance, and all are important.

1. **We understand what we feel, and why.** We stop trying to feel any different.
2. **We recognize our patterns** and stop trying to pretend they are different than they are.
3. **We accept the reality** (resources, situation, and problem) we have and decide to deal with it as it is and not how we would like it to be.

Working through all three layers of acceptance is hard and may take a long time for a complex Wall. That's okay; you can Climb the Wall (with difficulty) partway now and put a door in the Wall. Then, later, you can come back and finish the process.

Every time you accept, you let go of extra weight. You make climbing that much easier for the next time you face this Wall.

Once you see your Wall and your emotions clearly, spend some time accepting them. Again, acceptance does *not* mean that you are happy with reality, only that you agree it exists and have decided to be gentle with yourself about it.

2. Change Your Self-Talk

Now that you've accepted your emotions and reality, it's time to start doing something with them—taking action **(without smashing)**. The strategies in this section will help you Climb your Wall more easily, without causing damage.

For some of us, this will be a challenging step. We might not be practiced in self-talk. Doing it might make us feel silly. Or we might be *very* practiced at self-talk but only in a negative sense. Instead, we need to be a witness for the defense, defending ourselves against those negative thoughts. In either case, it's a worthwhile skill to develop because it prevents future Walls of Awful and keeps the ones we have from getting bigger.

Change How You Talk About the Problem

We've understood and accepted the reality of our Wall of Awful. Now let's address the way we talk to ourselves about our Walls. Oftentimes, the thoughts we have about them don't serve us. Thankfully, we can change those thoughts.

- It's not helpful to tell yourself, "**I'm so bad at this.**" Try reframing that to: "This is hard, but I can figure it out." (And remember that you can do hard things!)
- If you catch yourself thinking, "**This can't be done**," reframe it to: "This is just a problem to solve. What resources do I have to help me address it?"
- When you catch yourself thinking, "**I can't do anything right**," try changing that thought to: "I've done a lot of cool stuff in my life, but in this moment, I am struggling. Tomorrow will be different."
- If you catch yourself thinking, "**This isn't fair!**" reframe it to: "This may not be fair, but it also isn't personal. Sometimes bad things happen, and I get to choose how I respond."

When I was in the thick of my struggles during and after COVID-19, my friend and colleague Alan

P. Brown did a phenomenal reframe for my self-talk, almost by accident. As I told him about my family member's OCD and mental health challenges and my dad's battle with cancer, he validated it by saying, "Wow. You're really in a hard season." That word "season" really hit me. Because seasons are long, but temporary. They pass. That moment gave me hope. It helped me put down some of the weight I was carrying and made moving forward easier.

Challenge Your Feelings

I have good news for you: Feelings aren't facts, and they don't last forever. For example, my client's nine-year-old son, Elijah, *feels* like he's the worst test taker in the world at least twice a month. That feeling is probably not accurate—he's passing with C's—and it's temporary. The rest of the month he feels other emotions. But Elijah feeling defeated and ashamed of his test taking isn't helping him. His increasing Wall of Awful is standing between him and studying, and the *feeling* of defeat keeps him from asking for help from his dad to learn test-taking skills.

What if Elijah grows up and has to take a test at work one day? He might still have the defeat and shame in his thirties if he doesn't process those feelings and release them. And the feelings may not be at all accurate by then. If he learns skills in the meantime, he may become an expert test taker but still be convinced he's bad at it.

Feelings aren't facts, and they'll change. We also get to choose what we think is valid and what feelings still apply to us today.

Soothe Your Emotions

In the last chapter, I walked you through how to soothe anxiety before putting a door in the Wall of Awful. Those same strategies will work here if you need them. If you're feeling anger, humiliation, or disappointment, you may need to take a walk or take another action designed to calm down that emotion.

Again, as long as your brain and body see the Wall of Awful as a threat, your emotions may not go all the way to calm. That's okay. Just try to get them at a 4 or lower on the 10-point anxiety scale, enough that your prefrontal cortex can be back in charge.

Be firm but gentle with yourself. Comfort yourself enough to move to the next step.

3. Keep Moving Forward

Once you accept your Wall and your emotions about it, take a deep breath or two. Then commit—decide you will move forward anyway.

Your feelings may still be there and still be hard. (They may also have lightened.) But the feelings don't have to control you—you can still move forward and "do it afraid." Or you can act in a way you're proud of despite your frustration. Yes, it may be hard, and yes, you may need to get support or use strategies to *do the action.*

But the critical step here is to decide to *do it* rather than avoid it. Make the decision and commit. Do at least one small action immediately, even if that action is to ask for help.

Action is the antidote to anxiety.

Put Handholds in the Wall

If you make a decision to act and still struggle to take that first step, turn back to Chapter 6 and try putting a door in the Wall. Or try one of the following strategies to get traction for your climb.

Capture your thoughts in writing. It's often easier to process emotions, ask for help, or find and plan the next step by writing things down rather than keeping them in our heads. Here are some options to capture your thoughts:

- **Journaling**, to help process emotions.
- **To-do lists**, to write down next steps and keep track of details.

- **Calendaring**, to help find time for both processing and action and for making appointments for support or body doubling.
- **Text or email**, to vent to a trusted friend or ask for help.

Apply neurodiverse accommodations or other ways to work *with* your brain rather than against it. For example:

- **Timers**—Try the Pomodoro Technique or race a timer to see if you can do the task in ten minutes.
- **Obvious prompts**—Use reminders, signs, and sticky notes.
- **"Breadcrumbs"**—Leave a note for yourself when you stop work so you can find where you left off.
- **Take notes**—and plan in other ways.
- **Check out Chapter 9**—Get started and take action faster with the strategies here.

If none of these strategies help, reach out to a friend, counselor, coach, or other trusted person. Someone will help you talk through options and find a strategy that works!

4. Build Support Systems

We discussed this previously in Chapter 3 and will go deeper still in Chapter 9, but it's important to recognize the supports we have available to us. It's easy to feel stuck when we're ignoring our resources or too stressed and frantic to take a beat and consider other options.

Assuming you have access to them, here are a few things to keep in mind when you're climbing that might just make the whole process easier:

- **Therapy.*** The job of therapy is to help us get out of our own heads so we can look at our lives from new angles. It gives us the ability to change our perspective and see patterns in our challenges that we might otherwise miss. And those patterns potentially unlock new approaches and solutions.
- **Coaching.** Coaching is future focused, solution based, and pointed at specific outcomes. It is not designed to help us overcome mental health challenges, but rather to overcome the challenges of everyday life. A coach might be specialized in

* Again, some people get benefit from at-home therapy workbooks using ACT (acceptance and commitment therapy) or DBT (dialectical behavioral therapy).

a certain niche, like an executive coach, or in a broader area, like an ADHD coach.

- **Reflection.** Both therapists and coaches help us reflect on the challenges (Walls) we face. But not everyone has access to these resources. The good news is that we can also reflect on our challenges on our own. All we have to do is think about what we've experienced, whether they caused a Wall, and how we responded. We can think by journaling, talking to a friend/confidant, working in a mental health workbook, or even just talking out loud to your phone's Notes app. (But be careful not to get stuck in your own head.)

All of this is easier with the right mindset. Therapy, coaching, reflection, and all the ideas in this book boil down to two things: skills and resources. The more we keep in mind that building our skills and resources will help us overcome our Walls, the easier our climbs will become. (Hey! Turns out, the best way to keep that stuff in mind is reflection!)

The Good Stuff Is on the Other Side

Climbing the Wall requires discomfort. We have to get comfortable being uncomfortable. And—so much of life is on the other side of uncomfortable!

The life we want, the goals we have, are all on the other side of the Wall. We *can* climb it. We can be uncomfortable for a little while and then reach the things we want. It will be fine.

If we don't accept the hard emotions in the Wall of Awful, our lives become much harder. We won't be able to get to the other side of the Wall unless we're in really significant and acute pain. Because for us to move, doing the thing will have to hurt less than not doing the thing. We'll have practiced avoidance of pain as our primary motivator. We'll avoid problems until they get so bad we have no choice but to attend to them.

By avoiding discomfort, we're choosing meaningful long-term pain instead.

Even though it won't be fun to do this work, we can. We are strong, and we get stronger from hard things. Everything we want in life is on the other side of the Wall, and we can reach it. The struggle is real, but there is dignity in struggle—and in facing that struggle head-on.

Stick with me. On the other side of the discomfort are all the things we want. If we persist, we'll avoid bad outcomes, sidestep pain, and find our way to great things. It just takes a willingness to climb through the discomfort. Be patient and persistent—you can do this.

LEVEL UP (OPTIONAL): BECOMING A BETTER CLIMBER

Climbing is hard. Fortunately, with practice we can become both stronger and more skilled—so that our *experience* of climbing gets easier.

Developing Climbing Strength

Because climbing is emotional work, developing emotional strength and endurance makes that work easier. We have to be able to experience the powerful emotions that make up our walls and tolerate them, while still moving forward to address the task at hand—which takes strength. Sometimes our emotions lighten as we act, letting us see our resilience. But sometimes feelings linger. And that's okay. Recovering from lingering emotions makes us stronger in the same way that our muscles get stronger while we recover from a hard workout.

For additional strength building, try the following advanced exercises.

- **Reframe failure.** One of my mentors, Chandler Creedon, likes to say that he never fails if he learns something. I love that reframe. Another one that I've found in the various students I've worked with is that oftentimes their self-imposed conditions for success (straight

A's!) mean they're building Walls by seeing failure where it isn't. Personally, I've stopped using the word "failure" and replaced it with "struggle" because that way I can always grow from it. When you feel tempted to use the word "failure," how can you change that framing instead? What can you learn?

- **Forgive yourself.** Self-forgiveness requires that we recognize the negative feelings we've developed toward ourselves and then deliberately decide to let them go. Because some of us harness those feelings to Smash our Walls, letting them go can be scary. But releasing that burden will make Climbing much easier.
- **Take ownership.** Not everything in life is our fault, but when we take responsibility for our responses, we gain agency. We let go of being a victim, and can start acting—and that lets us become both calmer and more creative in addressing hard things.
- **Know your own patterns.** If we reflect on our habits, the things we do over and over without thinking, we learn our own patterns. We learn which Walls of Awful we face and when they pop up. Then we can deliberately interrupt those

patterns, make a plan to Climb our Walls, and grow. We can also get a realistic sense of how much we can handle at once and plan ahead so we don't get overwhelmed.

Developing Climbing Skills

Climbing the Wall of Awful is a skill. And like any skill, it can be trained. We can build on our inherent strengths and accommodate any weaknesses we may have. Many of the ideas I've introduced in other parts of the book can be applied to the process of climbing.

Just being exposed to the concept of the Wall of Awful is helpful (Chapter 1). That knowledge lets us understand what we're facing when we struggle to start on tasks we have difficulty with, and it lets us climb with intention. A good understanding of anxiety and some ways to manage/soothe it (Chapter 2) strengthens our foundation for climbing. Keeping our skills and resources (Chapter 3) top of mind gives us strategies to apply during the climb. And being aware of the strategies that don't work (Chapter 4) can keep us from falling into the traps that have plagued us in the past.

Here are a few more specific concepts you might want to play with:

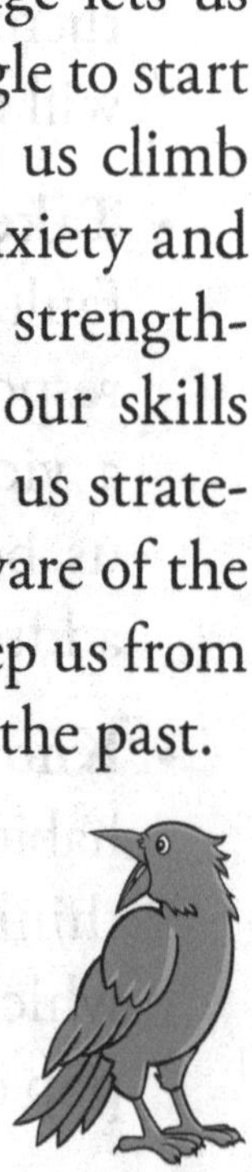

- **Use CCAW to soothe anxiety** (from Chapters 2, 6, and Appendix 3)—

reducing our anxiety allows us to better apply our executive function skills to solving the challenges we face.

- **Use INCUP to activate** (interest, novelty, challenge, urgency, or passion/values; see Chapter 6). Applying INCUP strategies makes activation easier because the signals are bigger and more obvious.
- **Allow more time to transition** (Chapter 8). Climbing our Walls is an uncomfortable period of transition. Accepting that it will take time and discomfort makes it easier to get through because we can prepare for it.
- **Create support systems** (Chapter 9). When things get especially challenging, we default to the strength of our systems. The stronger those systems are, the higher the floor of our performance will be.
- **Develop time wisdom** (Chapter 9). A common neurodivergent challenge is time blindness. We just don't perceive the passing of time well. Thankfully, we can build our skills in this area to make it easier to get things done.
- **Define the next step** (Chapters 9 and 10).

Often, we struggle to start because we're seeing our task as one overwhelming whole. Breaking tasks into their component parts can make them easier to engage.

- **Make a plan for your climb in advance** (Chapter 10). All of these things are easier to do if we plan ahead. Making a plan is one way to Climb the Wall of Awful. Having a plan puts a door in the Wall of Awful—especially if it's repeatable.

YOU CAN CLIMB

There's no getting around it—Climbing the Wall is hard. (It's almost like the Wall we're climbing is Awful!) We're processing emotionally. Our amygdala is activated, at least a little bit. Climbing requires us to regulate that emotional response intentionally. But the more emotional we are, the harder that can be.

Thankfully, if we know we're facing a Wall, there are strategies we can bring to bear to make that process easier. We can make time for soft fascination, allowing our minds to wander while processing emotions and working on problems in the background. We can climb actively by facing and processing our emotions. We can "put handholds in the Wall" by making and executing plans to Climb our Walls. Best of all, the more we Climb our Walls, the better we get at it, especially if we're working deliberately on building our strength and skills as we do so.

The best things in life are on the other side of the Wall—but to get there, to get the things we want, we will have to make changes. And while change is hard, it does get easier if we understand how the change cycle works.

CHEAT SHEET: CLIMBING

1 Climbing the Wall of Awful means sitting with our emotions, coming to terms with them, and moving forward—**while feeling those emotions**. If we're afraid, we move forward afraid. If we're anxious, we do it anxious.

2 Getting clear on **why we want to get to the other side of our Wall** is a critical first step. We need a strong "why" to counteract the negative emotions that make up our Wall. It can typically be **found by looking at the values** involved in the task.

3 Passive Climbing **happens in the empty spaces of our lives** when our mind is not focused on

things. These times allow us to process residual emotions, solve problems in the background, and consolidate the lessons we've learned.

4 Active Climbing is intentional. It happens when we do the hard work to **approach, accept, and address our problems** and the emotions that make up our Walls.

5 The most effective way to become a stronger, more skilled climber of the Wall of Awful is to **use both passive and active climbing strategies**. The blending of the two gives us a well-rounded, resilient strategy.

REFERENCE:

Appendix 4 in the back of this book gives you all the steps to Climb your Wall in one easy page.

ACTION STEPS:

1 Spend five minutes studying the Wall of Awful you've chosen for the book. What is the block? What emotions make it up? Do you know why the Wall exists?

2 Choose *either* the passive or the active climbing approach. Then go through the process to climb passively or climb actively. (If you get stuck, ask a friend or trusted person for help!)

After you've Climbed your Wall and done the thing, give yourself a reward.

PART 3

SYSTEMS AND CHANGE

CHAPTER EIGHT

HOW CHANGE WORKS

> This book is about change, but change is hard. Fortunately, when we understand how change works, we can start and maintain change intentionally. We can handle falling down, and get back up!

Welcome to the change chapter. It has always bothered me that so many self-help and mental health books encourage people to change but don't tell them *how* change actually works. So this book *is* going to talk about how change works. Now that we know *how* to overcome the Wall of Awful once, we'll need to put systems, habits (Chapter 9), and plans (Chapter 10) in place to let us do it again and again. But to make long-term changes successfully, we'll have to embrace the change cycle.

Of course, like a lot of things that are worth doing, it's going to be challenging.

CHANGE IS UNCERTAIN

The reality is, change is uncertain. Uncertainty leads to anxiety, and the higher our anxiety, the more our brains put the amygdala in charge. The more our amygdala is in charge, the less we can think clearly with our executive function—which is what we need to *make* the change in the first place. In other words, our brains are set up to resist change and keep us in the status quo. (It's lower energy and less stressful.)

Fortunately, while our brains and bodies push us to the easy path, we can teach ourselves to do the hard thing instead. If we consistently push ourselves to do hard things, over time we increase our tolerance for adversity. We learn to push ourselves and level up. But change and challenge take effort, and both require fighting the tendency of our brains—and the modern culture around us—to do what's easiest.

When we understand how the Wall of Awful works, we can overcome it more easily. The same goes for change. When we can point to the stages of change and understand where we are, the uncertainty gets smaller. When we can name what's happening, we feel more in control—which means we have more ability to make change happen and are far more likely to persist through that change to reach our goals.

Of course, we may face a Wall of Awful at any

point in the cycle. But that Wall, like any Wall, can be climbed.

Emotions That Let Us Know We Need to Change

Typically, our emotions are trying to tell us something. We just have to know how to interpret them.

Guilt, **shame**, **regret**, and **inadequacy** push us *away* from the behaviors that cause them, letting us know it's time to do something else instead.

Ambition, **competitiveness**, **excitement**, and **envy** encourage us to take action and point us toward a better life. If unmanaged, though, they can drive us back into feelings of guilt, shame, and inadequacy, even if we make our desired changes.

Hope, **motivation**, **curiosity**, **engagement**, and **inspiration** show us the kind of life we want to live or a possible path to get there, with fewer downsides. But they can be harder to notice if we aren't mindful of their presence.

(See Appendix 1 for information on what the emotions that make up our Walls might be telling us.)

TRANSITIONS ARE A KIND OF CHANGE

All change requires some kind of transition. And transitions are more complex than most of us realize.

Recognizing this complexity can help us to navigate them more easily.

Imagine you're in a room and want to go to another one. In order to do that, you'd have to leave your current room, walk down the hallway, and then enter the next room. So each transition has three parts—(1) where we are, (2) a gap or hallway, and (3) where we are headed. Each transition, then, is secretly two transitions. We have to transition—(1) out of where we are, and (2) into what's next.

Further complicating this is the fact that we always transition in more than one way. Physical transitions are obvious: We walk from the living room to the kitchen to eat dinner, open a laptop to get started on work, or drive from our home to the gym to exercise.

But there are two other kinds of transition, and they're less obvious because they happen internally: mental and emotional transitions. When we go from one thing to another, we often have to let go of certain ways of thinking and feeling. For example, the commanding mentality a parent might have at work may not be useful during family dinner. Similarly, the aggressively competitive attitude a kid uses to play video games online with their friends isn't appropriate for family dinner. (And if both parent and child fail to make their necessary transitions before dinner, it's not going to be a fun meal!)

Transitions apply in both large scale (major life changes) and small scale (moving from one task to another). The larger the transition, the longer the hallway/gap will be. And the longer that period of transition is, the more opportunities there will be for the Wall to pop up. It can arrive at any point in the hallway (gap) and can even happen more than once during a single change.

WHAT IS THE CHANGE CYCLE?

According to researchers Prochaska and DiClemente,[1] all change goes through five distinct stages. Researchers Raihan and Cogburn[2] have added a sixth stage to the cycle to explain what happens when people relapse. Here's how the model works.

- In the first, **precontemplation** stage, you may or may not be aware that a problem exists. Either way, you do not plan on changing your behavior.
- In **contemplation**, you see the problem exists. You are considering making a change but are not yet committed to it. You may feel ambivalent, uncertain, or unsure of whether you even *can* make a change.
- In **preparation**, you want to take action to correct the problem, but you're moving in at most small steps forward. The job of this stage is to build confidence and to turn resources and skills into a solid plan for change, ready to take action. (Reading this book is a sign you might be in this stage.)
- In the **action** stage, you have a plan for change and are implementing this plan. Your actions lead to clear patterns of new behaviors. As your actions continue, you see gains, and change begins to feel real. (When you apply the things you're reading in this book, you'll be in the action stage.)
- In the **maintenance** stage (typically after about six months for major changes), new behaviors

are reliably replacing old ones. You are taking consistent, committed action and conscious steps to avoid relapse. After some amount of time in the maintenance stage (about five years for major changes), the change cycle is considered complete, and the change is permanent. You may cycle through contemplation, preparation, and action over and over again until it becomes a habit.

- **Relapse** is a natural part of the change cycle and can interrupt any stage. If you relapse and return to your old behavior, you may experience frustration, disappointment, or feelings of failure. But relapse is only an interruption! By returning to an earlier stage in the change cycle and applying the lessons you learned about your patterns and triggers, you become that much closer to your goal of lasting change. (Relapse can also feel like facing a new Wall of Awful!)

Hey, What's with All the Relapse Talk?

As you may notice, the word "relapse" will keep coming up in this chapter. Just to be clear, I don't mean to imply addiction when I use it. I just mean "falling back into old habits."

I talk about relapse (or falling back into old habits) so much in this chapter because it's a possibility we should be aware of. It's NOT that I expect you to fail. It's because if you do struggle, if you relapse as you work to change, it will feel much harder if you don't know it might happen. Giving you the heads-up means you are more likely to have the awareness and ability to weather the storm and get back on track to make the changes you want to make.

If you're awesome out of the gate, though, that's great, too!

CHANGE IS MESSY

The change cycle graphic looks tidy. From the picture, it's easy to think that you should move smoothly from stage to stage in one cycle. But that's not how change works. In practice, we tend to bounce around from one stage to another, often out of order. We can visit any stage and return to previous stages over and over again.

No matter how messy the cycle, we can and *will* complete the change if we keep going.

THE WALL OF AWFUL AND SMALL-SCALE CHANGE

The change cycle and the Wall of Awful are interconnected. In fact, we often go through a small-scale change cycle whenever we face a Wall of Awful.

We begin precontemplation when we hit the Wall. We contemplate when we recognize the Wall and understand the problem. We might prepare by asking a friend for help, hiring someone, or just making a plan for how we'll climb. Eventually, we take action, either by facing our emotions and doing it anyway or putting a door in the Wall—and finally completing our task.

In small-scale change, like when we're trying to get past a Wall for checking our email, this whole process might only take several minutes to an hour. If we're able to zip through it consistently in only a few minutes, odds are we've entered the maintenance stage for that Wall.

Of course, we can relapse at any point in dealing with our Walls of Awful. Relapse is normal! And when it happens, we should return our attention to the Wall, reentering the contemplation stage and making plans to get past our Wall. After a few attempts, if we remain resolute, we'll overcome that Wall and do the thing.

Decisiveness

I was recently talking with my friend Jessica McCabe (of *How to ADHD* fame) about the Wall of Awful and transitions. I told her about my hallway metaphor and how we have to leave the thing we're doing and travel through contemplation and preparation before we act and move on to the next thing. She said something then that blew my mind: "There is no hallway, though."

"What do you mean there's no hallway?" I asked her, astonished.

She was serious. "There's no hallway. You just leave one and go into the other. You make up your mind and you're decisive, and there's no hallway to get stuck in." That's how Jessica works. She learned years ago that indecisiveness only makes the process worse: By making a decision and moving immediately, she skips the hallway. She also, as a result, gets to skip most of the opportunities for the Wall of Awful to pop up.

The more indecisive we are, the more opportunity we allow for double thinking and strong emotions. If we go through the process of decision making and change slowly, we make room for our Walls to show up again and again. On the other hand, when we make a decision and move on it quickly—even if it's deciding in advance to only eat sandwiches at restaurants or not to skip two gym sessions in a row—we eliminate analysis paralysis and leave much less room for anxiety or a Wall of Awful to show up.

LARGE-SCALE CHANGE

Large-scale changes work the same way as small-scale changes. It just takes longer. And a big change requires more steps and more skills over a much longer period of time, so it's harder to do.

With large-scale change, we often spend much more time in the *early* stages of the change cycle. We have to consider what we want in a larger sense. Do we want to quit smoking? Do we want to sell our house and move to Portugal? Do we want to start an exercise habit? Are we prepared to do the work?

To get out of contemplation and into the preparation stage, we have to make the decision to move forward to solve the problem or to make that big change in some way. Making that decision may be complex and take days, weeks, or months to settle—and we might face a Wall of Awful around that decision for any number of reasons.

Many Small Tasks

The further into the change cycle we go, the more significant our uncertainty and anxiety may become. Large changes are built of *many* small tasks, and each of these tasks can be an opportunity for a Wall of Awful to show up. Planning is often the first big barrier. For example, eating "healthier" could mean anything! Eating fewer premade meals and more salads, for example. Or increasing our protein intake. So a Wall of Awful around planning could show up midway through the process. Even if we don't mind planning, we may face a Wall as we carry out the plan—for spending extra money on healthier food or learning to cook new kinds of meals. Any action can trigger a Wall. They can even arrive during maintenance if we've eaten the same salad too many days in a row or if we impulsively eat fast food for lunch one day.

It's easy to get stuck in contemplation or in preparation when big emotions bring on a Wall of Awful. We might putter or try to go around the Wall, getting stuck in the procrastination of learning or doing "just one more thing" before we take action. Sometimes our Walls derail our change, maybe without us even realizing it, adding a new problem to solve. That's normal! It's all part of the change process (and what makes it hard).

The strategies that work for overcoming our Walls of Awful will work regardless of when they show up during the change cycle. The key is not to be surprised when they arrive, so we can better manage our emotions in those moments. Change is hard, and the uncertainty around it makes Walls far more likely—but with resilience and the strategies discussed in this book, we can overcome each Wall as it happens.

Over time, as our actions become more consistent, they'll be less uncertain. Our negative emotions will reduce, and our Walls will show up less often. Even better, we will have developed the skills and the endurance needed to climb them when they do, so that we're less bothered by the effort. And we will have developed more confidence and resilience, so that even if we fall back into old habits, we'll know we can get back on track.

Relapse Is Normal

The Wall of Awful model exists because I think it's important to normalize struggle. Everyone struggles, and we need safe ways to talk about it. Relapsing, falling back into old habits rather than finishing the change, is normal—and the harder and bigger the change, the more likely we are to relapse before we figure it out. The keys are to get back up and to learn something every time.

Those of us who are neurodivergent might have to go through more cycles of starting change and falling back into old habits than others do.* It's okay. If we fall down six times, we'll get up seven. We'll learn what we need to learn and eventually get the change to stick.

Of course, we might get mad at ourselves when we relapse—that choice is always available. Strong feelings are part of being human. But if we keep condemning ourselves when we make normal mistakes, we're only adding more bricks to our Wall. It's better to forgive ourselves and start again. We'll get further if we spend our energy on the change, not useless self-recrimination.

Change is hard enough. We don't need to make it harder than it is!

HACKING THE CHANGE CYCLE

Some change is harder by its very nature—life transitions, quitting an addiction, making a new network of friends, and changing your health will all take months or years of effort. That's okay. Knowing that the change

---

* Our trouble with executive function means we will fail to inhibit our impulses slightly more, may struggle more to stay consistent while habit forming, and might not learn as quickly from our mistakes. Plus, many neurodivergent people report habits are harder to establish in the first place and may be much harder to break afterward. Again, it's okay! We get it, even if it takes a few more cycles.

cycle exists helps us feel normal as we go through each of the stages. It helps us have self-compassion when facing hard moments or relapse. And it helps us keep going.

It may be hard—but we can make change a little easier by using the knowledge and the skills we build to "hack" the change cycle intentionally—making the process more predictable and faster to complete.

Make a Plan

By far the best hack for change is deciding and committing to what you'll do and when, in concrete, bite-sized steps. Better preparation often creates a more successful "action" stage. Choosing a time and a place to do a specific action makes change far more likely.[3]

Planning times and places isn't enough, though. As I'll talk about more in the next two chapters, those of us who are neurodivergent can't just assume we'll remember to do the action. No matter how motivated we are or how much we believe in ourselves, relying on memory is as silly as relying on willpower. Instead, we need to set up external supports, like people, reminders, and timers.

Then we have to figure out how we'll get the support to both establish and maintain our new habits. (Chapter 10 will be helpful with specifics.) Most of us need support throughout—and there's no shame in that. It's better to make the change we want with support than to struggle and get stuck without it!

Smashing Is a Clue

If we're Smashing through a Wall of Awful more than once, there is something on the other side that's important to reach. Otherwise, we would stare at the Wall, go around the Wall, or accept not reaching whatever is on the other side. We wouldn't pay the price to smash.

Smashing, then, is a signal that there's a problem—and the problem is worth solving even at a high cost. But if we *keep* smashing, we keep paying that cost over and over again. We keep getting angry or stressed or anxious, and we have to keep accepting the damage to ourselves and our relationships. Instead, we should try to solve that problem in more sustainable ways. Can we put a door in the Wall (see Chapter 6) for now or Climb the Wall (see Chapter 7)? Can we create systems and habits (see Chapter 9) or plan (see Chapter 10)? Or do we need to commit to begin the change cycle?

When we smash more than once, it's time to figure out the path to change.

On Timing and Time Wisdom

Many neurodivergent people are time blind, meaning that to us, a minute doesn't feel like a minute and an hour doesn't feel like an hour.* Our experience isn't even consistent from day to day, since we often mix up time and emotions.[4] A task that is fun and makes us feel engaged and entertained might take an hour but only feel like ten minutes. A task that is tedious and makes us feel bored might only take six minutes but feel like hours. We can't rely on our internal processing of time to let us know.

Because of this time blindness, we have to deliberately develop "time wisdom." Not only do we have to set a time and place to work on a goal, but we also have to figure out how long it will actually take by measuring.

For example, I know that making pancakes in the morning for my kids takes about forty minutes. A few times we had thirty minutes, and I thought that was enough time. But all of a sudden I was partway through making pancakes and we had to leave the house to go somewhere, with uncooked pancake batter and hungry kids. So I timed it and learned that pancakes take forty minutes.

---

* Time blindness is most commonly seen in ADHD folks, but there are anecdotal accounts of people with other flavors of neurodivergence with this issue.

Because of time blindness, the Wall of Awful can lie to us about how long a task will take. If we have a Wall of Awful for something, we will often feel like it will take longer than it actually does. Here's another example from my life: I have a Wall of Awful for mowing the lawn. It's not a chore I enjoy; it's loud, tedious, and triggers my allergies. So, because of my strong negative emotions around it, in my head, mowing the lawn takes all day—except it doesn't. The front yard takes about forty minutes. The backyard takes about an hour. My Wall of Awful is lying to me by letting my emotions expand how long the task *feels* like it will take to do. Similarly, the longer we put off a task because of our Walls, the bigger that task will feel—but if we know it will only take an hour, we can start it more confidently.

Once we know how long our tasks actually take, that time wisdom makes us far more likely to be successful. Even if the task is tedious, it becomes easier if we pick a time, set a timer, and get it over with. (Don't forget to add 50 percent to your estimate if you can.)

Supporting Growth

Professionals in both counseling and educational circles talk about the "zone of proximal development." It's basically the Goldilocks theory of personal growth. If a task is too hard for us to accomplish on our own, we'll get frustrated and give up. If a task is too easy, then we're not really growing anymore. It's not a challenge; it's Tuesday. (And therefore it's not a change that will make any impact on our lives.) To get better or stronger, then, we have to work within our zone of proximal development.[5]

But life isn't a video game. It doesn't always show up at the right level of hard, and we can't always choose our challenges! When work or school is more challenging than we can handle, or we're being asked to do something at home that's beyond our skill set, we might fail. And the more we fail, the more bricks get added to our Walls.

Here's the secret, though. When we're being asked to change and grow in a way that we are not currently able to, it doesn't mean we won't ever be able to do it. It just means we need more skills or more resources as we level up. Support groups and professionals like counselors, coaches, teachers, and even supportive friends can help us learn the skills or provide extra support, so that we're able to rise to the challenge in front of us and grow stronger. We can always do more and even increase our zone of proximal development if we have a support system enabling more effort or an expert showing us how.

Take a moment to think about this: When you're stuck, who can you ask for help? What resources can you use? These are key parts of your tool kit.

Moving from Emotional to Cognitive Processing

We can use what we know about the change cycle model to help us move from emotional processing to cognitive processing—speeding up the process of change and decreasing the number of times we relapse.

"But, Brendan," you say, "that sounds like magical thinking! Woo and hooey, even." Hear me out.

Processing emotionally is a minefield. We don't like the change, it feels hard, and we don't want to continue. Or we feel lost and uncertain, or overwhelmed, and want to pull away. Emotional processing isn't intentional—we get caught up in it, and soon we're making decisions that may or may not get us what we want in the long term.

Cognitive processing, on the other hand, is intentional. We're thinking on purpose, steering our thoughts and decisions toward the goals we want. Cognitive processing is *far* more effective when it comes to change than emotional processing.

When we feel lost and uncertain (because change is hard), we can always pause and figure out what stage of the change cycle we're in. That lets us orient ourselves. Then we can determine the steps we need to take to successfully leave that stage and move to the next one. Instead of feeling frustrated without any direction, or assuming that relapse means we've failed somehow, we can find our way back to the change cycle and continue making progress. This might mean performing a task necessary for moving to the next stage or falling back to a previous stage to get our bearings. (See "What Is the Change Cycle" earlier in the chapter.) Regardless, we'll have a general idea of what to do next.

Find the Pause

Mindfulness people talk about "the pause." (Heck, I just talked about a version of it in the paragraph above!) When something happens to us, we can react immediately. Or we can pause, and then respond. Generally, a considered *response* will be better than an instinctive *reaction*. We can respond with more intention and control, with more focus on the relationship with the person in front of us. Of course, mindfulness people make this sound easy, and it's not.

Finding the pause takes both practice *and* emotional regulation. (Both of which are harder for neurodivergent people.) But the pause is always available to us. The best case is to find the pause before we react emotionally, so we respond cognitively instead. But we might find it in the middle of our reaction, or even after the fact! Regardless, the pause will be there if we look for it.

For example, if my wife says something that upsets me and I immediately start ranting, I missed the pause. I had the opportunity to hear what she said, feel offended and upset by it, and then pause. Instead, I ranted. I didn't say, "That really hurt my feelings," or "I find that deeply concerning," or respond in some other measured way. I just started ranting. But if I catch myself mid-rant, I can choose to pause there. I can change course and say, "Oh man, I'm being a jerk. I'm sorry. Let me try again." Or I can go back in an hour and apologize and try to talk it through the right way. Neither approach is as good as finding the pause the first time, but both are far, far better on relationships than no pause at all. (Note: Pausing in the middle is usually hardest because the behavioral momentum is strong, and our ego can get in the way of us interrupting ourselves to admit our mistake.)

The same goes for quitting smoking or starting a gym habit: When we find the pause, we're catching ourselves before we make the wrong decision. If we catch ourselves halfway through smoking the cigarette, we can put it out and refocus on quitting. If we catch ourselves after the smoke break, we can make the cigarettes harder to get next time or ask a friend to walk around the office with us during our next break instead. If we skip a workout, we can pick up a smaller one at home, or make an appointment for a group fitness class next time to add accountability. Finding and using the pause allows us to act more in accordance with our goals.

Of course, self-care plays a role, as well. If we didn't get enough sleep or we haven't eaten in hours, we're less likely to find the pause and more likely to react. Our brains are tired, and our executive function is compromised. All of us mess up sometimes, but taking steps to care for ourselves can make finding the pause easier.

Find the Pause by Changing the Environment

Changing our environment also helps us find the pause and make better decisions. My client Anjuli avoids sending impulsive emails. She made a rule for herself that if an email makes her angry, she has to immediately take a walk, so she doesn't say anything she'll regret later. I try to keep cookies out of the house, so that I'm forced to stop and ask myself if I want

a cookie bad enough to go buy one at the store. (Usually it's no, and I eat the apple instead.) Adding space for a pause makes change easier and gives us a better chance of following through on what we *say* we want. Responding rather than reacting puts our best selves back in charge, rather than our emotional (or impulsive) selves.

Willpower Is Overrated

Those of us with neurodivergence have no business relying solely on willpower to make our changes happen. In fact, I would argue that even neurotypical people don't accomplish most things out of willpower—the people who run around getting hard things done consistently are far more likely to have strong motivation and values than superhuman willpower. If they can say "no" to tempting things over and over, their values are pulling them in the opposite direction with stronger force.

In the same way, our motivation to change should come from our values. *Why* are we making this change? What pain got us here, and what hope lies on the other side? Getting clear on our values and our *why* allows us to persist when things get hard—and they will!

As an example, my client Jonathan decided one day to quit smoking by sheer force of will. I asked him why—what was his reason for wanting to quit? If he didn't know, he was going to end up in trouble when he had a craving. But if he *knew*, he could decide again in the moment that his value was far more important. In the end, Jonathan figured out he wanted to be healthy for his daughter. And just like in the old commercial, he suggested putting a picture of his daughter on the cigarette pack so he sees it before picking up a cigarette—and I suggested throwing out the pack and putting the picture of his daughter on the gum pack he'd chew instead. Quitting was still hard, and he still relapsed several times, but now he knew *why* it was worth trying again. He made it to the end of the change cycle eventually, and we are both proud of him.

Change Your Language

Changing the language we use to talk (and think!) about a problem is a small hack that can have a big impact. For example, a few years ago, I had a client who would constantly say "I can't do that," when she actually meant "I'm not willing to do that." We worked on changing her language, and even that small change helped her feel more empowered. It wasn't that she *couldn't* make the change she said she wanted; it's that she was *choosing* not to. As we worked, we were able to determine the reasons she wasn't willing to change in certain ways (despite telling me she wanted to). Knowing why helped us figure out both the ways she *was* willing to change and the things she was willing to do to make the changes. Her path to change was much smoother this second time!

Changing our language has another benefit. It helps us tap into the power of cognitive processing. When we process emotionally, we may feel overwhelmed because we "don't have any money," but if we can stop and respond intentionally, we can choose to "not spend money on that right now." See the difference in how the two approaches feel? One is reactive, and one is proactive. The reality may be the same, but the second approach gives us more agency and certainty.

Of course, the biggest hack is starting again when we relapse. Let's talk about how to do that more effectively.

Getting Back on Track

One of the biggest obstacles to successful change is having rigid expectations. Progress isn't linear! So many of us believe that either we do the change perfectly or we don't do anything. If we expect to "keep the streak alive forever" or follow our difficult plans to the letter despite changing circumstances, then we will despair if we fail to meet such a lofty (if not impossible) standard.

Change isn't easy—we will make mistakes. Far better to grant ourselves forgiveness, realizing that any progress is good progress. Eating a vegetable—even one!—is better than not eating a vegetable. Smoking a few cigarettes a week is far better than smoking a pack per day. Every improvement is still an improvement. When we fall down, we can pick ourselves back up, reconnect with our *why*, and continue the messy, nonlinear process of change.

Smokers *normally* take six or more attempts at quitting[6] before change sticks permanently. But the efforts along the way are what give them the information they need to complete the cycle in the end. Nobody picks up a football and becomes an NFL player the next week, nor do they expect to. Whatever skills you need to add to create big change in your life may also be complex and take time and practice to master. That's okay! Be willing to be a beginner and to learn.

Temporary Priorities

In Chapter 2, we talked about the amygdala and its role in the anxiety response. When we are in fight-or-flight, our brains only understand *now*.[7] Similarly, when we're hungry, tired, or facing something tempting, we risk focusing more on immediate needs or rewards than on our long-term goals. Humans are constantly battling between our present and future selves. While it's tempting to choose the easy path or familiar treat over the harder actions that lead to our long-term goals, when we do, we often make mistakes we regret. And the push-pull between long- and short-term goals is always present—and always more challenging for those of us who are neurodivergent.

It takes discipline and determination to do something harder (even a little harder) now in order to make things easier for ourselves in the long term. But that's what's required for change, even in something as simple as organization. Until my late twenties, I didn't file papers or take the time to put anything away in the right spot, because I didn't want to deal with it—but then I'd constantly have trouble finding anything I needed. At some point I realized that putting things away in the right spot is a love letter to future me. It takes a few minutes longer now, but it saves me five hours of digging for that tax document when I'm under the wire. Reminding myself of that fact helps me catch up with filing and tidying when I fall behind even now.

When we lose our rhythm and mess up on change, it's our present selves undermining our future selves. Instead, remember the love letter: Value your future self, and go back to the habits that will support future you, even if you do them imperfectly.

Leaving Wiggle Room

When my dad got sick a few years ago, I was already in the middle of a personal growth season. I was trying to add a bunch of new habits and skills all at once—so I continued with that effort even though he was sick. I thought, for some reason, that I could both care for him and reach all these new goals at once. In retrospect, that was a terrible idea. Walls of Awful popped up like mushrooms after the rain. Eventually I couldn't move forward with anything until I dramatically lightened my load and focused on my family.

No matter what our ambitions, life *will* get in the way. Those of us with neurodiversity also face an executive function shortage; we can only do so many new things at once without shorting out. Given that something is going to disrupt our lives fairly regularly, whether we see it coming or not, it's in our best interest to leave room. When we limit the amount of change we try to go through at once, we create opportunities for flexibility. Sooner or later, we will need the wiggle room.

With wiggle room, we are more likely to be able to absorb the extra stress and continue to move forward, even if we need to do it more slowly than we'd like. If we insist on maxing out our capacity before life even happens, though, we set ourselves up for anger, disappointment, resentment, and eventually risk dropping everything.

Use the Power of Reflection

The last hack to support our efforts toward change is reflection. What realistic problems might show up, and how can we plan for them? This kind of planning prepares us for likely roadblocks and gives us a guide for navigating them. In the same way, after a relapse happens, we can reflect back on what happened and why. That way, we can figure out what triggered the unwanted behavior and learn how to avoid it in the future.

I find that the SHRED (sleep, habits, relationships, exercise, diet) model (from Chapter 3) is a helpful lens to use when change gets difficult. If we relapsed because we were tired, hungry, or hadn't exercised lately, those problems can be addressed with better self-care habits. (See more about habits in Chapter 9.) If our relationships influenced us in a negative way, we can push back by setting better boundaries in those relationships or seeking out positive people who support our journey.

Of course, change can be derailed by *many* things. That's why learning through reflection is so useful. If something else got in the way of the change we wanted, what was it? Do we need to try a new approach or find a new time and place for the change we want? Do we need support to break a pattern? Do we need to add resources or skills for the next time around? We may have to make hard decisions, and we may not like them, but learning and moving forward will empower us.

If we learn from each relapse, over time relapses become shorter, less frequent, and much less impactful. We know ourselves better and learn the skills we need to cement change permanently. Reflection can be difficult, but it's a consistent, effective hack to make change happen faster and more sustainably.

Awareness is the first and most important task of the change cycle. Use reflection as necessary to build awareness to drive the cycle forward.

PERSISTING PAST OUR WALLS

Deciding to change is a hard thing to do—and carrying out that change is even harder. But as we come out of our emotional processing and frustration and come back to the reality of the change cycle, we know the process is normal. Change may not be linear, but change is possible! Setbacks are a given, but they do not define us. Neither do the Walls that inevitably rise to block our way. However many times we need to bounce around the change cycle, if we persist, we'll make the change we want last.

The problem-solving skills we learn along the way are priceless. Once we've made a change happen once, we can apply those skills to make the next change that much easier to navigate.

CHEAT SHEET: HOW CHANGE WORKS

3 Change is uncertain, which means it always carries with it at least *some* anxiety. That's okay!

4 Change has several stages, from **precontemplation** and **contemplation** (thinking about the change), to **preparation** and **action** (where the change is in process but hasn't stuck yet), and finally **maintenance**, where the change has become permanent and simply needs to be maintained.

5 For small changes, we can move through this process in an hour; for large ones, it can take as long as months or years. **It's normal to bounce around between stages many times before permanent change.**

6 **Relapse—or falling back into old habits—is normal** and nothing to be scared of. We often fall back several times before we figure out the path to real change. Learning from our relapses tends to make the process faster.

7 Neurodivergent people can't rely on willpower for change. Instead, **we need to set up external supports, like people, reminders, and**

timers. We also need to leave **transition time** and **wiggle room** for the unexpected.

8 Developing **time wisdom** can help us start and manage change more effectively.

ACTION STEPS:

1 Think about the Wall of Awful that you've been playing with. Because it's a Wall you're still struggling with, odds are you keep landing in the relapse phase of the change cycle.

2 As you reflect on the Wall, consider the things that are keeping you from moving on to the maintenance stage in the change cycle. (In other words, what are the traps that are keeping you stuck?)

3 Brainstorm some completely new ideas to overcome your Wall. (You could even think back to the examples shared in earlier chapters, especially something you wouldn't ordinarily do.) Use that strategy the next few times you encounter your Wall.

4 Stay curious. See what works and what doesn't, and adjust from there.

CHAPTER NINE

SYSTEMS AND HABITS, AND WHAT GETS IN THE WAY

> Good systems and habits get us past the Wall of Awful with much less effort. But be careful—neurodivergent people need to establish systems and habits differently.

Before we start, I have bad news. If you're looking for this chapter to provide you with the perfect morning routine that will solve all your problems and make you a millionaire, it's not going to happen. (Spoiler alert: You haven't found it because that morning routine doesn't exist!) Instead, I'm going to talk more broadly about how systems and habits work and what trips them up. These are the tools that help you build the life you want, one step at a time.

I'll start with me. For years, I had a habit of not

going to the gym. I habitually did other things with that time instead, and as a result I didn't go. I *said* I wanted to be healthier and to get stronger. Every now and then I'd make a deliberate effort to walk in those doors. But I was in the habit of not going to the gym, so I didn't go to the gym. And I wanted that to change.

To do that, I got clear about why getting into better shape was important to me: not just being healthier for my family long term, but feeling stronger and smarter in the moment. I also had a looming kempo black belt test I needed to be in shape for. So I hired a personal trainer. The trainer would keep me accountable to show up twice a week, and I prepaid to meet with her for a year. I knew that after a year I'd have the rhythm down.

I also precommitted to 7:00 a.m. sessions. Research shows working out can help us focus for hours afterward.[1] I wanted to get that focus during the workday, and I did. I felt smarter, more "with it," and more connected to my body the whole day. Paying attention to that immediate positive effect acted as a reward for my brain and made the whole process more motivating.

I also found a second source of motivation. I'm easily motivated by my kids; parenting them is a value for me. So I took them to the gym after school to show them how to exercise and how to get stronger. Soon I was going four to five mornings and three afternoons or more per week—and I found my days went better. Of course, sometimes I'll get undermined by the weather, a damaged knee, or a cold, but I always get back on the horse. I'm in the habit of going to the gym now, so I go.

SYSTEMS AND HABITS FREE UP ENERGY

We tend to do the things we're in the habit of doing. We get up, go to work, come home, and eat dinner. We solve problems mostly using the same systems we've always used. A big part of our lives operates on autopilot, and there's a reason for this. Humans evolved to conserve energy to survive. New, intentional actions are energy intensive, so our brains and bodies try to avoid them as much as possible. Thinking is fine, but starting a completely new series of actions takes valuable executive function we'd rather not spend except in an emergency. So we use habits to keep things happening on autopilot.[2] That's good news and bad news.

THREE STAGES OF EVERY TASK

The tricky thing about habits is that they're going to happen whether we want them to or not. That can make it hard to create good ones, because we have to do it intentionally. I didn't have to put any effort into my habit of *not* going to the gym. But I had to work hard to create my new habit of going to the gym with intention—and persist many times before it stuck.

Part of how I did that was by using a lesson my friend and marketing expert Ryan McRae taught me—every large task has three stages.

- Set it up.
- Do it up.
- Clean it up.

Neurodivergent people—and especially those of us with ADHD—often like the *doing* stage. We're less excited about setting up and cleaning up. But if we don't set things up correctly, it will be much harder for us to do the task. If we don't clean it up, we'll be stepping over pieces of the task for weeks. Both add friction to our lives, and that friction may add to a Wall of Awful, or even create one.

So, as you create habits in this chapter, you may naturally want to jump ahead to the *doing*. We still need to set up the habit or system and clean it up for it to stick. (Setting up may also look like planning, which we'll cover in Chapter 10.)

Examples of Setting It Up and Cleaning It Up

The other two steps really do matter! For example, let's say I need to mow the lawn. The first step to mowing the lawn is turning on the lawn mower—only it's not. It's making sure there's gas in the lawn mower, getting any rocks, dog toys, or big sticks from the yard, and moving the lawn furniture out of the way. If I jump right into starting the lawn mower, I might run out of gas a third of the way through mowing. If I don't have gas in the gas jug, what should have been a quick hour task now involves the gas station, maybe Home Depot, and a lot of frustration. If I don't pick up the rocks and things, I could ruin a kid's toy, or the blade could hit that rock and drive it into my leg. Now the day also includes a trip to urgent care.

The same goes for getting rid of the bag of cut grass and putting the lawn furniture back at the end of the process. If I don't clean up now, I'll have to remember to do it all later. If I forget or don't have enough time to do it later on, I'll just be adding bricks to the Wall of my lawn mowing future self.

In this chapter we'll spend a minute setting up the task of making habits before showing you *how* to do it exactly. But because I understand the need to jump ahead, here's a quick preview.

SET HABITS UP FOR SUCCESS

To make an action or behavior more likely and to make a habit or system more likely to stick, we can:

- Increase our motivation by connecting the action to our values
- Make the action easier—consider systems!
- Increase our skill or comfort level with the action
- Reduce any friction that may exist related to the task
- Reduce the space between the cue and the action as much as possible
- Set a new reminder or prompt if the action is too far in the future
- Hook the habit onto other habits
- Add resources or ask for help

→ **Those of us who are neurodivergent absolutely *can* establish excellent systems, routines, and habits that make doing what we want and need to do much easier. We just have to do it differently.**

Systems are Shortcuts

So how do we turn good intentions into actual working systems and habits in practice? Let's start with systems, because systems are the building blocks of habits.

What are systems? They are sets of actions we do to accomplish something. Systems mean we don't have to figure everything out from scratch, using willpower to solve the same problem over and over. Instead, when the problem arises or the goal comes up, we apply our system to get the goal we want. It becomes automatic.

Setting up a system can be like setting up a line of dominoes. It takes time and effort to figure out where each of the pieces goes. But once it's set up, we can knock over the first domino with minimal effort, and the rest will fall. Thankfully, with systems, the dominoes reset themselves. We can knock over the first domino as many times as we want, and follow the cascade straight to our goal.

We can't do everything in our lives by willpower or by executive function alone. Everyone needs systems. And because neurodivergent people have weaker executive functions than average, we need more systems. Our support systems may look a little different from those of neurotypical people—but that's fine!

Simple Systems

The specifics of a good support system are individual to each person and take time to build. But the best ones tend to have similar elements:

- **Remove the option.** If we don't want to do something, we can change the environment so it's no longer an option. For example, if I don't want to eat cookies, the easiest way to do that is to simply not buy them. Not having cookies in the house means I eat an apple for my snack instead. (Even if it's not as good.)

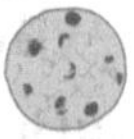

- **Spreadsheets and checklists.** Adding external lists can help us remember the steps of a routine or keep track of too many details. For neurodivergent people, a key part of using spreadsheets and checklists successfully is to *put them where the task is.* If the task is on the computer, leave the spreadsheet open where it's the first window you see.
- **Space as memory.** Rather than assuming we'll remember to take an item with us, we can put it in front of the door or in the location we'll need it. For example, when I took my kids skiing the other week, I put our ski tickets in the front seat of my car. That way, when I forgot to bring them to the check-in, I only had to walk back

to my car—not drive two hours home to get them. (And yes, I did forget them. But because I planned ahead, that didn't matter.)

- **Sticky notes.** A sticky note on the computer screen, bedside table, or other location reminds us in the exact place we need the information. If we leave ourselves a sticky note on the computer when we leave work, we'll see it when we return to remind us where we left off.
- **Direct questions.** Having simple systems in communication can also help. For example, at the beginning of a conversation with someone talking about a problem, we can ask, "Do you want to be listened to or helped to solve the problem?" Knowing which makes the conversation much better for both people.

The simplest support systems happen when we need them. They remember for us, and they put the supplies we need within easy reach. Take a moment to think about the simple systems you already have in place.

It's Okay to Take the Easy Way

We all get low, and we all have days we struggle. Depression, illness, a bad ADHD day, anxiety, or just too many demands can drain us. If that's you, I'm here to give you permission to do it the easy way. There are no rules—if it works for you, it works.

In the mental health community, there's a famous internet meme by Kate Scott[3] called "run the dishwasher twice." At one of the lowest points in her life, she was crying to her therapist about being overwhelmed. She didn't even have the energy to stand at the sink and rinse her dishes before putting them into the dishwasher. Her therapist told her to run the dishwasher twice—the dishes would still get clean. When she couldn't stand for a whole shower, he told her to sit on the shower floor and get clean there. Later she got better and rinsed the dishes and stood in the shower again, but she never forgot. If we can't do it the "right" way, we can run the dishwasher twice.

For another example, ADHD people often struggle with folding laundry. Instead of trying to keep up appearances, what if socks and towels just lived in the laundry basket? What if we hung up the clothes that would wrinkle on pegs next to the laundry basket? No one sees whether we do laundry the "right" way. We can meet our needs in whatever way works, even if our way is "unusual."

Friction: the Hidden Enemy

My favorite way to create systems for clients involves one simple idea: friction. Friction is the force that bogs us down, and it's the secret to most effective systems for neurodivergent people.

The less friction there is when beginning a task, the easier it is to start. So we want to **create more friction for the tasks or actions we don't want**, and **reduce friction for the tasks that we do want**.

Examples of Using Friction

Another client, Patrice, wanted help cleaning her house. She knew she needed to do it, but starting felt impossible. We worked together, adding easy cleaning wipes with nice scents to every room and putting the other cleaning supplies for certain rooms in easy reach. Now Patrice just wipes down a mess quickly when she sees it. Having to go downstairs to get the supplies meant that cleaning rarely happened—removing the friction made it happen naturally as she went through the day.

Of course, we can also use friction to *keep* us from doing things we don't want to do. (Not buying cookies fits into this category.) Similarly, if I catch myself checking the phone instead of working on the computer, I can put my phone in a box in a different room.

Now it's harder to use. I could also delete distracting apps or get software that puts a delay timer on those apps to prevent me from using them.

I've even seen people use negative friction as motivation. I had a client who had trouble getting up. He decided to set his coffeemaker to go off five minutes after he should be awake—without the coffeepot under it. If he didn't get up, the coffee would flood his kitchen countertop. He found it very motivating.

Friction Hides

Neurodivergent people often feel like everyday tasks take huge effort to accomplish. If something feels like it takes more effort to start than it should—but we're able to start sometimes—we should consider creating a system to help. *Why* is it so much effort? Getting to that answer can take work, but it's the only way to set up an effective supportive system. There's probably some hidden friction we need to address.

For neurodivergent people, the hidden friction is often **sensory issues** we aren't aware of.

My client Muhammed, a teenager, hates doing the dishes. He likes contributing to his household and having a job to do, but the sensory experience of doing the dishes is gross to him. It takes an incredible amount of willpower for him to push past that sensory experience and do the dishes. His support system for that task is simple: rubber gloves. If he wears gloves, washing the dishes is suddenly not slimy and gross. He also listens to music he likes when he needs to wash the dishes—all of that removes his friction in doing the task.

Of course, there are many other sources of hidden friction that neurodivergent people struggle with. Here are a few common ones. (Any of these can turn into a Wall of Awful over time.)

- **Sensory issues.** It's too loud, too gross, too hot, too scratchy, too smelly, too bright.
- **Location.** The environment doesn't help us start. (The tools are too far away. There's too much sensory input. There are too many distractions.)
- **A skill gap.** We don't have the skills to do what we're being asked to do.
- **Lack of clarity.** It's too hard to figure out. We don't know what we're supposed to do or where to start.
- **Overwhelm.** There are too many steps, too many demands, or the expectations are too high.
- **Forgetfulness.** If we can't remember that we're supposed to do it or how to do it, we're not gonna do it. (Duh!)
- **Regulating our attention.** Phones, other people, and our own thoughts can keep interrupting our focus. It's hard to bring it back.

- **Regulating our emotions.** Frustration, anxiety, and other emotions just get in the way sometimes!
- **Dealing with change.** Just when we know what we're doing, something changes!
- **Social challenges.** People-ing is hard. (And they cause at least half of the stuff above.)

When you hit a Wall of Awful, look for hidden friction. **And wonder if the friction itself could be your Wall.**

Regulating Friction

Once you know what the friction is, how can you reduce it? Can you get more clarity, skills, or reminders to help you? Can you develop skills to change the way you approach change or social challenges? Consider what the problem might be and how to address it. (There are practical suggestions for most of these problems throughout the book, and later in this chapter. I'm sure you can figure out any problems that aren't directly covered here!)

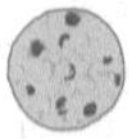

In the same way, if you find yourself doing something you *don't* want to do, how can you *increase* the friction to make the task harder? Often moving the phone to another room or not buying the cookies is enough without the need for willpower.

Successful systems for neurodivergent people use

friction to our advantage, even if they add additional elements like calendars, sticky notes, and checklists. Make the system as simple and low friction as possible, and it will happen more often. Add friction and complication to make it happen less often.

DON'T FORGET THE THREE STEPS TO A TASK!

As you create systems for your own task, take the time to plan for setting it up, doing it up, *and* cleaning it up. Where is the friction in each step? How can that friction be reduced? By planning for all three steps, you've kept yourself from being derailed by flying rocks and empty gas tanks.

FORGET THE SNOWBLOWER

I live in Massachusetts. It doesn't just snow; IT SNOWS! I have a snowblower, but I rarely use it because there's too much friction. The snowblower is complicated to start, and I only use it two to three times per year, so I often forget how to start it. And if I'm covered in snow, I'm not going to track it through the house so I can read the directions that I've invariably left inside. The up-front friction is huge. The friction of using it isn't any better, almost all of which is sensory-based. It's loud, it rattles around with a ton of vibration, and when the wind gusts, the snow gets thrown right back on me. The snowblower might clear my driveway in a third of the time, but I'd generally rather use a shovel. It's a stance that puzzles my wife.

Reflecting on my stance with the snowblower taught me a lot about how the Wall of Awful affects the decisions we make. If there's enough friction related to a task, even if it's friction we can get past but remains a part of the experience of the task, it will affect how we approach it. I'm willing to trade an hour to an hour and a half of physical labor to avoid five minutes of frustration and twenty minutes of sensory overwhelm. To the outside observer that might seem bananas because they only see that I'm working harder than I need to. They don't know what the experience is that I'm avoiding.

When I build systems with my clients, I try to take these ideas into account. What are the aspects of this task that you want to avoid? Are you trading a resource—like time or money—to make the experience better for you? Is that a resource you can afford to trade? How can you reduce or eliminate the parts you want to avoid? For me, I could laminate the instructions to my snowblower and glue them to the machine. I could also get a shield to put on the back of the snowblower to block the wind and snow while I use it.

How to Decrease Friction with Common Challenges

Neurodivergent people often struggle with recurring tasks we find tedious, unpleasant, or difficult to start. The best ways to make these tasks easier are to decrease the unpleasantness, decrease friction, and add INCUP strategies (interest, novelty, challenge, urgency, or passion/values, see Chapter 6, and see discussion in habits later in the chapter). Here's a quick guide with ideas for making useful systems for some common challenges.

- **Self-care.** If you don't know where to start, focus on good sleep. It's critical. Next move on to the rest of the SHRED model (sleep, habits, relationships, exercise, diet) to make sure you're effectively satisfying your basic needs. Then add the strategies and systems that are unique to you. Be sure to pay attention to how you feel after practicing self-care. That way, you can determine which options are most effective for you.

- **Personal hygiene.** Address sensory issues as much as possible; get a toothbrush or showerhead that makes brushing teeth or showering less unpleasant. Then add novelty, for example with multiple toothbrushes and toothpaste flavors. Or listen to a playlist of songs that get you motivated.

- **Task management.** Rather than "doing the hard thing first" like so many gurus say, start with an easy win. Then follow the momentum forward. Keep task management lists short to avoid overwhelm (put extra tasks/ideas in a "parking lot list" to get them out of your head), and set up time blocking or body doubling to get important things done. Leave extra time for transitions and break times in case you need it. (You're going to need it.)
- **Emailing.** I approach emailing as a competition with myself and the clock. I got a click counter. Every time I do email, I open the email box and tell myself I only have to do five emails, or ten, and then I can stop. Sometimes I set a timer and see if I can beat my current click record.
- **Emotional regulation.** The best way to manage the emotional friction that comes at the start of some tasks is to accept that it's going to happen. The more we fight against it, the worse it will be. After acceptance, we can use the soft fascination ideas shared in Chapter 7 to help with processing and releasing the emotions.

If your challenge isn't on this list, or these ideas don't help, use the ideas in the rest of this chapter (and the rest of the book) to build your own solution! Test it and adapt until it works.

Habits Make Actions Automatic

Once we make a new system, if we repeat that system enough times, we'll make a habit. Habits are actions that happen over and over, without the need for conscious thought. Habits can be one action or a set (system!) of actions.

Conscious, deliberate actions take willpower and executive function, as well as time to think. Habits don't. For example, let's take toothbrushing. We might have to remember it's time to brush our teeth, or we might not. But once we're standing in front of the sink, the habit kicks in. We go through all the steps involved—getting the toothbrush, toothpaste, squeezing the toothpaste on, brushing the left and right side of our upper teeth, and so on—without conscious thought. The toothpaste and toothbrush go back where they belong, and we move on with our day.

Habits are a double-edged sword: Once they're set, the brain is highly resistant to changing them. We tend to do the same action over and over in the same circumstance unless we change that habit with a large amount of deliberate effort. In other words, when I was in the habit of *not* going to the gym, I didn't go to the gym. I had to establish a new, replacement habit of *going* to the gym—and spend money on a trainer to get that habit going—to see real results.

All of us have habits, even neurodivergent people. How we establish and reestablish those habits is a little different, but how habits work in general is the same.

How Habits Work

According to Charles Duhigg's *The Power of Habit*,[4] there are three parts to a habit: the cue, the behavior, and the reward.

Cue

All habits—good or bad—start with **a cue**, a signal to the brain that it's time to do the thing.

A cue can be internal, like a smoker's craving for a cigarette, or external, like the alarm I have set to tell me when it's time to take the boys to school. A cue can be literally anything.

- **The environment.** My office is where I work, so if I sit down at my office desk, I focus and think critically. If I try to work while sitting on my couch, I struggle.

- **Sounds.** In the classic story, physiologist Ivan Pavlov trained dogs to associate the sound of a bell with being fed. Eventually, they started drooling every time they heard the dinner bell.[*] We've all been there.
- **Rituals and clothing.** If I'm struggling to work that day, I put on a collared shirt and a professional mindset. Alex lights a candle when starting to write.

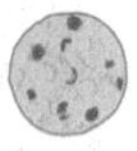

- **Physical cues.** If I'm used to eating a cookie in the afternoon when I get hungry, then getting hungry in the afternoon is my cue. The same goes for locking my car every time I get out and close the door.
- **Thoughts.** Yesterday, I was wandering in the woods and thinking about my upcoming black belt test. Soon, I was doing techniques as I walked.

---

* Well... that's what both Alex and Brendan were taught in textbooks in school and what's still taught to students in many classes today. Turns out the reality is more complicated, but the example is a good one, so we left it.

For one interesting discussion on why this isn't a thing, check out:

Michael Domjan (Jun 28, 2021). *What's Wrong with This Picture?: Just About Everything.* APS Observer. Association for Psychological Science. Retrieved June 25, 2025, from https://www.psychologicalscience.org/observer/revisiting-pavlovian-conditioning.

- **Another habit ending.** Routines are built of several habits "daisy chained" in a row. If an existing habit is already there, using that habit to cue another one is easier than creating a new cue. For example, a morning routine might start with waking up, showering, making coffee, taking medicine, eating breakfast, and so on... One habit follows the next naturally.

However the cue is triggered, unless we go out of our way to use willpower to interrupt the process, the cue will naturally lead to the behavior.

Behavior

After the cue, we will do the behavior at the center of the habit. If my client sees a cupcake in the break room, he'll eat that cupcake. If I hear the 7:00 a.m. alarm, I'll text our carpool buddy and get in the car to take the boys to school. If I put on my gi, I get mentally prepared to practice martial arts.

Reward

Every habit that continues in our lives carries with it a reward of some kind. When we brush our teeth, we have minty fresh breath. Over time, we've probably come to associate the mint taste with being clean and happy. The reward for sitting on the couch *for hours and hours* is that it feels indulgent and restorative, and that we avoided the pain of doing something harder. The reward for me going to the gym is how strong and accomplished I feel when I'm done.

How We Make Habits

Once we know how habits work, we can design them or hack them to get more of what we want. We form a new habit by repeating **cue**, **behavior**, and **reward**.[5] How many times we need to repeat the cycle depends on the habit and our specific neurodivergence. But eventually the habit will set and become automatic.

How We Change Habits

To change a habit, Duhigg says that interrupting the path from cue to behavior is hard—very hard. If we try to stop the behavior through willpower, we'll fail most of the time. Instead, to change habits, we'll be better off replacing the *cue* or the *behavior*.

For example, if my client Michael wants to stop eating sweets, he should probably avoid the company break room, which often has cupcakes and doughnuts available. If he still wants to socialize with colleagues, he can do so at the water cooler or take short walks for meetings instead.

When another client wanted to start her work-from-home day earlier, we replaced her habit of sitting on the couch and doing nothing with a habit of sitting on the couch with the laptop. She still went to the same location at the same time every morning, but her *behavior* in that location was different. **Changing the behavior in the middle of the habit is often the fastest, easiest way to get what we want.**

Sometimes we can also change habits by making the *reward* more (or less) satisfying. When I walk out of the gym, I really try to pay attention to how good I feel in the moment. The better I can remember those good feelings, the stronger the craving for them will be. To stop a bad habit, sometimes stopping the reward is enough. A new drug for alcoholism takes away the buzz of a drink; alcoholics can still drink, but they then experience all the negative effects of the alcohol with none of the benefits. For many, that's enough to slowly break the habit cycle over time—without the buzz, they simply don't want it anymore.[6]

All of us have habits, both good and bad. The key is to intentionally set up habits that serve us rather than harm us.

Another Way of Seeing Habits

BJ Fogg, author of *Tiny Habits*, has a different way of seeing habits.[7] He still believes in cues (he calls them "prompts"), behaviors, and rewards, but he adds two additional steps that neurodivergent people can use to change habits more easily.

Fogg says that before a new behavior can happen consistently, there are three things that need to be present:

- **Motivation.** How much do we want to do the behavior? Motivation is great when it's present, but it's fickle.
- **Ability.** How skilled are we with regard to that behavior or how comfortable are we with the behavior?
- **Cue or prompt.** Is there an obvious internal or external signal to start?

Most of us over-rely on motivation, but motivation comes and goes. By adjusting the cue in our environment and the skills and confidence we have around the behavior, we can make motivation much less important. Adding resources, asking for help, and increasing our skill all make the habit more likely to stick. Making the task easier also makes it more likely.

We can improve our follow-through as neurodivergent people by doing things as soon after the prompt as possible. (This is my favorite way to use my impulsivity for good!) If we go to a meeting and take notes, the cue and the action are immediately connected. We can also habit-stack and immediately send a summary email afterward. But if we walk back to our office, anything in the hallway might distract us. Even if we just stop to get a cup of coffee, the prompt and the action may be too far apart for us to do what needs to be done.

Make sure the prompt is obvious and can be acted on almost immediately. If we can't act on it soon enough, we have to set another reminder as a cue to do the thing in the future.

BEING REALISTIC

If we have a Wall of Awful for a task, odds are our motivation is limited. So, to make the task possible with low motivation, we need to pay attention to (1) our ability level and (2) how comfortable we are with the task. Making ourselves more comfortable or skilled with the task—often by asking for support or finding useful resources—helps us be more likely to do the task successfully. The same goes for (3) decreasing the friction around the task and (4) ensuring that our prompt for the task is as close to the actual doing of it as possible. Being realistic about what we need lets us make the task easier and not have to rely on motivation.

We're Going to Mess Up

Ever heard of the "don't break the chain" productivity system? It's attributed to Jerry Seinfeld, who supposedly said that comedians should write at least one joke a day every day and cross the day off on the calendar.[8] As the days add up, you won't want to break the chain.

Yeah... That's a terrible system for neurodivergent people.

Those of us with ADHD, autism, anxiety, depression, or any other neurodivergence *will* mess up. We will break the chain. It's going to happen. Rather than giving in to despair and walking away from the habit forever, we can just plan for interruptions and mistakes. Neurodivergent people need to build forgiveness into habits. Not only will it make us more resilient and more likely to actually set a solid habit, but it's better for our mental health. It gives us permission to learn from our mistakes and correct them over time.

Rather than starting a big "all or nothing" side hustle productivity habit, start smaller. Begin the habit by sitting in your chair and opening your laptop at a certain time in the evening. You don't even have to work right away—just set the habit. Once it feels set, create a to-do list, or work on getting one client. By starting small and building up from there, then being kind to ourselves when we mess up, we'll be more likely to return to the habit if we drop it. Something is better than nothing. The easy habit you do *sometimes* is better than the hard one you don't ever do again.

When you mess up, forgive yourself. Learn. And start again.

DIFFERENT HABIT MAINTENANCE FOR DIFFERENT BRAINS

Because our brains are different, neurodivergent people need to establish and maintain habits differently. While we can easily engage in preferred tasks, we tend to be less internally motivated toward nonpreferred tasks (like those behind the Wall of Awful). So, we often need more external cues. We may need to be prompted to *start* a task or system of tasks more obviously than someone who notices the time of day or a similar cue more easily. We may need more support to build a habit in the first place—starting smaller and making the process easier—than someone who can depend on willpower.

Remember, neurodivergent people often need more repetition to cement a habit. But when we have a (flexible) habit in place, it often sticks better! Put in the time to create the habit you want, and you'll free up energy for other projects later.

Let's review how to establish and maintain habits as a neurodivergent person.

- Set up a clear external cue that will start the habit you want, with a reminder as to what the habit was if you need it.
- Make the first steps of a task as simple and easy to implement as possible.
- Find and decrease friction.
- Repeat, repeat, repeat, until it sticks.
- Set reminders for more complex tasks. Use a checklist if you need one.
- Build in forgiveness. Plan for how to absorb mistakes or start again, right from the beginning.
- Tie habits to values, and set up external cues (including decorations!) to remind you of the connection to your values.

- When possible, hook new habits onto the end of old habits.

- Use INCUP (interest, novelty, challenge, urgency, or passion/values; see Chapter 6) and CCAW (Chapter 2) to activate and soothe as needed.
- Use or change your environment to support your habits. Put needed supplies close to hand and distractions far away.
- Pay attention to how changes in routine and environment affect you, and adjust as needed.
- Set a timer, or try Pomodoro sprints. (Look it up on your favorite search engine.) The urgency of trying to beat the timer can be focusing and helpful.
- Play is the antidote for anxiety, so be sure to add as much fun as possible!

Dealing with Disruption

Sometimes disrupted routines and other "small" changes can be hard for neurodivergent people. We can struggle to navigate changes in routines, work, or, for example, the learning curve that comes with getting a new phone. When the *way* we do something has to change, we need to be gentle with ourselves as we learn the new way.

Sometimes routine changes can mess up things we don't expect. We were writing this chapter as my teenagers were home from school on break, and having them home took up a lot of extra processing space in my brain. When I went to eat lunch, I made them lunch. On breaks I asked myself several times a day how much I needed to check on them and renegotiated the schedule to spend more time with them.

When I taught middle school, I saw kids get in trouble in math class consistently on the days they had a delayed opening for school. On those days, they would go to math at the time they were usually in my English class. I was chatty, so they were subconsciously expecting to be chatty at that time of the morning—something they weren't supposed to do in math. So they got in trouble.

When something changes your routine, expect the change to put you off-balance. Be gentle as you adjust, and add additional sources of comfort if you can. Then come back to your habits when you can.

HOW TO MAKE A HABIT FUN

Making habits neurodivergent friendly means we work *with* our brains instead of against them. That means using INCUP (interest, novelty, challenge, urgency, or passion/values; see Chapter 6) to make our habits more engaging and therefore easier to activate. Establishing habits is easier if they're fun! And the same goes for *doing* the habit, especially if it's linked with an emotionally difficult Wall of Awful.

For a quick recap, for those of us who are neurodivergent, "important" isn't always good enough to get our brains to activate. So if we want to create a habit around paying bills, for example, instead of yelling at ourselves about how important paying the bills is—especially if there's a Wall of Awful involved—we should make the process more interesting or novel. Maybe when it's time to pay the bills, we can light candles around the computer and play opera loudly. We can feel dramatic and "go off to war" to get the bills paid, because it feels confrontational. By changing the circumstances around the action, we make it more engaging and more fun. (Of course, after a few months, ADHD people may need to swap candlelight and opera for flashlights and movie scores to keep the habit novel, and that's totally fine!)

My suggestion to Alex and her daughter about their bedtime routine at the beginning of Chapter 6 was in this same vein. When in doubt, set up the environment and the music to make it easier and more fun to do the habit. Create a time, a distraction-free space, and a fun reward at the end. Can we bake cookies on bills day and eat them once we're done? Can we set up a bill-paying race with a friend? What engaging INCUP strategies might we use?

The more fun the action is, the more likely we are to repeat it and the more likely the habit will stick.

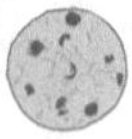

DECREASING FRICTION 2.0

Again, doing the work to identify friction points and figure out how to address them can be hard. Creating a system of habits to do so may take more thought and energy than just solving the problem in the moment—but that effort will more than pay off over time. The starting cost for that task will reduce every time we do it, and it will start to happen more naturally.

Neurodivergent-friendly support systems add elements that make a task easier, and so make it more likely that we'll do it. They decrease friction. They add certainty, connection, agency, and well-being to our lives. They decrease our anxiety and reduce the need to rely on executive function or willpower to get things done.

People with neurodivergence *can* create healthy, effective habits that increase our bandwidth (or at least use less of it!) and help us do more. We just need to do things differently, applying more varied support systems than our neurotypical peers. And that's fine!

CHEAT SHEET: SYSTEMS AND HABITS

1. **Systems and habits are an investment.** Creating them burns a lot of executive function and energy, but using them takes the pressure off our lives and gives us far more energy back over the long term.
2. There are three parts to any project or large task: **(1) setting it up, (2) doing it up, and (3) cleaning it up**. Skipping the setup or cleanup makes our lives much harder later, so all systems and habits need to include all three steps.
3. For systems, use the environment to reduce friction and make the right actions easier. Keep an eye out for "hidden" sources of friction like sensory issues.

4. **Neurodivergent people *can* make habits, but we need to do it differently.** Among other tricks, we need to make the cue and the action as close together in time as possible, and add music, novelty, and fun.
5. **Better habits may take a while to form.** We may even fall down while forming them—but they will stick if we persist! And better habits *will* make our lives easier in the long term.

ACTION STEPS:

1. Return to the Wall of Awful you've chosen. Take about twenty minutes and **create a system** that either (1) prevents that Wall from happening as often, and/or (2) decides in advance how you will put a door in it, with steps.
2. You may want to refer back to the earlier part of this chapter for how to create systems. If you're working on the (2) task, you might also want to flip back to Chapters 6 or 7 and scan headings to remind you what you need to do to put a door in the Wall or Climb the Wall.

Note: This action step is much harder than others in the book so far, and it's okay to ask for help from a friend, coach, therapist, or mentor!

CHAPTER TEN

PUTTING IT ALL TOGETHER WITH PLANNING

> The difference between an idea and something fully accomplished is a plan. This chapter ties all the information I've given you together by showing you how to plan, not only to overcome likely Walls of Awful when you need to but also to get to the big, important goals you have on the other side.

The year was 2016, and in a month I was supposed to leave for Reston, Virginia, to present the Wall of Awful at the ADHD Coaches Organization Conference. My extended family was sitting around the kitchen table at my dad's house, talking. Since my dad lived close to the airport, I had asked to leave my car at his place and have him drive me there.

It turned out that everyone else in the family was driving down to Washington, DC, to visit my nephew in college the same weekend I would be in Reston. So my dad wouldn't be at the house when I got back from the conference. I saw a problem.

"Hey, Dad, before you leave, I need you to make sure that the spare key to your car is hung up next to the door," I said.

"What?"

"Your car is blocking my car in the driveway. There's no space to get around it, and you're taking Lauren's car to DC. If I come back and you guys are still in Washington, then I'm not going to be able to get out of the driveway because I won't be able to move your car without keys. Then I can't go to the job interview and definitely won't get the job. If you leave your spare key on the hook, then it's not a problem if the car is still there."

Lauren, my older sister, looked at me, baffled. "Who are you?"

"What do you mean?" I asked.

"You just planned ahead! Like, you just saw a problem a month from now and knew how to solve it. When did you start doing that?"

"Oh," I said. "That's literally my job now. Part of ADHD coaching is helping people solve problems before they happen. I was just doing a pre-mortem, figuring out what could go wrong and trying to make sure it doesn't."

"Well, it was pretty cool," she said, clearly proud of me. I smiled and changed the subject.

I didn't get that job. But I did make it to the interview early—because my dad left the key on the hook next to the door.

MAKING IDEAS REALITY

To make the ideas in this book come to life—to get to *any* goal we want to accomplish—we have to make a plan. So in this chapter, we'll talk about planning. We'll think through how to make a plan. We'll consider what might go wrong and how to plan in advance to stop it and build in accommodations and strategies that make our plan work for our unique neurodivergent brains.

The more intentional the planning, the more effective this book will be in helping you create the change you want.

Three Parts of Any Task

Remember the three parts of a task from Ryan McRae in Chapter 9?

- Set it up.
- Do it up.
- Clean it up.

The fact is that those of us with neurodiversity tend to jump to the "doing it up" part but avoid setting it up or cleaning it up, often causing problems.

While you might be tempted to skip planning because it's boring, I encourage you to slow down. Remember the example from the last chapter about lawn mowing? Setting up and cleaning up for the lawn mower prevented a huge mess, a trip to the store, and a bleeding leg. It cut the time of the task in half and prevented a lot of future frustration and misfortune. In the same way, planning is a necessary "setup" stage of any large or complex task or project. Reflecting and learning from what happened is the "cleanup" stage. (See the sidebar at the end of this chapter.) Both planning and reflection make our lives much easier in the long run.

If you have a small task that takes less than thirty minutes, you may be able to avoid planning and just jump in. But any task longer than thirty minutes—and any task you have a Wall of Awful for—should be planned.

PLANNING MAKES THE REWARD REAL

Those of us with neurodiversity sometimes struggle to know what we want. Luckily, planning can help us visualize our end goals more clearly, so the change we want can feel more real and attainable. The clearer the visualization, the more we'll crave that desired result.

Creating a plan also lets us take our own needs into account. Rather than defaulting to the mainstream approaches we've been taught, we can set up systems that work for our unique brains. Neurodivergent people *can* plan and *can* achieve big things (like writing a book), but we often have to do it differently than others (like hiring a co-writer). Just like with habits, we also have to be strategic about when and how we plan. If we're going to use up our executive functions now, we want to be sure we're freeing up resources for later.

Planning Decreases Anxiety

In addition to the other benefits of planning, the *process* of planning actively fights anxiety. Creating and following a plan increases certainty and agency and is soothing to the brain. It keeps thinking and decision making in the prefrontal cortex, reassuring the amygdala that the executive functions have the situation under control. Sometimes having a plan decreases anxiety to the point that it puts a door in the Wall, and we can get the task done easily. But even when it doesn't, making the plan helps us solve problems and Climb our Walls of Awful.

If we create a good plan that takes our neurodiversity into account, we're able to separate the deciding from the doing (as friend and fellow ADHD coach Dusty Chipura says). It helps us take action more easily in ways that are far less exhausting.

What If I Have a Wall of Awful Around Planning?

Odds are you don't have a Wall of Awful for planning. It's far more likely that you have a Wall for whatever it is that you're planning about. So start there. But if that *doesn't* help, let's assume you do have a Wall for planning. How do we get past it?

Once your nervous system is calm enough to move forward, the first thing to do is figure out what the cause is. Planning requires a commitment to action. Could your Wall be related to that? Do you think you might get distracted or forget? Are you worried that you might fail to execute your plan and look foolish? Have you struggled with creating plans in the past?

Identifying the root of a Wall gives an idea of the problems we have to solve, increasing our certainty and agency. If we're afraid to fully commit to the plan, we can build in flexibility so it feels less confining. If we think we might forget to execute the plan, we can set up reminders. If we struggle with creating plans we can follow through on, we can research ways to plan or take a class on project management to develop the skills we're lacking. Knowing the exact problem means we can brainstorm solutions.

A DOUBLE-EDGED SWORD

Unfortunately, planning requires the one thing that neurodivergent people often struggle with: executive function. So planning itself can be a double-edged sword. It can be difficult for us to plan because it requires energy and effort that can feel hard to find. But if we don't plan, we end up exhausting our executive function *more* in the long run.

If we don't plan ahead, we're forced to plan and decide as we go—and that leads to traps, because eventually we exhaust our executive function and get stuck. Or we act foolishly from exhaustion and impulse and have to bail ourselves out of the problems that result.

But if we plan at the start of our week, our day, or even at the start of a task, we spend executive function now. And that means we can turn off our "thinking brains" later and just run through the list, which can feel much easier and smoother for a neurodivergent brain.

I'm not going to pretend that planning isn't demanding at the start. I've had clients who were so exhausted after detailed planning, they said they had to go lie down—and yet the plan we made together freed up mental resources for days or weeks afterward. They knew what to do when their Wall of Awful came up—and were able to Climb that Wall much more easily.

The good news is that planning, like any skill, gets easier and less effortful over time. We'll also get better at deciding when and where to plan, so that we get the most benefit from the executive function we spend.

HOW TO PLAN

"Planning" sounds vague, because it's a big topic. Planning is like a multitool; it's useful in a wide variety of situations. We might have to plan for:

- a complicated project at work
- any large task, like checking email every day for an hour, researching a topic, or organizing the kitchen

- how to get past a *specific* Wall of Awful, like a Wall for doing reports, paying bills, or talking to our kids about sex
- how we'll overcome Walls of Awful more generally as they appear in our lives
- how we'll use a day, week, or month

In nearly all of these cases, we'll go through the same general set of steps.

THE SIX STEPS OF A PLAN

1. Figure out what you want.
2. Determine your motivation.
3. Consider your resources.
4. Create a "rough draft" of your idea.
5. Plan for problems.
6. Stay flexible.

Step #1: Figure Out What You Want

It's an old saying, but it's true: If you don't know where you're going, any road will get you there.

Neurodivergent people—especially those of us who

are people pleasers—often struggle to tune out the noise and figure out what *we* want. But the more **concrete and specific** our goals are, the easier it is to make a plan to reach them.

More on Good Goals

Goals can be small: eating two salads a week, getting past a Wall of Awful to pay bills on the fifteenth, or finishing the TPS report at least two hours before the deadline. Or **goals can be huge:** training for a marathon, writing a nonfiction "how to" book, or supporting our child's study skills and emotional health through middle school.

We'll know we have a concrete and specific goal when we can see what reaching that goal looks like. We either ate two salads this week or we didn't. We either did the activities needed to support our child's study skills and emotional health consistently through middle school (once we have defined what those are), or we didn't. Notice how in the last example, we can get a partial score if we did some activities *inconsistently*—many goals are like that, and we may want to consider what is "good enough."

➜ Once you know what goal you'll be planning, write it down. Then write down how you'll know you achieved the goal. Can you get partial credit? If so, how?

When You Don't Know

If you don't yet know what you want to plan, take a moment to consider your overall life priorities. How are you doing in the following areas?

- **Basic daily needs.** Are your basic needs met? Do you have access to safety, food, water, survival, a workable living space, reliable income, and predictable routines?
- **Social connection (and lack of conflict).** Humans are social creatures. We need warm, supportive, or loving relationships with friends, family, coworkers, neighbors, and others. But relationships with too much conflict tend to drain us, and need to be addressed.
- **Your job.** Do you have concerns about productivity, income, office politics and dynamics, long-term career growth or fulfillment, and work-life balance? (If you're a student, all this applies, too!)
- **Your kids.** Do your kids have the care and guidance they need, along with education, support for their growth, and healthy independence?
- **Your well-being.** This refers to anything else directly related to you—your physical,

mental, and emotional health, financial budgeting or spending, and spiritual growth or maintenance.

How are you doing in each life area, in terms of your actual behavior patterns? Which area or areas are the most important to improve *right now*? Rank them in order, and think about how the different priorities may conflict—then pick only one or two immediate things to work on.

➔ Then take a moment to make that desire a specific and concrete *goal*, something to work on *next*. What's a good milestone to work on? How will you know you have succeeded, even if the goal is big? Go back to the previous area to help refine your thinking if necessary.

Do Fewer Things

Given that many neurodivergent people struggle with executive function and related challenges, I recommend choosing **no more than two** concrete goals or changes to work on at a time. Once you've moved a goal through planning and action and turned it into a repeatable system or habit, you can consider that goal to be in the maintenance stage of the change cycle (Chapter 8) and can pick another one to actively work on.

Also discussed in Chapter 8, it's important to build in "wiggle room" so that we can handle unexpected life events when they show up.

Step #2: Determine Your Motivation

It's important to connect with your motivations and emotions. *Why* do you want to make this change or reach this goal? For example, you may want to start an exercise routine and eat five salads a week (two separate goals) for the same reason: getting healthy.

Connecting to Values

We neurodivergent folks are often driven by our values, for example, in the form of justice sensitivity. Actions we take in line with our values feel better and are easier to do. Actions against our values can feel painful—and lead to Walls.

Because of this, I recommend connecting goals with multiple values if possible (discussed more in Chapters 7 and 9). For example, we could connect the "getting healthy" motivation from our earlier example with another value, like "getting healthy so we can see our kids grow up" (family) or "getting healthy so we can better give health advice to our patients from a place of integrity" (professionalism and integrity).

→ What values are connected to your goal? How might you leverage them to accomplish it?

Making the Goal Immediate

Since many of us with neurodiversity struggle with connecting to long-term motivations, it's important to add **short-term goals and motivations** that connect to the same values as our long-term ones. For example, "seeing our kids grow up" values family and parenthood—but so does "being able to keep up with our kids on the playground," which is much more immediate and concrete. Having both reasons in mind will more effectively help us connect goals to actions when things feel hard. If we take our kids to the playground every week, we have weekly motivation and accountability to remain consistent.

Complex Goals, Values, and Motivation

The same goes in reverse. We may have an ambition to run a 10k sometime in our life, and now seems a good time since our brother-in-law wants to run one with us early next year. That's great. Unfortunately, a goal that far away may feel overwhelming, particularly if we only see the big picture. On the other hand, if we can break the larger goal down into the smaller, more immediate next steps, it will feel more doable. We might even be able to keep up our motivation by texting achievements to our brother-in-law along the way.

Active Challenges vs. Passive Ones

Life is full of challenges—some that we choose (active challenges) and some that other people or circumstances throw at us (passive challenges). According to psychiatrist Alok Kanojia,[1] when we feel overwhelmed, it's often because we have more passive challenges than active ones.

The solution to overwhelm, then, surprisingly, is generally not to do less—because often doing less means we drop the challenges we chose first, which leaves us with only passive ones! That strategy leaves us even more overwhelmed. A better solution is to do some work to turn passive challenges into *active ones*.

Maybe we're overwhelmed and struggling to finish a boring project that was given to us at work. If we can connect it to a value, finishing what we started, for example, or we can decide to take on the project out of integrity or because we want to be a good worker, it will become more of an active choice. Choosing a challenge decreases the overwhelm! The same principle applies to swapping out other passive challenges for active ones, *even if the active ones are harder.* Luckily, we don't have to choose the situation for this strategy to be effective. We can choose who we want to be and how we want to act *in* the situation.

Of course, we can't get rid of passive challenges entirely. But we *can* often turn enough passive challenges into active ones that we no longer feel overwhelmed. And *that's* worth doing.

Step #3: Consider Your Resources

I recommend looking at resources early in the process of planning. Resources give us different solutions to the potential problems we could face and different potential paths to consider to get to our goal.

For this setup step, it's worthwhile to consider *all* the categories of resources and skills discussed in Chapter 3. (You may also want to go through the neurodiversity problem-solving exercise from Dusty Chipura on page 65 in that chapter.) But just as a reminder, here's a quick list of common resources.

- **Time.** How much of it do you have, and how do you get more if you need it?
- **Money.** Will you be able to solve problems or make your plan easier by using money? Can you

hire someone or buy a service or product that frees up time or helps make something easier?

- **People.** Who do you know who might be able to help you in this area? Make sure to consider your neighbors, coworkers, and other connections—even ones out of state or on the internet.
- **Materials.** We often have more physical resources than we realize. Everything from those old cans of tuna fish to the extra bedroom might provide creative solutions or help.
- **Community resources.** Don't ignore community resources, workplace and professional organizations, charities, and systems of support provided by schools, state, and local governments. When in doubt, find your local library and ask the librarians for help finding the resources you're looking for.
- **The internet and books.** The internet connects us. The internet and books both provide access to the world's information. Try to find books, forums, online communities, blogs, podcasts, YouTube, or other places giving good, balanced information on what you're facing—shoot for three or more sources. Also consider Udemy or Outschool for classes and professional and

support groups. (The book in your hand is a major resource!)

Whenever I'm facing a problem, especially one that feels overwhelming, I ask myself, "What resources are available to me to help me solve this problem?" (Sometimes I literally say that out loud.) Asking myself the question always helps me find a useful path forward.

Step #4: Build a "Rough Draft" Plan

Now that we've gathered all of our resources, ideas, values, and goals, we're ready to do the real work of planning.

The Main Goal

→ **Go back to your specific, concrete goal. Did you write it down?** If not, do that now.

Then double-check: What is your main objective?

- For example, we might want to get the kids to school on time in the morning—which is really a goal about leaving the house before a specific time.
- Or, if we have a goal of staying in better contact with our friends, we might now need to decide

how to stay in touch. Facebook might not count because it's not direct connection. Texting or calling may be better—and in person best of all. It may also make sense to decide how often to check in.

Subgoals

Start with the objective in mind and work backward, thinking critically about all the steps in between. **Are there any steps or subgoals that *have* to be done for our big goal to happen?**

For example, if we're trying to get the kids out the door in the morning to be at school on time, we'll need to:

- wake the kids up,
- feed them breakfast,
- get everyone dressed with shoes on,
- gather homework,
- have a nice morning chat,
- and brush hair.

(If we're leaving for work after dropping off the

kids, we *also* have to: get dressed in office clothes and get ourselves breakfast.)

For another example, if we want to run a 10k, we'll need to:

- put on sneakers and clothes we can run in comfortably,
- then run.
    - For many people, that means walking first... or developing a plan like a "couch to 5k" to run/walk until the body is ready to run for extended periods.
    - We have to make time to run consistently to get stronger.

We can't finish a 10k until we finish a 5k.

↛ Write down any subgoals that have to be accomplished to make your main goal happen. Identify which happen once (like the hook for keys) and which need to happen over and over (like feeding kids breakfast).

What Can Be Dropped?

Now, figure out which subgoals are optional. Being dressed in work clothes is critical, but we can skip the breakfast step if we put meal bars in the car for ourselves and the kids in advance. We can probably also skip the chat with family on a day when everyone overslept, without having to plan in advance.

↛ Mark the subgoals that you can skip without making arrangements, and then note what steps you'll need to take to drop others. Your plan should focus on only the critical subgoals. Add the steps (like the meal bars) that give you flexibility to drop subgoals later only if you have the time and energy to do them.

Do It Now or Write It Down

Do you have the energy to tackle the "extra" steps? Great. There are two ways to do that well.

1. Many neurodivergent people do best if they make a habit of "doing it now." If that's you, write down what you should do next in the planning process. Then write down your "extra" steps, like putting the meal bars in the car and installing the hook for the keys. Then go do the list in the order you wrote it down, while you're thinking about it.
2. On the other hand, if your brain works best when you don't interrupt it, just write down the immediate "extra" steps on a list to do later. Then continue with planning. When you're done planning,

you can get up and do these "extra" tasks without forgetting what you were going to do.

Find Your Tactics

Now that you know your goal and subgoals, think backward again. Let's start with the essentials of making a concrete plan.

- ***What* specifically do you need to do?** What steps are needed and in what order? Get as detailed as is useful, giving special focus to the initial steps.
- **Focus most on the actions that *must* happen to get you to your goal.** Only add others if you have time and energy.
- Are there any steps that **depend on other steps**? If so, those should be planned to happen first.
- ***How* specifically** are you going to accomplish each action or step? Make the barrier to entry as small as possible, both at the beginning of the plan and at any point where you might step away from it for a time and then resume.
- What **resources** (money, people, etc.) will you use to help you and where?

- ***When* and *where* will you do the actions?** Consider setting a schedule, estimating how long the various steps will take, and setting due dates for yourself. Put the schedule in your calendar. Then consider the environment you'll be taking action in and how that might affect things.
- **How will you remember?** Neurodivergent people should not rely on memory. Instead, use reminders, checklists, and other aids to help you. What will you use, and where and how will it remind you?

Do not neglect the decisions on specifically when and where to do each step. Choosing a time and place for action makes accomplishing your goals more likely. So does setting an effective reminder system!

For advanced planners, you might also consider the following questions.

- Can you create a *system*? And can you build in a *cue*, *behavior*, or *reward* to make some actions easier and encourage them to become habits (Chapter 9)?
- What will you do to activate or begin key tasks? Use INCUP strategies (interest, novelty, challenge, urgency, or passion/values; see Chapter 6) to make that process easier.

DEFINE THE NEXT STEP

Sometimes we can get lost in the process and lose track of what to do next. Sometimes the Wall of Awful plays tricks on us and obscures the next step. In both cases, the best thing to do is identify *any* step in the process (X). From there, we can move on to the next step (Y), or work backward from X. I typically do this by saying, "Before I can do X, I have to do W. And before I can do W, I have to do V. And before I can do V, I have to do..." You get the idea.

Productivity Gains

Once we get to the other side of our Walls, we may still have to handle our work differently. While a full treatment of productivity for neurodivergent people is beyond the scope of this book, here are some common strategies to get more of the things *we* want done:

- **Time blocking.** Neurodivergent people often have a fuzzy relationship with time. So blocking out *when* we will do the thing, with a longer block than we think we need, can dramatically improve our odds of doing it. Of course, we'll need to follow through!

- **Increasing transition time.** As I've said before, those of us who are neurodivergent usually need a lot more transition time than we think we do. So it's critical to allow for that transition time in our calendars. This means not only planning for time to Climb a common Wall but also blocking out recovery time after stressful conversations and being realistic about the number of transitions we can handle in a day.
- **Doing less.** Hustle culture says filling every minute of our lives with effort gets more done, but the opposite is true for us. We make better progress by choosing a *very* small number of important things (one to three) to work on in any given day, week, or quarter.*
- **Theming your days.** In the same way, because we have a bigger task switching penalty (look that up in your favorite search engine), neurodivergent people often get more done if we work with fewer things. Try to group like tasks into a single day, or work on a single document or project over two or more days, rather than

* This is well-established wisdom in the ADHD and productivity communities. Christina Wodtke makes a great case for the concept (saying, in fact, you should do ONE big thing only at any given time) in her book *Radical Focus.*

constantly switching between different tasks or projects, which exhausts us.

- **Separating the deciding and doing.** As friend and fellow ADHD coach Dusty Chipura says, we can get further if we separate the executive-function heavy work from the "carrying it out" work. Do the planning, prioritizing, and coordinating ahead of time and the "doing" part another day.
- **Balancing focus, hyperfocus, and breaks.** Pay attention to how different types of focus affect you. Some people will need planned breaks to prevent hyperfocus from going too deep, and others will do best with longer deep-focus blocks followed by longer recoveries.
- **Learning by trial and error.** There is no one right way, as different people will need different approaches to find their happy place. Try things and pay attention to the results, taking notes if possible. Over time, if you do more of what works and less of what doesn't, you'll get more output for the same effort. But be patient! You may have to find your way through a long period of trial and error.

For more on productivity strategies that work for neurodivergent people, check out Alan P. Brown's *Zen and the Art of Productivity*, Dani Donovan's *The Anti-Planner*, and (for goals) Christina Wodtke's *Radical Focus*.

Consider Task Stages

I've already mentioned setting it up, doing it up, and cleaning it up from Ryan McRae (Chapter 9 and earlier in this chapter). While planning is the "setup" task of any habit or big project, it's often only the first step. We will still have to plan for both the setup and the cleanup of any given task moving forward.

➻ Have you accounted for the setting up and cleaning up stages in your plan? If not, go back and figure those out now. Then find out where and when you'll do those steps.

Simplify the Plan

Fair warning, it's often really fun to make a complex plan in the moment! Designing lots of steps and complicated moving parts *feels* fun to the planning brain. But then we can't execute the plan because it's too complicated.

For example, if we are taking the kids to see their grandparents, we might create a complicated travel plan. We'll leave at 7:00 a.m. and drive until 9:00

a.m., then stop at the breakfast place we've all been wanting to visit forever. Then we'll get back in the car and drive for a few hours, stop at the batting cages for a fun outing with the kids for an hour, grab a quick lunch, and then get back on the road to arrive at the grandparents' around dinnertime. It's a fun-seeming plan, but there are too many places it could go wrong—particularly with kids, who won't want to leave the batting cages after an hour! One delay early in the day (leaving the house late or hitting construction) will tend to cascade into a *series* of frustrations, and soon we're arriving at the grandparents' at 2:00 a.m., or stopping at a hotel overnight because we're too tired to drive.

Instead, we should take a look at the plan before we move on, and simplify it to something that's reasonable. We should build in buffer time. And then we should ask ourselves what problems could come up and try to address those, too.

Step #5: Plan for Problems

I tend to do this step and the previous one—Creating a Plan and Planning for Problems—at the same time. After you've practiced the process several times, you may be able to do the same, especially for smaller

> tasks/plans like getting past a single Wall of Awful. But for now, do steps #4 and #5 in order.

Now that we've finished the rough draft of the plan, it's time to consider what could go wrong. Planning for problems helps to prevent bad outcomes.

The Pre-Mortem

> Note: If you have severe anxiety, approach this exercise cautiously and skip it on a bad day. Or do the exercise **with** your therapist, a trusted friend, or an adviser.

Doctors and software coders learn from their failures in a systematic way: They get together afterward as a group and analyze what happened. But we don't have to wait for something to go wrong to learn. In fact, we can usually see failure coming—if we look.

To do a pre-mortem, we imagine ourselves in the future. We pretend that we have already executed the plan we're currently working on—only things went horribly wrong. It blew up in our faces!

Now we ask ourselves:

- What did we imagine would go wrong?
- What are some likely reasons for *why* those things went wrong? For example, our behaviors or the

behaviors of others, areas we typically struggle in (including neurodivergent challenges), and typical obstacles like heavy traffic or a kid needing the bathroom at an inconvenient moment.

- What can we do *now* to prevent these worst-case scenarios or to make their impact less bad?
- What areas or obstacles can't be prevented or managed? How will we respond to those obstacles, and how will we cope with the big emotions that may result? (The tools in Chapter 7 for strong negative emotions and Appendix 3 for managing anxiety may be helpful.)

A pre-mortem may feel like one extra step, but it pays off, as you saw in my story at the beginning of the chapter with the car keys. By planning in advance, we make our lives easier. We also take the weight off our nervous systems in the moment, because we know what to do when hard things come.

The Fallback Position

Assume that your plan will not work out as well as you hope—what's the bare minimum you need to do for success? What's the best version of events you can imagine? What are the gradations in between? Many people like to create different plans for "good days" and "bad days" to allow them to keep making progress even when they can't reliably do as much. Would a "bad day" minimum plan make sense for you to create?

Common Neurodivergent Challenges

Now we'll do a double-check to make sure that we've planned for our neurodivergent needs. How can we make the plan more likely to succeed? What accommodations can we build in?

- **Decrease friction** to make tasks and projects easier to start, especially when starting or restarting tasks, or when you will likely be dealing with big emotions (Chapter 9).
    - Consider friction that might result from impulsivity or your own choices, such as staying out all night at a party before a big work presentation. (That would make giving a good presentation much harder! Thinking about it in advance and choosing to stay in instead will avoid that friction.)
- **Identify sensory issues** and make plans to mitigate them, such as wearing rubber gloves when doing dishes so the soapy water and food gunk doesn't feel icky on your hands.

- **Be honest about what tasks you will find boring**, and brainstorm ways to make them more interesting or engaging. Some ways might include focusing on an exciting *result* of the plan or including music or INCUP techniques (interest, novelty, challenge, urgency, or passion/values; see Chapter 6).

- **Introduce soothing, regulating, or grounding techniques** that help your specific flavor of anxiety or mental health. Your needs may vary, but some ideas for nervous system regulation are in Chapter 2 (and Appendix 3). When in doubt, consult a mental health professional for help with more ideas.

Make Sure You're Solving the Right Problem

I had a client who had been going through a challenging time, and we were trying to rebuild his life. One of the first things we focused on was improving his physical health. In order to do this, we set up a plan for him to go to the gym two to three times per week. (It seemed like an easy win because he had been a gym rat when he was younger.)

In the session following that first week, he told me that he thought he had a Wall of Awful for going to the gym. Based on his past, that seemed unlikely. So we played with the idea that something else might be getting in the way for the rest of the session. As it turned out, he was encountering Walls of Awful, just not for going to the gym.

The first Wall was leaving the house in general. He worked from home and hadn't gone out much since the pandemic. That Wall was something he could usually push through, but it got harder if a second Wall of Awful was involved. That's why he assumed he had one for the gym.

I was still doubtful of his hypothesis. We spoke some more, and we discovered that the other Wall regarded his appearance. He had gained weight, so his shorts were too tight and his T-shirts rode up to show his stomach when he raised his arms over his head. To address the issue, he got some gym clothes that were one size up from his old gear. It worked. He was soon back to exercising regularly, which proved critical to getting his mental health back on track.

Sometimes we plan for what seems like an obvious problem, but it doesn't get us anywhere. When that happens, it's worthwhile to see if there's something hiding underneath that actually matters more—a lagging skill, a missing resource, or (like in this case) a hidden Wall of Awful.

Plan for Walls of Awful

If you're reading this book, it's likely that a Wall of Awful will come up for you *at least once* in any large project. Good planning, then, means identifying any potential strong emotions that are likely to come up and the Walls that may come with them. *Where* are Walls likely to arise? What are the Walls about? (See Appendixes 1 and 2.)

Clues that a Wall is likely:

- You have to do something you don't want to do.
- You know something will make you feel uncomfortable.
- You have a task that you typically leave for last or try to avoid it completely.
- You've struggled and failed in a specific area in the past. Walls will happen in that area far more frequently.

Once we identify potential Walls, we need to plan for how we can overcome them. It's usually wise to both (1) plan on *which* tactics to use from Putting a

Door in the Wall (Chapter 6) *and* (2) put aside extra time for Climbing (Chapter 7). We may also need additional transition time or recovery time after particularly challenging tasks. (This principle is even more true for those of us with mental health challenges!)

Encountering a Wall of Awful doesn't mean you're doing it wrong. You're allowed to struggle or find a certain kind of task harder to start. You can be uncomfortable and do it anyway—but if you want or need to do the task, it's a good idea to plan for those feelings and for how you'll cope with them. It's also smart to allow for more time than you think you need to deal with your Wall and to decide *in advance* how you'll put a door in it or climb it.

➻ Make a plan for each Wall or mental health challenge you can predict in as much detail as is helpful. (Bonus points if the plan is repeatable!) Then leave extra time in the plan for the emotions and Walls you *can't* predict.

Plan Ahead to Get Past Your Wall

When we encounter a Wall of Awful, we're at least partially processing from an emotional state. That means we may have some trouble accessing the problem-solving skills we need to make a plan. So it's useful to plan ways to get past our Walls in advance.

To make the plan, you'll need to first consider the specific kind of Wall you're dealing with and where it comes from. (See Chapter 7 for help on that thought process.) To move on, you'll need to be able to answer three questions:

- What kind of Wall is this, and what emotions make it up?
- What has worked for this kind of Wall (or these emotions) in the past?
- What is the clearest next step to take once you're on the other side of the Wall?

Once you can answer these questions, use Chapter 7 to help you collect strategies to soothe and activate, or Chapter 6 to help you strategize how to put a door in your Wall.

Step #6: Stay Flexible

Plans *will* change. We all know that. We move to a new home, relationships evolve, jobs change, cars break down, and things come up! We can't become so rigid with our plans that we can't handle that reality. We have to remain open and mentally flexible.

Planning well means planning for change—which can take several forms. We can always acknowledge change, adjust our plan, or make a new one at any point. Or we can choose to adopt a strategy *for* change. For example, we can create a plan A and backup plans B and C. We can plan for contingencies and emergencies. Or, if we're good at improvising, we can leave portions of our plan flexible and adjust as we go.

Executing on a plan is a lot like driving across a big city. We have a plan for how to get from point A to point B, but then we hit major traffic on the highway. We *could* stick to the plan, stay in traffic, and arrive two hours later than planned with a headache and a nasty mood, or we can take a look at the GPS and find another route. The change in plans might lead us through back roads or have us dodge traffic along side roads. Or, if the whole city is overcome with rush-hour traffic and we have the time, we can just find a restaurant. (I always enjoy avoiding the stress of bumper-to-bumper traffic and having a nice, relaxing meal while I wait for traffic to dissipate. It makes me feel like I outsmarted the world for a few minutes.)

All of this is to say that something *will* come up that affects our plan. Just like in traffic, how we respond may be different every time.

Planning for Change

Here are some practical things to consider to help us remain flexible and plan for change more effectively:

- **Plan ahead.** Anything that's likely to go wrong should be done early in the plan, to allow for time to solve those problems.
- **Don't count on the best-case scenario.** Do your pre-mortems carefully, and make plans to avoid the worst outcomes. (But if you have an anxiety disorder, *don't expect the worst case to happen* either—most likely the reality will be something in between.)
- **Allow for "wiggle room" and extra time.** Plan for at *least* 20 percent more time in any schedule than you think you need, even over and above transition time and time for Walls. (If you have ADHD, are bad at estimating time, or are time blind for whatever reason, plan for *twice* as much time as you think you need. After you've successfully done the task several times, then you can drop to 20 percent after that.)
- **Plan for other kinds of "wiggle room."** Allowing yourself to have several "off" days or having extra money is just as useful as extra time. In fact, I even brought one extra friend to help me move—and he turned out to be needed!
- **Figure out when to start over.** Decide in advance when you know it's time to make a new plan and how you'll do that.

- **Play to your planning style.** If you're good at planning *and* like structure, try to plan for the most likely challenges with a plan B and a plan C. Otherwise, take steps to keep the plan flexible and expect to improvise as you go. Then try the other strategy with the next plan to see what works best for you.

Values Conflict

Our personal values aren't the only critical information we need to know. We also need to understand the priorit(ies) of our values *in the situation* in order to know what to do when something goes wrong. For example, if we're working on a client advertising campaign and something goes wrong, what is most important: the campaign going out on time or the relationship with the client? The two lead to very different actions!

If we believe that the campaign going out on time is most important, then we'll stay all night trying to fix the issue and get the campaign out on time and try to get our coworkers to do the same, even if it costs us. On the other hand, if we have a good relationship with the client at that point, we can call them and tell them the situation with honesty and integrity. Maybe the client still needs *part* of the campaign immediately, but by communicating well, we've ensured we keep the client. An all-nighter where no one talked to the client might have caused damage to that relationship.

↠ **Think about your priorities** and the values that are most important to this situation. Talk to your boss, your spouse and kids, or other important people to get their input. Knowing what your value priorities are gives you more options and makes problem-solving easier.

POST-MORTEM REFLECTION

Remember our discussion at the beginning of the chapter? If planning is the "setting it up" stage of any large project or task, "doing it up" involves doing the actions until it's finished. Then, at the end of the project or task, we should "clean it up" by reflecting on what has just happened.

Sure, we *could* move on to the next big project or task, leaving messy trails of thoughts scattered on our mental lawn to melt away in the rain. But doing that prevents the good stuff that reflection would give us.

Doing a post-mortem reflection is an act of learning. It's metacognition (thinking about thinking). When we reflect, we can formalize what we've learned by writing it down. Then we can include what we've learned in the next plan.

To reflect, ask:

- How did this project or task go?
- What actions did I take, and what were the results?
- What went well, and what went badly? Why?
- What was hard about it? Did it feel uncomfortable, and in what way?
- Were there friction points? If so, what can we do to reduce those points?
- What was easy about it?
- What could be easier next time?

Next, spend a little time finding one to three "takeaways." We may want to give ourselves credit for something that went well so that we do it again next time. Or we may want to notice something that went badly or was excessively hard and figure out another approach that's better for next time.

By looking backward, we learn lessons from the past in order to apply them to the future. In this way, a post-mortem reflection makes us better at planning and better at carrying out our plans. We become *better* and *smarter* over time.

THE STRUGGLE IS WORTHWHILE

Overcoming the Wall of Awful is, at least in the beginning, very hard. But just because it's hard doesn't mean it can't be done!

As you start applying the ideas in this chapter and the ideas in this book, you'll get a new perspective on your Walls of Awful. As you use the ideas to make plans, you gain more control over your struggles and gain more certainty. Over time you'll find that you really *can* do hard things. You can accomplish so much more than you realized—and that the hard things you want are worth doing.

Your efforts are worthwhile. There is dignity in struggle, and you are worthwhile. I believe in you. But even more importantly, I hope that *you* believe in you. By working through this book to this point, you're showing that overcoming your Walls is important to you—*and it's something you can do!*

Moreover, you're showing yourself that you're worth it, that your efforts matter and are of significance. The way in which you want to change, the way you want to address the challenges you face matters. You're showing that you'll keep trying until you get it. You'll keep climbing and putting doors in your Walls until you get to the other side.

Imagine how proud of yourself you'll be.

CHEAT SHEET: PLANNING

1 Planning decreases anxiety because it increases certainty and agency and keeps processing in the prefrontal cortex. (So the amygdala doesn't take over!) Because of this, plans also sometimes put a door in the Wall.

2 Planning is often hard for neurodivergent people, because it requires us to use our executive function. Luckily, planning is a skill that can be developed through practice and training.

3 **A good plan includes six parts:**

Figure out what you want.

Determine your motivation.

Consider your resources.

Create a "rough draft" of your idea.

Plan for problems.

Stay flexible.

4 **Friction is the silent killer we must find and remove from the plan.** Look for friction like: sensory challenges, boring tasks, distractibility, and likely big emotions.

5 Walls of Awful might interrupt us halfway through a task—and that's normal and fine. We can plan how to get back on track.

6 Some kinds of tasks will make us struggle more than others. We're allowed! Even after overcoming the Wall of Awful, we may feel uncomfortable for a little while as we engage with the task. It's worth doing.

ACTION STEP:

Choose a goal, ideally one that's related to the Wall of Awful you've chosen. (But any goal will work.) Now, go through each of the six planning steps in this chapter to make a plan to reach your goal.

Note: Again, it's okay to ask a friend, coach, therapist, or mentor to help with this process, especially the first few times. Planning takes practice.

CONCLUSION

YOU *CAN* DO THIS

There are two ways we can treat the Wall of Awful: as an excuse or as a reason. Only the second is healthy.

If we use the Wall of Awful to validate our struggles and see that validation as an excuse to give up, we defeat ourselves. We tell ourselves we can't and become stuck behind the Wall. Soon we're avoiding hard things as a habit, and avoidance slowly takes over our lives. That's not the point of this book—in fact, it's the antithesis. That "can't do" attitude is a trap.

We want to use the Wall of Awful as an explanation—a reason for our struggle—so it can be a source of comfort, courage, and empowerment. Understanding *why* empowers us to act. It teaches us how to confront hard things in useful ways. Rather than giving up when we encounter difficult negative feelings, we learn to face them. We learn to struggle well and to overcome.

We learn to feel our difficult emotions and do the thing anyway.

The mission of my Wall of Awful model is to help explain why getting started is hard. We can name and understand our challenges, and—here's the fun part—play with those challenges. We can start to manipulate them and work around them. We can define our sandbox and work within those boundaries to achieve our goals in sustainable, healthy, actionable ways. So we get to the places we want to be in our lives.

Sure, it'll be hard at times, but we can do hard things!

THE BEGINNING

The Wall of Awful is not the endpoint; it's the beginning. Everything we want in life is on the other side. And with time and work, we can get there. Our struggle can become the obstacle we can climb at need. We can lose our fear of it.

When we understand that truth, we can use the skills we've learned to get past the Wall of Awful reliably. We can put a door in it. We can climb over it. We can use resources to get past it, create systems and habits to go through it, and on occasion, if things are very hard, we can deliberately choose to harness our anger (or anxiety) and smash through it. We are *not* helpless.

We have *power*. When our Walls rise up, we'll know what to do, and the climb will get easier.

I can't say specifically what is on the other side of your Wall of Awful. I don't know what goals you have and what milestones you'll accomplish. But I can tell you the emotions you'll feel when you get there. You'll feel accomplished and effective. You'll have a sense of power and agency over your own life. Every time you get to the other side of the Wall of Awful, celebrate that accomplishment! Even if the moment is small, it's important to establish those good feelings. You have done the hard thing! You have overcome. Over time, as you celebrate, you'll anchor the good feelings to the other side of the Wall, and that will put a permanent door in that Wall.

The Wall of Awful is made of awful feelings. Positive feelings of celebration and power help defeat it.

NOTHING WILL CHANGE UNLESS YOU ACT

I have read many books like this one. The only ones that changed anything were the ones I *applied* to my life.

I see it all the time: people who use learning as a way to avoid taking action. They take classes, read books, and even hire a coach, but don't *do* anything with the material they've learned. That's not what I want for you. I want you to apply the ideas in this book to your life, one step at a time.

PICK ONE THING

Right now, pick one thing from this book that feels like it will help you (two at the most).

When in doubt, pick the thing with the most potency for your life, and then apply it to your life today. Put the idea up on your bathroom mirror. Talk about it with your kids. Reread that part of the book, and make plans to apply that thing every day until it sticks.

If you can find one thing that will make three or four areas of your life better, choose that one. Or pick the idea that is most likely to bail you out of a pressing problem. If you're about to lose your job if you don't change, for example, you might want to put doors in the Wall at work.

Just take action. It's better to take action and mess up than do nothing. "Nothing" is stagnant, and nothing will result from it. Taking action imperfectly and badly, on the other hand, gives you immediate feedback. It may hurt, but that pain is learning. You'll know how you failed and can adjust accordingly for next time. Jump in on your one thing, and see what you can learn from the process of doing.

Feel free to pick any idea or practice from this book to try first, but here's a quick list of some possible options:

- Identify when you have a Wall of Awful vs. when something is against your values (Chapter 1).
- Figure out how you can apply the CCAW strategies to reduce anxiety (Chapter 2).

- Consider how you can apply resources to help you solve problems (Chapter 3).
- Add a new skill or ask for help when you face a Wall (Chapter 3).
- Identify when you're churning, puttering, or procrastinating, and take action instead (Chapter 4).
- Catch yourself wanting to smash and use another strategy instead (Chapter 5).
- Put a door in the Wall by using INCUP methods to make it more engaging or fun (interest,

novelty, challenge, urgency, or passion/values, see Chapter 6).

- Practice applying one of the climbing strategies to the Walls you face (Chapter 7).
- Apply the change cycle to your next attempted change (Chapter 8).
- Deliberately add or replace a habit to make something easier for yourself (Chapter 9).
- Do a pre-mortem and post-mortem the next time you do something hard (Chapter 10).
- Plan ahead to Climb your Wall more easily (Chapter 10).
- Of course, there are many others!

Change is hard at first, but don't give up. Keep practicing until you're doing things consistently. Get help to learn the skills attached to it if you need help. In the beginning, you'll apply your thing cautiously and awkwardly, with lots of thinking. Over time, you'll begin to feel more natural at what you're doing, until eventually you apply that thing instinctively.

When you've put your change into action and can use it easily under pressure, add a second practice to the first.

START SMALL

For everyone (but especially for those of us who are neurodivergent), big, sweeping change is usually a bad idea. Better to start small and be consistent, adding to the habit over time, than to try to change everything all at once. Large-scale, sudden change tends to be difficult to maintain.

A single big change might have differences for a week or a month, but six months later you will have abandoned the change and be back in the same spot. Instead, start with one thing (or at most two), and start small.

If you want to eat more vegetables, eating a salad every single day for lunch might be hard to maintain. But one salad per week is easy, and over time you can expand to two salads a week and then three. Eventually you're eating salad for lunch most days, and the difference doesn't feel hard.

Understanding Leads to Action

Pay attention to your life, and notice your patterns. Then think about the ideas in this book. If you continue to do both, you'll find action (and change) becomes easier once you're ready. Some change may even happen naturally in the meantime, as understanding leaches into your actions.

I see this with my parent groups. The understanding and the noticing happen long before the change does. Many parents come to my groups thinking they're supposed to be acting like a boss to their kids, and they assume the worst of them. The group and the discussions slowly change how they think about their role and the way they should be interacting with their kids. That new understanding slowly works itself out in action, day by day, week by week. They start treating their kids as teammates instead of employees, stop assuming laziness and start assuming the kids are trying their best but lack skills or resources. Soon they're looking for opportunities to provide their kids with those skills and resources! In many cases, the parents haven't created a master plan for formal change, but by the end of the group, they've changed anyway. They've noticed, tried, and changed in small movements over an extended period of time—and ended up with success.

When you know and understand your patterns, and you can see your Walls of Awful, you've done half the work of change already.

BE GENTLE WITH YOURSELF

The parents in my parenting group get farther with their kids when they don't assume their kids are being lazy or defying them on purpose. In the same way, you'll get farther on your journey if you give yourself more grace along the way. If something isn't working, don't call yourself lazy. Don't assume the worst of yourself. Instead, see if you can add skills or resources, or find a different way past the Wall. Don't try harder—try differently.

It's Okay to Do It Differently

If you're reading this book, you might be managing anxiety, OCD, or depression. You might be navigating ADHD, autism, or have other things going on that affect the way you interact with the world. Regardless of your flavor of neurodiversity, the strategies you've learned up to this point may or may not work for you. That's okay. Part of the job of this book is to give you permission to do stuff differently: If the way you've been doing it up until now hasn't worked, you're allowed to change it up. You're allowed to do things differently, even if your uncle or mom or spouse doesn't do it that way.

For example, I work with college kids with ADHD. They've often heard years of advice that they should "eat the frog," or do the hardest thing first. The theory is that if we do the hardest thing first, everything after that is easier—which is true *if* we can activate. But many of my clients find the hardest or biggest task to be intimidating. They feel too overwhelmed to start with the hardest task—and the overwhelm only gets worse if they have a Wall of Awful for it. So instead, we look for a small, easy win: a simple worksheet or reading a chapter. When they get that easy win under their belt, they gain momentum for moving into the harder stuff.

I've talked about creating accommodations in our living situations: giving up on folding laundry and living out of laundry baskets and hooks, if that works better. Allowing (clean) clutter to build up rather than insisting on an Instagram-worthy house that looks like no one lives there. Or delibrately *using* planned visual clutter to remind us to do tasks, like the unopened mail sitting on the table or the winter coat next to the door. Maybe our favorite pan lives on the stove, and we return it there after we clean it, to make it more likely that we'll cook a healthy meal at night.

There is no wrong answer, as long as the strategies work and we satisfy our goals.

PLANTING SEEDS

It's okay to not remember everything in the book. It's okay not to notice or apply all the ideas at once. (In fact, it's probably a good idea.) Get what you can out of it, and reread the book later when you're ready. Take what you need, and the rest can land in your subconscious. You're planting seeds.

Some people reading this book will be aggressive learners. They'll take a million notes, put sticky notes everywhere, and go bananas. (Alex waves hi to fellow banana learners.) Other people will act more like standard readers. They'll read all the way through and will find the book interesting and engaging but then not know what to do with it. Still others will jump around and get ideas they'll apply to their current struggles. (Brendan waves to his fellow jumping learners.) Hopefully, whichever category you fall in, this conclusion will have helped you figure out where to start.

That being said, the stuff that you're not sure how to use right now is still useful. It's a seed. It may turn out to be helpful at another time in your life. You may be able to help a friend. Or it may not apply at all. Any of that is okay. But if you think of the ideas as seeds, when your life takes a turn, suddenly an idea may take root. And it may grow into something that bears fruit.

If an idea from this book is stuck in your head but you don't know what to do with it, think about what's going on in your life. Does anything in your life connect to that idea? If not, it's okay to let the idea go for a while. We don't have to hold on to ideas too tightly; we can pack them in the loose soil of our minds and see if they grow into something.

YOU CAN DO IT

The best part of Climbing the Wall of Awful, and doing it over and over again, is that you learn you are capable. You learn to accept wherever you are and to use creativity and effort to get where you want to be. You learn that, if you persist, you can find the resources and skills that you need.

If you are facing something hard, it doesn't mean you're a failure. It doesn't mean that you're less than. It just means that this thing is hard right now! You're worth the effort of getting past it. You'll get stronger for having done it. And eventually you'll develop the skills to move through it more easily and sustainably.

You can do it. I believe in you!

ACKNOWLEDGMENTS

Grateful appreciation to the following people who have generously allowed us to quote from and reference their work:

- Alan P. Brown
- Dusty Chipura
- Dr. William Dodson
- Dani Donovan
- Charles Duhigg
- BJ Fogg
- Jonathan Hassall
- Lynn Lyons
- Caroline Maguire
- Ryan McRae
- Dr. Alice Nicholls
- Dr. David Nowell
- Jessica McCabe
- Phil Pritchard

BRENDAN'S ACKNOWLEDGMENTS

BOOK TEAM:

I want to begin by thanking my book team, starting with my co-writer, Alex Hughes Capell. Her knowledge and experience are the only reasons this book reached its full potential. The whole process went more smoothly thanks to her, and she is a joy to work with. She has been an outstanding partner in all of this, and her expertise is apparent on every page. I'm looking forward to our future collaborations.

My agent, Michele Martin, made the process of finding a publisher go much faster and more easily than I ever expected. She believed in this project from the start, connected me with a few agents in the process of getting a deal, and sold the book at auction, a feat that was well beyond my expectations.

I was happy when I learned that Renee Sedliar would be our editor. When we first met, her intelligence, calm enthusiasm, and clear expertise really struck me. I'm glad to say that my positive impression from our first meeting has borne out over the long hall. She's been understanding of my first-time author anxieties, accommodating of my ADHD when necessary, and her keen eye and insight made this book better than I could have hoped. In a word, she's awesome!

I'd also like to thank the rest of the team at Hachette:

Alexandra Hernandez, Alana Spendley, Jessica McKenzie, Nana Twumasi, Anjuli Johnson, Becky Maines, Penina Lopez, Bart Dawson, Jim Datz, Melissa Mathlin, Sara Schaller, and Victoria Roddam.

I contacted Jesse Lundberg pretty late in the game to illustrate, but he stepped up like the pro that he is, and his outstanding work has added an important graphic element to the final product, which I know will help many of the ideas in this book resonate more with readers.

I want to acknowledge our beta readers—Clifton and Leslie Capell, Mahdi Gharavi, Tanith Korravai, Amy Mahan, Steve Messenio, Emily Shugarman, Shane Thrapp, and Lollie Weeks. Thank you for taking the time to help make this book the best it could be.

Finally, my friend E. Christopher Clark came in early to serve as our first draft editor and has been supporting us the whole way through. His experience and talent as both a writer and professor of writing helped us get this book ready to submit to publishers, and he listened to my updates and questions about the project with positivity and good humor. I deeply appreciate having him on my team.

FAMILY:

I am eternally grateful for my wife, Amy Mahan. My career has not been a typical one, and it has had plenty of ups and downs. Her patient support throughout is the only reason I managed to get this far. There's no one I'd rather be dancing through life with. I Love You.

My sons, Nathan and Gavin, are two of the most intelligent and resilient people I've ever met. I'm proud of the men they're becoming, honored to be their dad, and grateful to them for helping me to remember that I'm allowed to take a moment to feel happy and proud about the things I accomplish (whether it's a black belt or writing a book), instead of just moving on to the next thing on my list.

I want to thank my sister Lauren Mahan for believing in me, often when I didn't. I'll never forget standing in CVS, worrying to her on the phone about being let go from yet another teaching position, and her saying, "Yeah, but you're resilient. You'll figure this out. You've always bounced back from this stuff." That conversation helped me see something in myself that I haven't lost sight of since.

And thank you to my sister Mary Casali, her husband, John, and my nephew and niece, Jack and Riley. I appreciate you listening to me yammer on about this book adventure whenever we get to see each other. (And a bonus thank-you to Riley for helping us figure out the cover.)

I'd also like to acknowledge my in-laws, Lou and Peggy Schoen. I appreciate your interest in and excitement about this project. And thank you to my sister-in-law, Debra, and her husband, Alex Wiessman (and their son, Ari), for their support as well.

Finally, this book doesn't happen without the help of my dad, William Mahan. He's been supportive of my writing since I started figuring out I was good at it in high school and has been promoting my career in ADHD since I started the *ADHD Essentials Podcast*. I can't wait for him to see it in the bookstore.

FRIENDS AND COLLEAGUES:

Jessica McCabe has been a champion of my Wall of Awful model since 2018, when she attended a workshop I did on it. The next thing I knew, I was on her YouTube Channel, *How to ADHD*, talking about it with her, and we've been friends ever since. I'm grateful to have her on my side. There wasn't anyone else I could see writing the foreword, so I'm glad she agreed!

My friend Caroline Maguire, author of *Why Will No One Play with Me?* and *Friendship Skills for Neurodivergent Adults*, has been an incredible help to me through some of the most challenging parts of getting published. She guided me with skill, aplomb, and a level of enthusiasm that very few have.

Thank you to Dr. Ari Tuckman, Dr. David Nowell, and Dr. Zach Gershon for being willing to put their names behind this project when it was only in the proposal stage. I appreciate your belief in me, and I'm glad to have seen it through.

Thanks to the Men's ADHD Support Group board—Marc Almodovar, Shane Thrapp, Sam Coyer, Kristian Moton, and John Hazelwood for letting me ease off the throttle a little bit while I worked on getting this done, and for being incredibly supportive of this project.

I'm sure I'm going to miss someone here, so apologies in advance. I want to acknowledge my many friends in the world of neurodiversity who have been supporting me and my work—Kate Barrett; Dr. Raffael Boccamazzo; René Brooks; Alan P. Brown; Dusty Chipura; IngerShay Colzie, MSW, LSW; Will Curb; Dani Donovan; Lucia Miri Echavarria; Cameron Gott; Jon and Monica Hassall; Dr. Carolyn Lentzsch-Pacells; Dr. Tamara Rosier; and Dr. Sharon Saline. I am better for having met each of them, both professionally and personally. Thank you for being in my corner.

I also want to thank Jarrett Beeley, Drea Catalano, Kerri Deschaine, Matt Karas, Becky Pollinger, Mstr. Phil Pritchard, Ryan McRae, Kris Moody, Aaron Morse, Will Serwetman, and Adam Wilson, not just for listening to me babble about this book, but for being the best cheerleaders a guy could ask for, and for helping me see the significance of this. It's easy for me to get caught up in the doing of the thing and lose sight of what it means. Thank you for breaking me out of my tunnel vision at various times when I needed to over the last few years and helping me see that what I was doing was pretty special.

Finally, thank you to my friend Shane Thrapp. There's a lot more to writing a book than just writing the book, especially once the book comes out. Shane has been helping me figure out, plan, and build the infrastructure for those next steps. Any cool social media posts or videos you see from me in the future are purely because he pushed me when I needed it.

ALEX'S ACKNOWLEDGMENTS

First of all, I'd like to thank my parents for their unwavering support and encouragement for my writing from the time I was eight. This career would never have happened without you. Moreover, your incredible insight and notes for the beta read of *this* book made it better. Thank you, Mom and Dad. I love you.

I, of course, have to thank my co-author, Brendan, one of the smartest people I know, a true expert, and a dear friend. We've geeked out about mental health, neurodiversity, and the brain for so many years on Twitter before this project ever started, and I have been honored and excited to be part of it from the first minute I was asked. Moreover, I am deeply grateful to be given a seat at the table and allowed—and encouraged!—to add my own knowledge and experience to the book in the moments they fit. Thank you, Brendan, for an amazing working relationship and one of my favorite books I've ever written. I'm incredibly proud of us both.

I'd like to thank our editor, Renee Sedliar at Hachette, whose keen eye and amazing input helped shape this book into the powerhouse that it is. Many thanks to Michele Martin of MDM Management, who believed in the project from the first moment and sold it faster than I thought was possible. And to all the people, named and unnamed, who were a part of bringing the book to print—and from print to the bookstore. Your work is so appreciated and needed.

I'd also like to thank Dusty Chipura, my ADHD coach, and Tanith Korravai for her extraordinary insight and beta reads. Finally, I'd like to offer my profound gratitude again to Tanith, as well as Ann Decker, Karen Lacey, Loriane Parker, Hannah Johnson, and Janice Hardy, who have all made me the writer that I am. I love you guys.

APPENDIX 1

WHAT THE EMOTIONS OF THE WALL OF AWFUL™ ARE TELLING US

> You might want to sticky note this page, since we played with emotions throughout the book.

Some emotions are hard to feel. But no emotion is completely bad. Every feeling has a purpose, and every emotion has *something* it's trying to tell us. Here are some common feelings that make up the Wall of Awful and what they're normally trying to tell us. (This is by no means an exhaustive list.)

EMOTIONS THAT DRIVE US TO ACTION

and what they tell us

- **Anger** is telling us: *A boundary has been crossed.* (We need to address this boundary in a healthy way.)

- **Frustration** is telling us: *We're being prevented from doing something.* (Our Walls can make us frustrated with ourselves.)
- **Anxiety** is telling us: *Something bad might happen. We need to handle that NOW.* (The more we fight anxiety, the more it increases our suffering.)
- **Guilt** is telling us: *We made a mistake, and we need to plan how to not do that again.* (It's hard with neurodiversity to avoid the follow-up of shame, see below.)
- **Regret** is telling us: *We wish we had done something differently.* (It shines a light on our core desires or values and drives us to act differently in the future as a result.)

EMOTIONS THAT SLOW US DOWN

and what they tell us

- **Overwhelm** is telling us: *We have too many problems to tackle, and we don't know where to start or how to cope.* (We can decrease overwhelm by changing any of those three things!)
- **Shame** is telling us: *We not only did a bad thing, but we are bad and are stuck being bad forever.* (Shame is almost always unhelpful, and

is usually lying to us—can we turn it to guilt instead?)

- **Embarrassment** is telling us: *We're vulnerable to the judgment of others.* (This may or may not be true.)
- **Depression** is telling us: *We're sad and unable to move forward.* (Ironically, the best treatment is often recapturing our faith in our ability to move forward, which can take time.)
- **Rejection** is telling us: *We're in the wrong place or wrong role.* (Rejection can be painful for neurodivergent people, but it can help us find our people.)

Our emotions scream at us, but what they are screaming may not be what we need to do. Instead, if we listen more closely, we can find their deeper message. Then we can act in an appropriate way to move forward.

APPENDIX 2

HOW DO YOU KNOW IF IT'S A WALL OF AWFUL™?

People sometimes ask me how they can identify their Walls of Awful.

The best way to look for our Walls is to apply the URPU model. **If a task makes us feel Uncertain, Rejected, Powerless, or Uncomfortable, we're likely to have a Wall of Awful for it.**

MANY WALLS WERE BUILT IN THE PAST

Since many of our Walls are built in the past, take a moment to reflect on past struggles. Think about your patterns and habits. Where do you struggle? Feel free to go back to your childhood experiences, as many Walls begin to form in middle school. But don't ignore recent examples—even earlier today! Recent examples can point to the Walls you're facing in the present.

Ask yourself:

- Where have you typically failed in the past?
- What types of tasks or behaviors have given you the most difficulty?
- What kinds of situations have led to the most conflict or struggle?
- What aspects of your life have held the most challenge?
- What are the things that you have found consistently hard to start?

Once you've found the answers, look for what they have in common.

- What are your patterns with the *kinds* of tasks or situations you struggle with?
- Are there any tasks that lead to you engaging in behaviors that look like staring at, going around, or Smashing through a Wall of Awful?
- What do these challenge areas have in common?

OUR WALLS AFFECT THE PRESENT

The behaviors and patterns you identified from the past can help you identify Walls in the present. If you catch yourself engaging in these behaviors, odds are you're facing a Wall of some kind.

As a general rule, if you often find yourself struggling to start a certain task, assume that you have a Wall of Awful for it. Then take steps to Climb that Wall or put a door in it. (I tell you how in the next Appendixes.) Even if you later determine you were wrong, your actions won't hurt the situation and will likely help you to start that task in the future.

THE COMMON PATTERNS REVEAL OUR WALLS

Finding your patterns and the things your challenges have in common can point to areas where you may have a Wall. For example, I have a client who hated to check his email, got anxious whenever his wife texted, and struggled to follow up with new professional contacts. As it turned out, the common denominator in all these things was that he had a Wall for having demands put on his time when it was already overtaxed, which it often was.

Thankfully, not all Walls are that sneaky. Usually our Walls are much more obvious, like having a Wall for dealing with finances, risking rejection, having vulnerable conversations, or being in noisy environments.

As you continue to identify your Walls, use the worksheet in Appendix 5 to get past them. You've got this!

QUICK-START REVIEW:

Try asking the following questions to help identify a Wall of Awful

- **Does it feel overwhelming?**
- **Is the task hard to do or hard to start?**
- **Are there broad categories that you struggle with?** Look for URPU!
    - Things that feel icky—doing the dishes, picking up dog poop
    - Things that risk rejection—job interviews, making new friends
    - Things that involve money—buying expensive things, asking for a raise
    - Things that are loud—going to a bar, attending a concert
- **Are you having big feelings about something that isn't really all that big?**

APPENDIX 3

DECREASE YOUR ANXIETY AND GET READY TO CLIMB YOUR WALL OF AWFUL™

> As a reminder, if you're regularly experiencing significant anxiety (7+ on the scale in Chapter 2), your needs are likely beyond the scope of this book. I advise you to seek out professional clinical support through your local mental health organizations or national organizations such as NAMI in the United States, CMHA in Canada, MIND in the UK, Mental Health Ireland in Ireland, and Mental Health Australia in Australia.

Remember the Anxiety Scale from Chapter 2? We can use the scale to help us to visualize our anxiety (or stress) level. Once we have an idea of where we are—either in the moment or overall—we can start working to reduce our anxiety level.

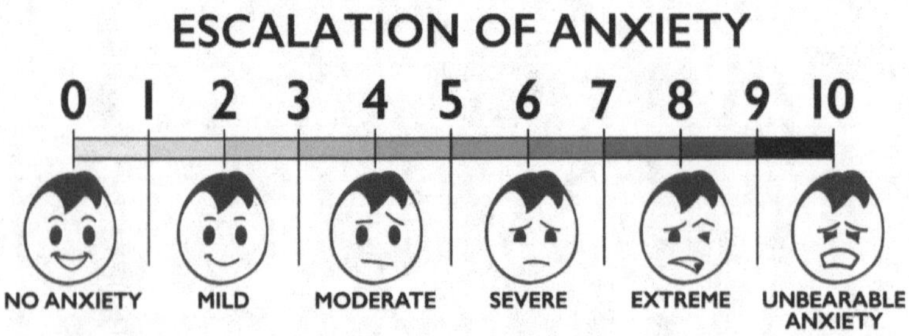

Once we know where we are, we can use the CCAW model to figure out ways to decrease our anxiety. As a reminder, CCAW stands for: Certainty, Connection, Agency, Well-being.

When we look at our current situation, we can (1) find where one of those areas is lacking, and (2) determine how to improve that area (or areas). Even if we can only improve things by a small amount, it will still help.

Strategies that help with anxiety management.

- **Certainty**
  - Identify your skills and resources related to the task at hand.
  - Determine your goals and write them down.
  - Clearly define when you will be done with the current task for the day (even if it isn't finished overall).
- **Connection**
  - Talk to a trusted friend
  - (in order of usefulness) in-person conversation > video chat > phone call > text > nothing.
  - Ask for help from a co-worker or an expert.

    - Join a support group related to your challenge
    - (in order of usefulness) in-person > online > nothing.

- **Agency**
    - Do something that has an obvious outcome, like cleaning or making something.
    - Practice breathwork or a similar body-focused activity.
    - Review past successes as evidence of your ability.
    - Make a decision, even if it's not perfect, and take the next action—you can always fix it later.

- **Well-being practices**
    - Cuddle up under a (weighted) blanket or with a pet or loved one.
    - Take a soft fascination break by walking in the woods or listening to comforting music.
    - Satisfy your biological needs—drink some water, eat a meal, get some sleep, etc.

The higher our anxiety, the more likely we are to be lacking in multiple areas. Connection and well-being strategies are best to start with at high levels of anxiety (7 or higher on the scale) because increasing certainty and agency often requires critical-thinking skills, which are undermined by the amygdala hijacking our processing at high levels of anxiety. The lower our baseline anxiety, the easier it will become to routinely Climb our Walls.

NOTE: Be careful not to increase one factor at the expense of the others. For example, deciding that you can't improve your situation may give the illusion of certainty, but it undermines agency and well-being.

BONUS TOOL KIT

- **Breathing exercises.** There are many kinds of breathing exercises, including yoga and meditation ones, box breathing, and breathing exercises developed for children (like "snake breathing" and "whale breathing"). All of them are designed to counteract fight-or-flight and come back to calm.
    - Here are the instructions for my wife Amy's favorite diaphragmatic breathing exercise: Get comfy, putting one hand on your chest

and the other on your belly. Inhale deeply through your nose, focusing on expanding your belly and keeping your chest fairly still, for a four count. Exhale slowly through your mouth for an eight count, letting your belly fall. Repeat several times, keeping the same rhythm, until you feel calmer.

  - Try Amy's breathing exercise first. Then, if you want to try others, do an internet search for breathing exercises, or try one of the other terms I listed.

- **The 5-4-3-2-1 Method.** Look around and ground yourself in your immediate surroundings by naming out loud: five things you can see, four things you can touch, three things you can hear, two things you can taste, one thing you can smell.
  - Another option: Look around and name, for example, six things that are blue. Helpful with kids!

- **Sensory regulation strategies.** Do something physical. Swinging on a swing, walking, petting a pet, deep pressure from hugs or lifting weights, squeezing a stress ball, any repetitive fidget, eating crunchy or soft foods, chewing gum.

- For more of these, find the sidebar for Dr. Alice Nicholls's sensory strategies in Chapter 6.

- **The Mammalian Diving Technique.** Fill up a clean sink with very cold water (try adding ice cubes!). Holding your hair back if necessary, take a deep breath and then put your face (and or head) into the water for thirty seconds to a minute. Hold your breath while underwater, and come back up for a break when you need one.
  - If you can't use a sink full of cold water, try an ice face mask.
  - After two to three cycles of cold, your body will forcibly calm down your nervous system—it's the same mechanism that lets whales dive deep!

- **Immediate distraction techniques.** Chew ginger or horseradish, play very loud acid rock or other strong music, hold an ice cube in your hand, eat a spoonful of honey or hot sauce, balance on one leg, smell vinegar, oranges, or other very strong scents, look at adorable pet GIFs.

- This approach is especially useful if you are caught in rejection sensitivity dysphoria (RSD, common in neurodivergent people—look up the term if needed).
- Note: These are intentionally brief distraction techniques. We want to avoid getting lost in a hyperfocus rabbit hole or having it turn into a numbing behavior.

Remember—anxiety, like all emotions, is temporary. Even chronic anxiety eventually ends. Use these strategies, as well as whatever ones you've already developed, to move through your anxiety and get to the other side of your Wall. Even when it's hard, there are great things on the other side of your Wall!

For more ideas, including ideas to help soothe strong anxiety, reread Chapter 6.

APPENDIX 4

HOW TO CLIMB THE WALL OF AWFUL™

> Note: At any point in the sequence below, you can: (1) **use soft fascination breaks to clear your head** and soothe your nervous system, or (2) go to Chapter 6 and figure out how to put a door in your Wall instead!

CLIMBING YOUR WALL

1. Realize you have a Wall. (*Oh no!*)
2. Study your Wall.
   a. Put a name to the emotion(s) the task is bringing up.
   b. Where is it coming from?
3. Accept your reality.
   a. Accept your emotions and the task at hand. (You don't have to like them.)
4. Change your self-talk.
5. Decide to move forward.

6. Build support systems.
    a. Apply skills as needed.
    b. Apply resources as appropriate. (Ask for help if you lack skills.)
    c. Include a reward if you are so inclined. (*Maybe cookies?*)

7. Do the thing. (*You can do this! I believe in you.*)

APPENDIX 5

CLIMBING THE WALL OF AWFUL™ QUICK-START WORKSHEET

> Note: At any point in the sequence below, you can go to Chapter 6 and: (1) **use soft fascination breaks to clear your head** and soothe your nervous system, or (2) figure out how to **put a door in your Wall** instead!

1. What situation is causing your Wall of Awful?

....

....

....

2. What emotions are making up your Wall?

....

....

....

3. Where might they be coming from?

....

....

....

4. <u>Action step:</u> Accept your emotions and the task at hand. (You don't have to like them.)

....

....

5. What are you telling yourself about this situation? Is it helpful or making things harder?

....

....

....

6. If it's making things harder, how might you change your self-talk so it serves you better?

....

....

....

7. What is the first thing you need to do to move forward?

....

8. What skills might you need to take that first step?

9. What resources might you need to take that first step?

10. Is there anything that would serve as a good reward for having completed the task?

11. <u>Action Step:</u> Take that first step. (*You really* can *do this! I'm rooting for you.*)

NOTES

CHAPTER ONE: WHAT IS THE WALL OF AWFUL?

1. Heinz Walter Krohne, Manuela Pieper, Nina Knoll, and Nadine Breimer, "The Cognitive Regulation of Emotions: The Role of Success versus Failure Experience and Coping Dispositions," *Cognition and Emotion* 16 no. 2 (2002): 217–43. doi:10.1080/02699930143000301.
2. Martin V. Covington, "Self-Esteem and Failure in School: Analysis and Policy Implications," *Social Importance of Self-Esteem*, edited by Andrew Mecca, Neil J. Smelser, and John Vasconcellos, University of California Press, 1990, pp. 72–124. https://doi.org/10.1525/9780520355033-005.

CHAPTER TWO: ANXIETY AND THE WALL OF AWFUL

1. Liesel Ebersöhn, "Adding 'Flock' to 'Fight and Flight': A Honeycomb of Resilience Where Supply of Relationships Meets Demand for Support," *Journal of Psychology in Africa* 22, no. 1 (January 1, 2012): 29–42. https://doi.org/10.1080/14330237.2012.10874518.
2. Ingrid Clayton, PhD, "What Is the Fawning Trauma Response? Caretaking and People Pleasing Through the Lens of Complex Trauma," *Psychology Today*, March 24, 2023. https://www.psychologytoday.com/us/blog/emotional-sobriety/202303/what-is-the-fawning-trauma-response.
3. Monica Hassall, RN, and Barbara Hunter, MEd, "Fight, Flight, Freeze… or Fib?," *ADDitude*, May 9, 2025. https://www.additudemag.com/why-lie-adhd-fight-flight-freeze/?srsltid=AfmBOooQAibYJKjtjP9czcG2q7-VFEjOhRCAgzRt9J4tSlbi_rQQXZL_.
4. Panagiota Koutsimani, Anthony Montgomery, and Katerina Georganta, "The Relationship Between Burnout, Depression, and Anxiety: A Systematic Review and Meta-Analysis," *Frontiers in Psychology* 10 (March 13, 2019). https://doi.org/10.3389/fpsyg.2019.00284.
5. UNC Health Caldwell. "Doom Scrolling and Its Effect on Your Mental Health," May 16, 2023. Accessed October 23, 2025. https://www.caldwellmemorial.org/blog/doom-scrolling-and-its-effect-on-your-mental-health/.

6. Sandra J. Llera and Michelle G. Newman, "Worry Impairs the Problem-solving Process: Results from an Experimental Study," *Behaviour Research and Therapy* 135 (October 27, 2020): 103759. https://doi.org/10.1016/j.brat.2020.103759.
7. Lara S. Franco, Danielle F. Shanahan, and Richard A. Fuller, "A Review of the Benefits of Nature Experiences: More Than Meets the Eye," *International Journal of Environmental Research and Public Health* 14, no. 8 (August 1, 2017): 864. https://doi.org/10.3390/ijerph14080864.

CHAPTER THREE: SKILLS AND RESOURCES HELP US GET PAST THE WALL

1. "Executive Function Deficits, Higher Level Employees, and Accommodations." Job Accommodations Network, 2016. https://askjan.org/articles/Executive-Function-Deficits-Higher-Level-Employees-and-Accommodations.cfm.
2. Damali M. Wilson and Deborah Gross, "Parents' Executive Functioning and Involvement in Their Child's Education: An Integrated Literature Review," *Journal of School Health* 88, no. 4 (March 2, 2018): 322–29. https://doi.org/10.1111/josh.12612.
3. Lana J. Williams, Felice N. Jacka, Julie A. Pasco, Seetal Dodd, and Michael Berk, "Depression and Pain: An Overview," *Acta Neuropsychiatrica* 18, no. 2 (April 1, 2006): 79–87. https://doi.org/10.1111/j.1601-5215.2006.00130.x.
4. Adam Km Woo, "Depression and Anxiety in Pain," *Reviews in Pain 4*, no. 1 (March 1, 2010): 8–12. https://doi.org/10.1177/204946371000400103.

CHAPTER FOUR: STRATEGIES THAT DON'T WORK

1. Rayne Whitington, "How Do You Deal With ADHD's 'Waiting Mode'?" *Healthline*, September 13, 2024. https://www.healthline.com/health/adhd/adhd-waiting-mode#:~:text=%E2%80%9CWaiting%20mode%E2%80%9D%20is%20a%20term,but%20it's%20commonly%20reported%20anecdotally.
2. Alethea Rachel, Xi Ern Lee, et al., "Fear of Failure Among Perfectionist Students," *International Journal of Evaluation and Research in Education (IJERE)* 13, no. 2 (April 1, 2024): 642. https://ijere.iaescore.com/index.php/IJERE/article/view/26296/13876.

CHAPTER FIVE: SMASHING THROUGH THE WALL

1. Leon F. Seltzer, PhD, "What Your Anger May Be Hiding: Reflections on the Most Seductive—and Addictive—of Human Emotions," *Psychology Today*, July 11, 2008, https://www.psychologytoday.com/us/blog/evolution-of-the-self/200807/what-your-anger-may-be-hiding.

2. Ingrid Clayton, PhD, "Caretaking and People Pleasing Through the Lens of Complex Trauma," *Psychology Today*, March 24, 2023. https://www.psychologytoday.com/us/blog/emotional-sobriety/202303/what-is-the-fawning-trauma-response.
3. "Chronic Stress Puts Your Health at Risk," Mayo Clinic, n.d., https://www.mayoclinic.org/healthy-lifestyle/stress-management/in-depth/stress/art-20046037.
4. Rodrigo Narvaes and Rosa Maria Martins de Almeida, "Aggressive Behavior and Three Neurotransmitters: Dopamine, GABA, and Serotonin—A Review of the Last 10 Years," *Psychology & Neuroscience* 7, no. 4 (June 2014): 601–607. https://doi.org/10.3922/j.psns.2014.4.20.
5. "Importantly, anger is associated with perceived task ease, a status that again diverges from other negatively valenced emotions, such as sadness, which are associated with greater perceived task difficulty." See Sarah N. Garfinkel, Emma Zorab, et al., "Anger in Brain and Body: The Neural and Physiological Perturbation of Decision-Making by Emotion," *Social Cognitive and Affective Neuroscience* 11, no. 1 (January 2016): 150–58. https://doi.org/https://doi.org/10.1093/scan/nsv099.
6. Nelly Alia-Klein, Gabriela Gan, Gadi Gilam, Jessica Bezek, Antonio Bruno, Thomas F. Denson, Talma Hendler, et al., "The Feeling of Anger: From Brain Networks to Linguistic Expressions," *Neuroscience & Biobehavioral Reviews* 108 (December 3, 2019): 480–97. https://doi.org/10.1016/j.neubiorev.2019.12.002.

CHAPTER SIX: PUTTING A DOOR IN THE WALL (AKA EASY MODE)

1. L. A. Barnett and B. Storm, "Play, Pleasure, and Pain: The Reduction of Anxiety through Play," *Leisure Sciences* 4 (2): 161–75. doi:10.1080/01490408109512958. **Also** Mercedes Díaz-Rodríguez, Lucía Alcántara-Rubio, David Aguilar-García, Celia Pérez-Muñoz, Jesús Carretero-Bravo, and Esther Puertas-Cristóbal, "The Effect of Play on Pain and Anxiety in Children in the Field of Nursing: A Systematic Review," *Journal of Pediatric Nursing* 61 (2021). https://doi.org/10.1016/j.pedn.2021.02.022. https://www.sciencedirect.com/science/article/abs/pii/S0882596321000646.
2. K. McRae, "Cognitive Emotion Regulation: A Review of Theory and Scientific Findings," *Current Opinion in Behavioral Sciences* 10, (2016): 119–124. https://doi.org/10.1016/j.cobeha.2016.06.004.
3. **Low blood sugar / hunger increases anxiety.** A good breakdown of some of the reasons, including a doctor's take here: Lisa Bowman, "Here's Why

You Might Feel More Anxious When You're Hungry," *Stylist*, August 7, 2023, retrieved June 25, 2025, from https://www.stylist.co.uk/fitness-health/wellbeing/feeling-anxious-hungry/800220. **Lack of sleep increases anxiety, and anxiety increases the effect of lack of sleep.** See: Cara A. Palmer and Candice A. Alfano, "Anxiety Modifies the Emotional Effects of Sleep Loss," *Current Opinion in Psychology* 34 (August 2020) 100–104. https://doi.org/10.1016/j.copsyc.2019.12.001. **Dehydration increases anxiety.** See H. A. Young, A. Cousins, S. Johnston, et al., "Autonomic Adaptations Mediate the Effect of Hydration on Brain Functioning and Mood: Evidence from Two Randomized Controlled Trials," *Sci Rep* 9 no. 1 (November 11, 2019). https://doi.org/10.1038/s41598-019-52775-5. Furthermore, there is *some* evidence to suggest that **other unmet biological needs and issues can also increase anxiety**. For example, constipation has been significantly correlated with anxiety in some studies—though of course that does not mean constipation *causes* anxiety; it could also be the reverse. (And the evidence is not overwhelming.)

4. **Music's ability to change emotion is widely observed.** Two perspectives on why and how it works: A. P. Stevens, "Music Has the Power to Move Us Physically and Emotionally. Here's Why," *Science News Explores*, July 19, 2024. https://www.snexplores.org/article/music-sharing-brain-health-emotions; S. Heshmat, PhD, "Music Can Be Seen as a Coping Resource That Enhances Internal Abilities," *Psychology Today*, November 8, 2022. https://www.psychologytoday.com/us/blog/science-of-choice/202211/how-listening-to-music-affects-your-mood.
5. J. Ratey, *SPARK: The Revolutionary New Science of Exercise and the Brain* (Little Brown and Company, 2013).
6. Eva Nowakowski-Sims, Mariah Rooney, Dana Vigue, and Savannah Woods, "A Grounded Theory of Weight Lifting as a Healing Strategy for Trauma," *Mental Health and Physical Activity* 25 (October 2023): 100521. https://doi.org/10.1016/j.mhpa.2023.100521.
7. Alice Nicholls, "5 Sensory Regulation Strategies for Autistic Burnout," Dr. Alice Nicholls, May 15, 2025. https://www.dralicenicholls.com/5-sensory-regulation-strategies-for-autistic-burnout/.
8. William Dodson, *The Recognition and Treatment of ADHD*, forthcoming.

CHAPTER SEVEN: CLIMBING THE WALL

1. J. J. Gross, "Emotion Regulation: Current Status and Future Prospects," *Psychological Inquiry* 26 no.1 (2015): 1–26. https://doi.org/10.1080/1047840X.2014.940781.

2. "From the Vault: Nutrient Rich Boredom with James Garrett of Brian by Design," *ADHD Essentials*, PodBean, podcast audio, May 21, 2021. https://adhdessentials.podbean.com/e/from-the-vault-nutrient-rich-boredom-with-james-garrett-of-brian-by-design/.
3. Phone interview with David Nowell, PhD; March 31, 2025.
4. For ADHD, see: Kelly A. Duffy, Keri S. Rosch, Mary Beth Nebel, Karen E. Seymour, Martin A. Lindquist, James J. Pekar, Stewart H. Mostofsky, and Jessica R. Cohen, "Increased Integration Between Default Mode and Task-Relevant Networks in Children with ADHD Is Associated with Impaired Response Control," *Developmental Cognitive Neuroscience* 50 (August 2021): 100980. https://doi.org/10.1016/j.dcn.2021.100980. To add autism, see: Ya-Yun Chen, Mirko Uljarevic, Joshua Neal, Steven Greening, Hyungwook Yim, and Tae-Ho Lee, "Excessive Functional Coupling with Less Variability Between Salience and Default Mode Networks in Autism Spectrum Disorder," *Biological Psychiatry: Cognitive Neuroscience and Neuroimaging* 7, no. 9 (September 2022): 876–84. https://doi.org/10.1016/j.bpsc.2021.11.016.
5. A. Basu, J. Duvall, and R. Kaplan, "Attention Restoration Theory: Exploring the Role of Soft Fascination and Mental Bandwidth," *Environment and Behavior* 51 nos. 9–10 (May 16, 2018): 1055–1081. https://doi.org/10.1177/0013916518774400 (Original work published 2018).
6. The Open Minds Foundation, "How Viral Social Media Posts Undermine Critical Thinking: This Viral Post About Elon Musk Highlights Our Predisposition to Thinking Badly," *Psychology Today*, July 16, 2025. https://www.psychologytoday.com/us/blog/the-art-of-critical-thinking/202504/how-viral-social-media-posts-undermine-critical-thinking.
7. Ahmed Mohamed Yousef, Alsaeed Alshamy, Ahmed Tlili, and Ahmed Hosny Metwally, "Demystifying the New Dilemma of Brain Rot in the Digital Era: A Review," *Brain Sciences* 15, no. 3 (March 7, 2025): 283. https://doi.org/10.3390/brainsci15030283.

CHAPTER EIGHT: HOW CHANGE WORKS

1. J. O. Prochaska, C. C. DiClemente, and J. C. Norcross, "In Search of How People Change. Applications to Addictive Behaviors," *PubMed* 47, no. 9 (September 1, 1992): 1102–14. https://doi.org/10.1037/0003-066x.47.9.1102.
2. Nahrain Raihan and Mark Cogburn, "Stages of Change Theory," StatPearls—NCBI Bookshelf, March 6, 2023. https://www.ncbi.nlm.nih.gov/books/NBK556005/.

3. As popularized in *Atomic Habits* by James Clear, the study is from Sarah Milne, Sheina Orbell, and Paschal Sheeran, "Combining Motivational and Volitional Interventions to Promote Exercise Participation: Protection Motivation Theory and Implementation Intentions," *British Journal of Health Psychology* 7 (May 2002): 163–184.
4. Surprisingly, **differences in the perception of time based on emotional state has been seen in studies of typical populations**—not just neurodivergent ones. It's a human thing! See a summary here: Joe Dawson and Scott Sleek (Sept. 28, 2018), "The Fluidity of Time: Scientists Uncover How Emotions Alter Time Perception," *APS Observer*, Association for Psychological Science. Retrieved June 25, 2025, from https://www.psychologicalscience.org/observer/the-fluidity-of-time.
5. For a decent summary of this commonly discussed idea, see "Zone of Proximal Development" by Saul McLeod, PhD, https://www.simplypsychology.org/zone-of-proximal-development.html.
6. M. Chaiton, L. Diemert, J. E. Cohen, S. J. Bondy, P. Selby, A. Philipneri, and R. Schwartz, "Estimating the Number of Quit Attempts It Takes to Quit Smoking Successfully in a Longitudinal Cohort of Smokers," *BMJ Open* 6 no. 6 (2016): e011045. https://doi.org/10.1136/bmjopen-2016-011045.
7. A simplification of the current understanding of the function of the amygdala, but a decent representation of what happens during an amygdala hijack event. This event is well understood. A good account of it is here: K. Holland, "Amygdala Hijack: When Emotion Takes Over," *Healthline*, April 18, 2025. https://www.healthline.com/health/stress/amygdala-hijack.

CHAPTER NINE: SYSTEMS AND HABITS, AND WHAT GETS IN THE WAY

1. For ADHD: Lasse Christiansen, Mikkel M. Beck, Niels Bilenberg, Jacob Wienecke, Arne Astrup, and Jesper Lundbye-Jensen, "Effects of Exercise on Cognitive Performance in Children and Adolescents with ADHD: Potential Mechanisms and Evidence-Based Recommendations," *Journal of Clinical Medicine* 8, no. 6 (2019): 841. https://doi.org/10.3390/jcm8060841. For the brain in general: Adilson Marques et al., "Bidirectional Association Between Physical Activity and Dopamine Across Adulthood—A Systematic Review," *Brain Sciences* 11, no. 7 (June 23, 2021): 829. https://doi.org/10.3390/brainsci11070829.
2. W. Wood, "The Role of Habits in Self-Control," in *Handbook of Self-Regulation: Research, Theory, and Applications*, 3rd edition, ed. K. D. Vohs and R. F. Baumeister (The Guilford Press, 2017), 95.

3. Later added to *Medium* by the author. See K. Scott, "Run the Dishwasher Twice," Forge, December 22, 2012, *Medium*. https://forge.medium.com/run-the-dishwasher-twice-e24ff24def60.
4. Charles Duhigg, *The Power of Habit* (Random House, 2012).
5. Duhigg, *The Power of Habit.*
6. Joseph Schacht, PhD, "Alcohol Use Disorder Can Be Treated with an Array of Medications—But Few People Have Heard of Them." *University of Colorado Anschutz Medical* (blog), May 23, 2024. Accessed June 20, 2025. https://news.cuanschutz.edu/news-stories/alcohol-use-disorder-can-be-treated-with-an-array-of-medications-but-few-people-have-heard-of-them.
7. BJ Fogg, "A Behavior Model for Persuasive Design," Persuasive '09: Proceedings of the 4th International Conference on Persuasive Technology, Article No.: 40, Pages 1–7. https://doi.org/10.1145/1541948.154199https://dl.acm.org/doi/10.1145/1541948.1541999.
8. Though according to some sources, he claims to have no hand in its creation. (See article from ToDoist, with one account of the system here: F. Adegbuyi, F. "Workflow Guide: Accomplish Your Big Goals with Don't Break the Chain," April 16, 2025, *Todoist Inspiration Hub*. https://www.todoist.com/inspiration/dont-break-the-chain.)

CHAPTER TEN: PUTTING IT ALL TOGETHER WITH PLANNING

1. HealthyGamerGG. *If You're Feeling Overwhelmed Watch This* [Video]. YouTube, May 20, 2023. https://www.youtube.com/watch?v=7VfSCQnGfk4.

ABOUT THE AUTHORS

ABOUT THE AUTHOR

Brendan Mahan, MEd, MS, grew up with undiagnosed ADHD. He has spent the last twenty-five years becoming the person he needed. Mahan draws on his experience as a former teacher, principal, and mental health clinician in his work as an esteemed ADHD and neurodiversity coach, consultant, celebrated podcast host, and speaker. He is on the board of the Men's ADHD Support Group and is director of professional resources for Calmer Con Boston. He has coached hundreds of clients with ADHD, autism, and anxiety through their most difficult challenges. Over that time, he has built a groundbreaking model that helps people understand and solve their challenges at a deeper level. That model is the subject of this book: the Wall of Awful.

ABOUT THE CO-WRITER

Alex Hughes Capell is an award-winning career writer of twenty-two book-length projects and numerous shorter pieces. Her ghostwritten books have earned clients accolades and speaking engagements, with one recent project being called "a delightful surprise in the world of business literature . . . with the sharpness of a seasoned strategist and the charm of a natural storyteller." She has worked on projects in the fields of psychology and behavior, neurodiversity and mental health, science, business, and the technology industry. Alex met Brendan on ADHD Twitter, and they became mutuals through discussions on mental health and neurodiversity before deciding to collaborate on a book. In addition to her expertise as a writer, Alex adds patient expertise on the mental health community, anxiety, and trauma-informed approaches to the book.

RAISING READERS

Books Build Bright Futures

Thank you for reading this book and for being a reader of books in general. We are so grateful to share being part of a community of readers with you, and we hope you will join us in passing our love of books on to the next generation of readers.

Did you know that reading for enjoyment is the single biggest predictor of a child's future happiness and success?

More than family circumstances, parents' educational background, or income, reading impacts a child's future academic performance, emotional well-being, communication skills, economic security, ambition, and happiness.

Studies show that kids reading for enjoyment in the US is in rapid decline:

- In 2012, 53% of 9-year-olds read almost every day. Just 10 years later, in 2022, the number had fallen to 39%.
- In 2012, 27% of 13-year-olds read for fun daily. By 2023, that number was just 14%.

Together, we can commit to **Raising Readers** and change this trend. How?

- Read to children in your life daily.
- Model reading as a fun activity.
- Reduce screen time.
- Start a family, school, or community book club.
- Visit bookstores and libraries regularly.
- Listen to audiobooks.
- Read the book before you see the movie.
- Encourage your child to read aloud to a pet or stuffed animal.
- Give books as gifts.
- Donate books to families and communities in need.

BOB1217

Books build bright futures, and **Raising Readers** is our shared responsibility.

For more information, visit **JoinRaisingReaders.com**

Sources: National Endowment for the Arts, National Assessment of Educational Progress, WorldBookDay.com, Nielsen BookData's 2023 "Understanding the Children's Book Consumer"

www.ingramcontent.com/pod-product-compliance
Lightning Source LLC
LaVergne TN
LVHW030725061126
851857LV00019B/1990

9781538786024